THE BIZ

THE BIZ

the basic business,

legal and financial aspects

of the film industry

SCHUYLER M. MOORE

SILMAN-JAMES PRESS | LOS ANGELES

First Edition

10 9 8 7 6 5 4 3 2 1

Library of Congress Cataloging-in-Publication Data

Moore, Schuyler M.
The biz: the basic business, legal, and financial aspects
of the film industry / Schuyler M. Moore.
p. cm.
1. Motion picture industry—Law and legislation—United States. 2. Motion picture
industry—Law and legislation—United States—Forms. I. Title.
KF4302.M66 2000   791.43'068'—dc21   99-089791

ISBN 1-879505-53-3

Cover design by Wade Lageose

Printed in the United States of America.

SILMAN-JAMES PRESS
1181 Angelo Drive
Beverly Hills, CA 90210

TABLE OF CONTENTS

Appendix

PREFACE

"In the beginning . . . "

When I marched out of law school, freshly scrubbed and brimming with legal knowledge, I looked forward to applying imperfect laws to a perfect world where the facts, at least, would not be in doubt. To be sure, the law was rife with latent and patent ambiguities forged in a fire of political reality, but my goal was to unravel the law through application to concrete facts.

By complete circumstance, the factual laboratory I was thrown into was the film industry, because it made up a large percentage of my new firm's business. I soon had a surfeit of film contracts floating across my desk, and my task was to sort out the legal issues. During this time, my vision of a perfect world rapidly disintegrated, as the contracts told a sad story of muddled facts, ambiguous relationships, and wild aspirations, all tied together with incomprehensible terminology. The complexity and confusion was, and is, compounded by the following factors:

- Films are based on copyright, an intangible asset, and it is possible to splinter that asset into a thousand pieces with little effort.

- Contracts are laced with unique jargon, much of which has no legal meaning even when translated into English.

- The entertainment industry is rife with dreamers and schemers. Dreamers have grand visions, but often lack the basic business knowledge necessary to implement their visions. Schemers think they have the knowledge, or worse, pretend they do, and attempt to baffle and bamboozle their way to success; to some, success is parting you from your money.

- The informality with which the entertainment industry does business shocks normal businessmen. Napkin deals do, in fact, occur. The majority of deals are documented by pathetic, sparse "term-sheets" which allude to some long form to follow. In those rare cases when the long form does follow, it is usually after the transaction is over.

When this chaos is stirred in a pot, it is not surprising that what is brewed is litigation, and lots of it. The badge of a successful film is the amount of litigation heaped upon it, from claims of ownership, to hopeful participants cut out of the process, to actual participants who wonder what happened to "net profits."

Ever since I started working as a lawyer in this nutty business in 1981, I have been looking for a good basic book to provide an overview of the business side of the film industry. There are a number of excellent, extraordinarily focused texts dealing with one aspect of the business or another, such as investment economics, the studios, taxation (for which text I am guilty), participations, and the history of the industry, yet I could find no book providing a basic overview of all the business aspects of the industry.

I started life as a tax lawyer, and my enthusiasm for the topic led to my publication of one of the narrow texts alluded to above, *Taxation of the Entertainment Industry* (Panel Publishers, New York). This is a highly specialized text that does not remotely address the broader picture that this book is aimed at. In 1995, I had the pleasure of teaching a UCLA Extension course, which, not coincidentally, I gave the same title as this book. As with this book, the course was aimed at a broad spectrum of people in the entertainment industry: executives, bankers, lawyers, accountants, and financiers. Of necessity, the course had a broad sweep. I was then unable to find a text to meet the needs of the course, so my text consisted of a compilation of numerous articles I had written.

From 1996 to the present, I have had the privilege of being an adjunct professor at the UCLA School of Law, teaching a course titled Entertainment Law (or some years, Entertainment Business Law). Every year, I kept expanding the text that originally started as the compilation of my articles for the UCLA Extension course, throwing in my lecture notes, a glossary, additional articles I wrote from time-to-time, and other odds and ends. Although that text is useful for my course, it is too specialized to be used as a basic book on the film industry.

All the while, I kept hearing the same refrain from students, clients, and colleagues: "Where can I find a basic book that will provide an overview of the business aspects of the industry?" I kept thinking to myself that perhaps I could and should write it. The catalyst for this book finally occurred when I read *All You Need to Know About the Music Industry* by Donald Passman (Simon & Schuster, New York). The author was in my identical position—a practicing lawyer who taught on the side and felt the need for a basic book. Donald Passman did a yeoman's job for the music industry, and I will be happy if I come close to providing the same for the film industry. My goal is for the book to be basic enough to be sold through general bookstores and read and understood by laymen, yet detailed enough to use as a text in an introductory course on the film industry in law school or business school. At least my students will be reading it, whether they like it or not!

1

JARGON TRANSLATION GUIDE

"When I use a word, it means just what I choose it to mean."
Lewis Carroll, *Through the Looking Glass*

Perhaps the most frustrating part of initiation to the film industry is being deluged with bizarre terminology and having to constantly nod your head as though you get it. Even worse, when you have the temerity to ask what a word means, you get several different definitions depending on who you ask. You often realize that knowledgeable insiders are completely mis-communicating, because they use a word as a shorthand, but each side is taking it to mean vastly different things. For example, insiders constantly banter about the concept that so-and-so is "attached" to a project. Some people take this to mean a contractual commitment, while others simply mean the actor or director has expressed some interest (at best) in a project.

It is impossible to write this book without using this specialized terminology, so to make sure we communicate, I offer my definitions right up front in this chapter (rather than being buried in the back in a glossary you will never read). If you are an insider, you can skip this chapter, or peruse it to see if your definitions match mine. Also, I will repeat many of the definitions the first time you stumble upon the word in the text. All capitalized words used within the definitions are themselves defined.

Above-the-Line: Motion picture costs that relate to the acquisition of rights and payments to Talent and the producer.

Accrual Method: An accounting method whereby expenses and income are reported when incurred or accrued, rather than when paid or received.

Actual Break-Even. The point in time when a motion picture's revenues reach Net Profits based on a full Distribution Fee. Compare to the definition of Cash Break-Even. Also see the definition of Rolling [Actual or Cash] Break-Even.

Adjusted Gross Receipts: Generally means Gross Receipts minus Off-the-Tops. However, many people use the term to refer to Gross Receipts less all distribution costs.

Advance: Advance payments for either (a) the license of motion picture rights or (b) compensation for services rendered. Also see Recoupment and Overages.

Answer Print: The first positive print of the completed picture that can be seen and heard, as it combines visuals from the original negative together with the sound, music, and effects tracks.

At-Source: A contractual provision requiring Royalties or Participations to be calculated based on Gross Receipts at a contractually defined link in the distribution chain, regardless of whether the licensor directly receives those Gross Receipts. Generally, At-Source Gross Receipts for various media is calculated as follows:

a. Film Rentals for theatrical;
b. Wholesale price charged to retailers for video;
c. Payments by broadcasters for television; and
d. Payments by manufacturers to licensors for merchandising.

Attached: Generally means that Talent are contractually committed (often with conditions) to a Project.

Back-End: Can refer to either a Royalty or Participation.

Below-the-Line: Actual production costs (excluding Above-the-Line costs and certain miscellaneous costs described under Negative Cost).

Berne Convention: A copyright treaty among a number of nations, including the United States:

Box-Office Gross: Gross Receipts collected by motion picture theaters.

Budget: See Negative Cost.

Cash Break-Even: The point in time when a motion picture's Gross Receipts reach Net Profits, but using a low Distribution Fee. There can be several levels of Cash Break-Even using progressively higher Distribution Fees until Actual Break-Even.

Cash Method: An accounting method whereby expenses and income are reported when paid or received, rather than when incurred or accrued. Compare to Accrual Method.

Completion Bond: A contractual commitment issued by a Completion Guarantor agreeing to either (a) complete and deliver a picture on time or (b) repay the bank if timely delivery is not achieved. The Completion Bond fee is generally calculated as a percentage (from two to five percent, depending on market conditions) of the combined Above-the-Line and Below-the-Line costs (usually excluding costs relating to acquisition of the rights and payments to lead actors).

Co-Production: In a technical sense, a joint production between two companies in two separate countries pursuant to a co-production treaty between the countries. Now, generally used to refer to any form of partnership or joint venture relating to production of a film.

Completion Guarantor: A company issuing a Completion Bond.

Cross-Collateralized: When Gross Receipts from one picture or territory are used to recoup losses from another picture or territory.

Deal Memo: A term sheet or letter of intent, usually binding.

Deferment: A fixed payment to Talent that is payable out of Gross Receipts, usually after reaching Cash Break-Even:

Delivery: Delivery of the physical film elements for a motion picture.

DGA: Directors Guild of America.

Distribution Fee: A retained share of profits by the Distributor, usually charged as a percentage of Gross Receipts, and confusingly referred to as a "fee."

DVD: Digital Video Disk.

Distributor: The owner or licensee of motion picture rights that licenses such rights to third parties. Compare to Sales Agent.

Domestic Territory: The U.S. and Canada.

Droit Morale: Moral rights of authors and directors, typically respected in Europe, but not the U.S.

E&O Insurance: Errors and omission insurance. Insures against claims by third parties relating to exploitation of a motion picture (e.g., copyright, defamation, or trademark claims).

Exhibitor: Owner of a movie theater.

Exploit: To use a motion picture in any manner that generates Gross Receipts.

Film Rentals: The portion of Box-Office Gross paid by the theatrical Exhibitor to the Distributor.

Final Cut: The final edited version of a motion picture.

First Dollar Gross: A Participation that is calculated as a percentage of *all* Adjusted Gross Receipts (i.e., Gross Receipts less Off-the-Tops), although it is almost always offset against any up-front compensation paid.

First Look: Either a right of first negotiation or an option to purchase motion picture rights.

Foreign Territory: The world excluding the Domestic Territory.

Green Light: A motion picture is approved for production.

Gross Participant: Someone who is entitled to a share of Adjusted Gross Receipts, either First Dollar Gross or after a pre-defined point, such as after Actual Break-Even.

Gross Receipts: All gross revenues from a motion picture at a specified link in the distribution chain, such as either At-Source or received by the Distributor.

Hard Floor: Typically, a producer's own Participation is reduced by Participations paid to Talent, and a Hard Floor is a contractually defined point at which all further Participations are borne by the Distributor. For example, a producer may be entitled to a Participation equal to 50% of Net Profits, reduced by all other Participations, subject to a Hard-Floor of 10% of Net Profits.

Home Video Royalty: Typically, a contractual provision whereby only a percentage, typically 20%, of home video royalties are included in Gross Receipts, and the balance is retained by the Distributor.

Hold-Back: A contractual provision prohibiting a Distributor from Exploiting a motion picture until a specified time.

Loan-Out Company: A corporation that loans out the services of its sole shareholder to third parties. Typically, Loan-Out Companies are used by Talent.

Long-Form Contract: A full agreement containing all contractual provisions, including all "boilerplate."

Main Titles: Opening credits on a motion picture.

Merchandising Rights: The right to sell tangible property embodying either trademarks or copyrights from a motion picture (e.g., games and T-shirts).

Negative Cost: The cost of producing a motion picture, including Above-the-Line and Below-the-Line costs and certain miscellaneous costs, which include financing costs, the Completion Bond fee, and a contingency reserve – generally 10% of the Above-the-Line and Below-the-Line costs.

Negative Pick-Up: An agreement whereby a studio acquires substantial rights (typically, at least Domestic Rights) in a motion picture in consideration for a fixed payment due upon Delivery plus Royalties.

Net Profits: Gross Receipts minus all imaginable costs relating to the motion picture, including the Negative Cost (and interest thereon), Distribution Fees, Residuals, Distribution Costs, and, typically, Participations.

Non-Theatrical: Exploitation of a motion picture on small-venue screens, such as schools, churches, and military installations. Non-Theatrical does *not* mean "any media other than theatrical."

Off-the-Tops: Specific deductions taken from Gross Receipts in calculating Adjusted Gross, namely checking, collection, currency conversion, trade dues, taxes, and Residuals.

Output Deal: A contract requiring one party to acquire all motion pictures produced by the other party.

Overages: Can refer to either a (a) Participation or (b) Royalty.

Overhead: An arbitrary mark-up (such as by 15%) that is added to either Negative Cost or Distribution Expenses in calculating Participations and Overages.

Participations: Contingent payments to Talent based on a percentage of Gross Receipts or Net Profits from a motion picture.

P&A: Prints and Advertising.

Pay-or-Play: A contractual provision providing that if Talent is not used in a motion picture for any reason, they will be paid their full compensation (other than a Participation).

Pre-Production: The preparatory work that goes on during the three months prior to commencement of principal photography.

Pre-Sale: A sale of particular motion picture rights for a fixed payment upon Delivery plus Overages, which sale is entered into prior to completion of production for the motion picture.

Prints & Advertising: The cost of film prints and advertising expenses: one type of Distribution Expense.

Project: Usually refers to the status of a film prior to commencement of principal photography.

Recoupment: The right of a Distributor to recoup any Advance prior to paying Overages.

Release Print: The positive film print used by Exhibitors.

Residuals: Contingent payments owed to Talent and unions pursuant to the provisions of the collective bargaining agreements entered into with the unions (e.g., DGA, WGA, SAG).

Rolling [Actual or Cash] Break-Even: A reference to "rolling" means that Actual or Cash Break-Even is re-calculated from time-to-time based on cumulative expenses, rather than being based on the initial occurrence of Actual or Cash Break-Even. For example, 100% of Gross Receipts after Rolling Actual Break-Even is the same as Net Profits.

Royalty: Contingent payments based on a percentage of Gross Receipts or Net Profits paid by a Distributor to the licensor in consideration for a license of motion picture rights.

SAG: Screen Actors Guild.

Sales Agent: A party that acts as agent for the owner of the rights in arranging for distribution or Exploitation of a motion picture. Contrast to Distributor.

Soft Floor: Like a Hard Floor, except that additional Participations come off-the-top, and are thus partially borne by the producer, as opposed to being borne exclusively by the studio.

Subdistributor: A party licensed by a Distributor to Exploit a motion picture.

Studio: One of the major U.S. film distributors (e.g., Warner Brothers, Sony, Disney, MGM, Fox, Universal, and Paramount).

Talent: Generally refers to writers, directors, and actors.

Trades: *Variety* and the *Hollywood Reporter*.

WGA: Writers Guild of America.

2

MONEY MATTERS

Most Films Lose Money!

Schemers and Dreamers

Money In, Money Out, and Control

Keep it Simple!

Contract Basics

Sources of Financing

*"How do you net $5 million in the film industry?
Start with $10 million."* Old Hollywood adage.

MOST FILMS LOSE MONEY!

At first, I was going to title this section something neutral, such as
"Basic Economics of the Industry," but the point is so important, I
want to beat you over the head with it—*most films lose money*. This
simple fact has profound implications throughout the film industry,
and I will harp on it over and over.

The fundamental reason for this phenomenon is simple; if you were
trying to impress someone at a cocktail party, what would you rather say:
"I make movies" or "I make widgets"? Face it, the film industry is sexy,
and people like sex. Even if not of the direct ilk (a not infrequent motivation), most people who produce films are driven by the conscious or sub-
conscious sexiness of the industry. The law of supply and demand takes it
from there. For example, there is a wild oversupply of film productions—
approximately 600 to 700 per year—while only 200 or so obtain even a
decent release, permitting any return at all, much less a profit.

Comparing the film industry to the real estate industry is instruc-
tive. If a real estate developer built a $10 million building completely
on spec, the developer would hope to sell the building for a profit of
perhaps 50%. On the other hand, if a film is made for $10 million,
the film company considers itself wildly successful if it sells the film
for $10 million with the psychological comfort of a speculative back-
end net-profits interest that will never be paid.

The dire odds improve somewhat if the film company is also a
distributor, because it does not have to pay distribution fees to third
parties. Also, by controlling distribution, the film company can ensure the best chance for success of its films. The worst position to be
in is an independent film producer who hands over films to a third
party to distribute for a fee. Conversely, the best position to be in is

a distributor of other people's films for a fee, without paying any advance. It is commonly said that studios make money on distribution, not production. This is a different way of expressing the same thought: It is better to distribute your own films, and it is better yet to distribute the films of others.

The saving grace in the film industry is that when the rare blockbuster occurs, it can make up for the losses on a lot of other films. The film industry is a form of gambling, similar to wildcat oil drilling. The problem is that a lot of capital is required to make enough films to obtain the rare blockbuster, and few companies have the financial stamina to make it. This factor works strongly in the studios' favor, as they have the economic wherewithal to withstand a string of flops.

All of this has profound implications for the film industry, including the following:

• You develop a jaded eye when reviewing projections of future income. I have not yet seen projections for a new independent production company that did not show a rosy picture of ever-increasing profits. If the projections were honest, and were based on historical averages, they would show a downward spiral into bankruptcy.

• Independent production companies almost always have a finite life. In all my years of practice since 1981, every single one of my independent production clients (and there have been many) have gone out of business, often by bankruptcy. By the process of elimination, I have ended up representing more distribution companies, as they tend to stick around.

• You must be a wild gambler to invest equity in a single film only, or even in a small slate of films, particularly where the film company does not control distribution (unless, of course, my client is asking you to invest).

• You should be wary of spending a lot of time and money setting up a complex international tax plan to shelter all those boatloads of cash that will be rolling in. It would be wiser to spend the time and money setting up a structure that will permit the owners to deduct the tax losses that will inevitably occur.

- Never, ever, ever start production on a film without distribution locked-up in advance. Because of the vast oversupply of film productions, many films—even large-budget films—often can not obtain any distribution at all or obtain distribution only on pathetic terms.
- The film industry has a voracious appetite for money. Overall, the film industry could be viewed as a roving predator ever searching for the next victim to suck dry of cash.

SCHEMERS AND DREAMERS

Because most films lose money (have you heard that before?), the film industry is constantly searching for new and varied sources of capital to sate its appetite. This condition has let the industry fall prey to an endless parade of bottom feeders – the schemers and dreamers who purport to have the wherewithal to finance the film of your dreams. You *must* be able to spot the schemers and dreamers, or you will waste the majority of your precious time chasing chimeras. Let me suggest some time-tested techniques for identifying these idiots.

First, let's start with the dreamers – the pathetic individuals who honest-to-God believe that, through some scheme or another, they can raise all the financing in the world. These individuals are *far more prevalent* than the schemers (the frauds) and are much harder to spot, since they do not ask for money up front, so there is no obvious motivation for their actions. They are always, however, driven by less obvious desires: being "players," being treated like big-shots, the feeling of power, and hobnobbing with stars. They like being taken to lunch, and they particularly like being picked up by limousines. Even far short of that, they are more than happy to waste your time with important sounding phone calls and faxes. How to spot them:

- Look for a glazed-eye stare. No kidding.
- Question them in detail on what transactions they have *closed*. Demand references, and call them.

• Question them in detail on their alleged sources of financing, and insist on having some written proof (bank accounts, commitment letters, etc.) that the sources of financing are real. It may appear rude to request a bank statement of someone who is purporting to be a financial angel, but it must be done.

• Get on the computer and research news databases for any articles on them. Coming up empty will tell you volumes.

• Do basic background checks, such as verifying their résumés.

The schemers (the frauds), though less prevalent, are far more dangerous, because they are con artists out to steal your money. They usually have honed a professional demeanor, and they have their act down to a fine art. You can usually spot schemers because sooner or later their plans always boils down to this: Give them money now, and they will give you much more money later. Sometimes, it's as simple as a request for an advance reimbursement of expenses (I've seen it as low as a request for $400; fraud is cheap these days) to as elaborate as a request for perhaps up to $1 million, which is allegedly placed in escrow in order to release millions of dollars in financing. Whenever you hear a request for any payments prior to closing, you should immediately be on red alert. My early warning system for schemers includes the following:

• Undertake all the steps you would to identify a dreamer, listed above.

• Run litigation checks in the state and federal courts where they reside. All kinds of fun stuff can pop up.

• Whenever they get around to asking for the money up front, offer to double it if it is paid only upon a successful closing. If they refuse this offer, you know they are not willing to put their money where their mouth is.

The one thing in common with schemers and dreamers is that their financing schemes usually involve some elaborate multi-layered proposal that always reminds me of the old game of Mouse Trap: You drop the metal ball into a little basket, and after a series of related machinations all over the board, the plastic mouse finally gets trapped.

Whenever I hear how A will post collateral to B, who will issue a letter of credit to C, who will issue a guarantee to D, who will loan money to E, I always ask, "Why doesn't A just loan the money to E?" The truth is there is no good answer to this question, and you are being taken.

Curiously, most of the schemes involve the same buzz words; you should be wary if you hear the words "foreign bank," "bank guaranty," "letter of credit," or "escrow." Particularly be wary if you are told that your advance deposit is secured by any of the foregoing. If you hear all the words combined, run.

And please, never do what too many of my clients have done without telling me: commenced production or made contractual commitments to third parties based on the unverified promises of financing from schemers and dreamers. More than one film has had to have the plug pulled in mid-production because someone made the sorry mistake of relying on the words "trust me."

MONEY IN, MONEY OUT, AND CONTROL

Many transactions in the film industry do not fit within any standard paradigm. At the extreme, transactions can involve contributions of property, services, or money by a number of entities in different countries, all of which may end up owning various rights to recoupment, distribution rights, and profits in one or more underlying films. No matter how complex (or how simple) a transaction may be, it may always be understood if it is broken down into the three basic elements: Money in, money out, and control. Whenever I hear a highfalutin film financing transaction that I do not understand, I always ask for an explanation in terms of these three basic elements:

• *Money In*: Who is contributing money? What triggers the contribution? When do they contribute it? How much are they obligated to contribute? Who funds unforeseen losses? What is the legal mechanism for enforcing the contribution?

- *Money Out*: What is the order and priority for distributions of money? Are capital contributions returned first? Is there interest on the capital contributions? How are profits divided? Are the sources of distributions different for different parties?
- *Control*: Who has control? Is it joint, so any party can lock-up the others? Is it allocated (e.g., party A has creative control and party B has financial control)? Does one party have veto rights? Can control rights be transferred to a third party?

By asking these simple questions, you can have a basic understanding of any transaction in the film industry.

KEEP IT SIMPLE!

If you are doing the structuring, rather than trying to figure out the structure, keep it simple! You will have more than enough chaos without heaping it on yourself by starting off with an inordinately complex structure. The analogy is building the foundation of a tall building; cracks and fissures in the foundation will result in the entire edifice falling of its own weight. A well thought-out, solid, logical structure is far more important than the wording of the documents. Also, always remember the immutable law of quantum legal physics:

$$D = L^2$$

Which means that the number of *Days* it takes to close a transaction equals the number of *Lawyers* squared. Note that the relationship is logarithmic, not linear. This alone is adequate reason to keep the structure as simple as possible. Recently, a client decided to produce a film as a multi-country co-production in Europe on the theory that it would save money. So many lawyers were telling the client to do so many contradictory things that the film went vastly over-budget and ended up being taken over by the completion bond company. Not that these things never work, but forewarned is forearmed.

CONTRACT BASICS

The informality with which contracts are concluded in the film industry is staggering. Napkin deals do occur, and perhaps the majority of agreements are signed after the transaction is over, if at all. This informality is disastrous, and spawns the endless litigation for which the film industry is infamous.

The height of informality is the oral agreement, which should simply be thought of as an unenforceable moral promise, if that. Sadly, I have had many clients act in reliance on oral agreements, including commencing production, making pay-or-play commitments, and issuing press releases. DON'T DO IT! It ain't over 'til it's over, and it ain't over until a binding contract is signed.

One plague in the industry is the propensity to use "letters of intent," "term sheets," and "deal memos" (collectively referred to below as "deal memos"), instead of long-form binding contracts. This tendency is caused by the fast pace of the industry and the impossibility of closing the ponderous tomes that are used for the long-form contracts. However, most deal memos are rife with a number of fatal flaws, including the following:

• They are often ambiguous on the key issue of whether they are binding, which is inexcusable. At a minimum, they should clearly state whether they are intended to create legal obligations on the parties or are merely expressions of non-binding intent.

• They are invariably sloppy and ill-thought-out, because the drafters have the excuse that the "other issues" will be dealt with in the long-form contract. The problem is that the long-form contract rarely follows. The majority of the time, it is not even drafted; people simply rely on the deal memo and go on with their business.

• Quite often, the deal memo purports to incorporate one party's "standard terms and conditions" or, just as bad, incorporates "customary terms and conditions in the industry." In either case, the parties always argue about just what was intended by this ambiguous reference, as there are many gradations of "standard terms" and "customary terms."

Because of all of the foregoing problems, deal memos often end up in litigation, so they should be avoided at all costs unless absolutely necessary.

As alluded to above, the reason that people opt for deal memos is because long-form contracts can run fifty or more pages and include such absurdities as defining the words "and" and "or." In addition, long-form contracts often incorporate pages upon pages of boilerplate that merely restate the default rules that would be implied by law even in the absence of such language. The solution to both ambiguous deal memos and ponderous long-form contracts is to draft contracts that are short, concise, and final, which forces the drafter to think carefully about each word. The goal should be to give each contract the beauty and brevity of the equation, $E=MC^2$. Also, contracts are a whole lot easier to follow if they contain a table of contents and an alphabetical list of defined terms up front; it is inexcusable to force the reader to slog through the entire contract looking for the definition of every capitalized word they come across. Another suggestion is to drop all the long-winded recitals of facts, which don't amount to a hill of beans; every word in a contract should have legal significance.

The most important aspect of any contract is for your team to control the drafting, even if it costs more legal fees, because the battle can be won or lost at this stage. People usually negotiate off of what is in front of them, as opposed to what is not. They typically do not think about what is *not* in the draft. Also, by controlling the revision process, you control the wording of the resolution of each open issue, and ultimately you wear down the enemy.

And *never* accept that old saw: "This is our standard form contract; it can't be changed." The studios will always tell you this, particularly with respect to their lengthy exhibits defining net profits. (The best quip I've heard on these exhibits is from a producer who said that the top of each page should be labeled, "And here is another reason why you won't receive net profits.") Licensors, too, are fond of giving licensees a form license prepared by the American Film Marketing Association, and these licenses are grossly one-sided and unfair. Always attempt to be anointed as the drafter of every contract, but failing that, never accept a "standard form" contract at face; everything is negotiable.

Equity

So where do you find the money to make a film? Surely, you can just walk down to your local investment bankers and tell them how much money you want, and they will do a public or private placement for a reasonable fee. Right? Wrong. This is the least fruitful source of financing for the film industry. Unless you are a large company with a proven track record, do not bother calling an investment banker. You are far more likely to raise money from your family and friends than you are from an investment banker. In fact, family and friends are the source of most "seed" money.

Far and away, the most likely source of financing for any film project is film distributors, who are willing to pay for distribution rights. This can provide a direct source of financing – if the distributors fund production themselves – or, more likely, provides an indirect source of financing by permitting banks to loan against the distributors' commitments to pay on delivery. In other words, the distributors pay back the banks when the film is done.

Now and then, some film company or other comes up with what I refer to as "funny money" — money that seems to fall from heaven from some rich real estate or stock investor who is attracted by the sexiness of the industry and would like to go to a few wild Hollywood parties. This does happen, but rarely.

Foreign Financing

Foreign governments also provide direct and indirect film subsidies. One form of indirect subsidy comes from quota requirements. For example, the European Community ("EC") has passed a resolution requiring its members to implement legislation requiring a majority of television broadcasting time to be devoted to "European Works." This is a minimum requirement, and each EC country is free to be even more restrictive than this (France is clearly the leader). By establishing a minimum quota for "European Works," the legislation dramatically increases the value to broadcasters, and thus the sale prices, of qualifying films. For example, if there are two identical films, yet one of them qualifies as a "European Work," distributors in the EC will pay far more for the "European Work" because television broadcasters will, in turn, pay more.

A "European Work" generally requires the "authors" of the work to be European, and most countries interpret the word "authors" as the writer and director. In addition, the film must be shot within the EC. Some more restrictive countries, such as France, require the film to be shot in the local language. The requirements and procedures vary from country to country, so it is absolutely necessary to obtain a local advisor or producer to shepherd the project through.

Because it is so difficult to make a film meeting all the quota requirements of a single country, many countries have entered into co-production treaties permitting production activities within any of the signatory countries to count toward meeting the quota requirements. For example, a film produced in both France and the UK can qualify as meeting both the French and UK quota requirements, even if it would not meet either country's requirements separately. An important aspect of this approach is that it permits English-language films to meet the French quota requirement through the back-door of the co-production treaty. Heaven is when a film can somehow be produced in three co-production countries, permitting the film to meet the quota requirements for all three countries. This qualification will vastly increase the value of the film, as it can then be sold for a much higher amount in all three countries.

Over time, the word "co-production" came to be used to refer loosely to any arrangement where two or more parties were producing a film and sharing the costs. Thus, whenever you hear the word "co-production," you must be careful to identify what exactly is meant.

Other forms of government subsidies include the following:

• Some governments provide "loans" or equity contributions up to a percentage of production costs incurred in the country.

• Some governments permit free use of government production facilities or certain services or supplies.

• Some governments provide an indirect subsidy by providing tax benefits to resident taxpayers who fund production costs. These foreign tax shelters are not a pot of gold at the end of the rainbow; when the dust settles, they rarely fund more than 10% of a film's budget. Nonetheless, 10% of a budget is nothing to sneeze at. In most tax-shelter structures, the film is "sold" to a partnership of foreign taxpayers for a fixed sale price, and the partnership then "licenses" the film back to the producer in exchange for annual license payments. The producer is then required to deposit most of the sale proceeds into an escrow account to secure the producer's obligations to make the annual license payments, and the producer gets to pocket the balance (usually less than 10% after commissions). Some foreign tax shelters are a form of intentional subsidy for local production only. Other foreign tax shelters (e.g., in Germany) do not require any production in the local country, and are thus not designed to subsidize local production. In these cases, the tax benefits are usually an unintended loophole in the local tax system.

3

ENTITIES

Sole Proprietorship

General Partnership

Limited Partnership

C Corporation

S Corporation

Limited Liability Company

"If you want to study a Grand Faloon, remove the skin of a toy balloon."—Kurt Vonnegut, *Cat's Cradle*

To navigate the shoals of the business side of the film industry, you must have a basic understanding of the different types of legal entities. Every transaction—from the humblest to the noblest—involves a choice from the smorgasbord of entities, so it is important to know the basic business, legal, and tax distinctions between them.

SOLE PROPRIETORSHIP

A sole proprietorship is a legal nothing; it is merely an individual operating under a fictitious business name. These are often referred to as "dba's," because the person is *doing business as* so-and-so. The good news is that they are cheap and easy to create. The bad news is that because a sole proprietorship is not treated as a separate entity, it gives you no protection from liabilities. They are perfect entities to use if you are acting alone (they can only be owned by one individual) and if you would be responsible for all the liabilities anyway. The best example would be a consulting or other similar service business. Any lenders to the business would undoubtedly require your personal guarantee anyway, and you would be directly liable for any damage you caused, even if you operated through a corporation.

GENERAL PARTNERSHIP

A general partnership is deemed to be formed whenever two or more persons combine in a business enterprise to share profits and losses. It does not require any type of filing, and it is not possible to disclaim partnership status by contract (notwithstanding that almost every contract purports to do so). The broad definition of general partnership includes within it the ubiquitous "joint venture" and "co-production"—

the names many lawyers give to a film transaction when they do not know what else to call it. Since these arrangements will be characterized as partnerships anyway, it makes sense to structure and draft the transactions as partnerships to start with, to make sure that all the relevant issues are dealt with properly (i.e., money in, money out, and control).

In a general partnership, each partner has the ability to contractually bind the partnership vis-à-vis third parties, and the partnership is liable for acts taken by any of the partners in furtherance of the partnership's business. Worse yet, each of the partners is personally liable for all the debts of the partnership. For all of these reasons, it is not common to intentionally form an entity as a general partnership, although it is quite common to inadvertently do so by structuring a transaction as a "joint venture" or "co-production."

For tax purposes, general partnerships are treated as transparent; the income and loss of the partnership is passed through to the partners, who then deduct the losses (to the extent permissible) and pay taxes on the income.

LIMITED PARTNERSHIP

Limited partnerships are like general partnerships, with the following exceptions:

• To create a limited partnership, a filing must be made with the Secretary of State in the state where the partnership is formed.

• A limited partnership has two classes of partners—the general partners and the limited partners. The general partners have the right to manage and control the affairs of the partnership, and are liable for all the debts of the partnership. The limited partners do not have the right to manage or control the affairs of the partnership (although they typically have the right to vote on specific important matters), but they are not liable for any of the debts of the partnership.

In all other respects, limited partnerships are the same as general partnerships. For example, they are transparent for tax purposes; the income and loss of a limited partnership is passed through to its partners. Because the general partners are liable for the debts of a limited partnership, it is common to use a single corporation as the sole general partner of a limited partnership. This structure combines the limited liability of a corporation (discussed below) with the flexibility and tax transparency of a partnership.

Until the advent of limited liability companies (discussed later in this chapter), limited partnerships were the entity of choice for most film financing transactions.

C CORPORATION

A C corporation is just a good old-fashioned regular corporation. It is referred to as a C corporation to distinguish it from an S corporation, which is discussed in the subsequent section. The "C" and "S" refer to the Subchapter of the Internal Revenue Code that governs the respective corporations. Whenever a new client mentions owning a corporation, I always ask whether it is a C or an S corporation, as the answer has tremendous implications on almost any discussion that follows.

A C corporation is formed by filing articles of incorporation with the Secretary of State in the state where the corporation is formed. Ownership of a C corporation is evidenced by shares, and the owners are called shareholders. Unlike a partnership (both general and limited), none of the shareholders of a C corporation has any liability for the debts of the C corporation. For this reason, many lawyers to this day continue to blindly form C corporations, without thinking through the negative tax implications (discussed below), and without considering alternatives.

The shareholders of a C corporation elect a board of directors, who exercise ultimate control. The directors, in turn, appoint officers, such as the president, but the directors retain the ultimate power to replace the officers. Normal shares that are entitled to the residual profits of a C corporation are referred to as common shares. Shares that are entitled to some type of distribution preference over the common shares are referred to as preferred shares. For example, upon liquidation, preferred shares might be entitled to a preferential distribution equal to the initial amount paid to the corporation for the shares, but in return, the preferred shares might only receive a limited dividend during the life of the C corporation, similar to interest on a loan. Since it is all a matter of contract (evidenced by the articles of incorporation), it is also possible to have preferred shares participate in the profits like common stock, in which case the shares are called participating preferred shares.

In general, a C corporation is the *only* entity that can go public. However, if you have grandiose dreams of ultimately going public, you do not need to use a C corporation until that magic day arrives; you can and should use something else until then, and you can simply convert it to a C corporation when you go public.

Far and away, the single most important detriment of a C corporation is that it is *not* transparent for tax purposes, which results in the extraordinary burden of double taxation; the C corporation is taxed on income it earns, and the shareholders are taxed again when that income is distributed to them. In addition, any losses are locked-up in the C corporation and may not be deducted by the shareholders.

The *only* time that you would not be concerned with double taxation is when you are positive that you can bail out the income of the C corporation to the shareholders in the form of deductible compensation. The primary example is when all the income earned by the C corporation is attributable to loaning out the services of its sole shareholder, and these C corporations are referred to as loan-out corporations. It is quite common for talent (i.e., directors, writers, and actors) to use loan-out corporations to obtain various tax benefits, such as the ability to deduct numerous otherwise non-deductible expenses. As an example, assume that an actor renders services to his wholly-owned loan-out corporation, and the corporation loans out his services to a studio for $10 million. The loan-out corporation then pays the actor $9 million as deductible compensation, and pays another $1 million of deductible expenses (which would have been non-deductible if paid directly by the actor). In this manner, the loan-out corporation has no taxable income, and the actor has only $9 million of taxable income.

S CORPORATION

Except for their unique tax aspects and restrictions, S corporations are identical to C corporations in every way: They are formed under the same corporate law by filing articles of incorporation with the Secretary of State, and they are owned by shareholders who elect directors, etc. The big difference is that the shareholders must affirmatively elect to become an S corporation, in which case the corporation is treated as transparent for tax purposes, and the income and loss of the S corporation is passed through to its shareholders. Thus, S corporations combine advantages of both corporations and partnerships; the shareholders are not liable for the corporate debts, and an S corporation is not subject to double taxation, as a C corporation is. (However, some states impose a small tax on an S corporation's net income; e.g., California imposes a 1.5% tax.)

There are, however, numerous disadvantages with an S corporation, the most important of which are the following:

• An S corporation cannot have more than 75 shareholders. Thus, an S corporation cannot be publicly traded.

• With minor exceptions, all the shareholders must be individuals who are U.S. citizens or residents. This precludes ownership by any type of entity, such as a partnership, C corporation, or limited liability company.

• An S corporation can have only common shares. It cannot have preferred shares or any other type of preferential equity ownership. This restriction precludes every type of standard equity financing, as an S corporation cannot provide the equity financiers with any kind of preference on distributions.

All in all, it is like playing tennis in a straitjacket, and any footfault may result in the disastrous consequence of inadvertently becoming a C corporation, with its attendant double taxation. In general, therefore, it is best to steer far afield from S corporations.

LIMITED LIABILITY COMPANY

Limited liability companies ("LLCs") are manna from heaven. The owners are not liable for the debts of the entity, as with a corporation, and LLCs are taxed on a transparent basis, identical to partnerships. They thus combine the advantages of both corporations and partnerships, without the restrictions of S corporations. They are absolutely the entity of choice for almost every film company, with the limited exceptions discussed above under the various types of entities.

An LLC can be most readily understood by comparing it to a corporation. In fact, most LLC terminology is simply a modification of corresponding corporate terminology, as illustrated below:

LLC Terminology	Corporate Terminology
Articles of Organization	Articles of Incorporation
Operating Agreement	Bylaws
Member	Shareholder
Manager	Director
Membership Interest	Shares

An LLC is formed by filing articles of organization with the Secretary of State in the state where the LLC is formed. The LLC is either governed directly by its members, or its operating agreement may provide that the members elect managers (who may or may not be members), who in turn run the LLC. As with partnerships, LLCs have complete flexibility; whatever the mind of man can imagine can be written into the operating agreement (such as special allocations of income or control).

As mentioned above, an LLC is transparent for tax purposes. If it has two or more members, an LLC is characterized as a partnership for tax purposes. If it is owned by a single member, it is disregarded as a separate entity and is treated as part of the owner. This gets tricky: for *state law* purposes, a single-member LLC is treated as a separate entity, providing limited liability to its owner, while for *tax purposes* it is completely disregarded and treated as part of the owner. This is an extraordinary result that was not possible prior to the introduction of LLCs. Although California tax law follows this tax characterization, California does not currently authorize single-member LLCs. Thus, it is necessary to form single-member LLCs in another state, such as Delaware.

The only negative of LLCs is that some states charge a premium for using them. For example, in California LLCs are not only required to pay the same $800 annual minimum tax that corporations and limited partnerships are, but they are also required to pay an additional tax roughly equal to .16% of their gross income, with the tax capped at $7,785 in 1999. This is a small price to pay for all the advantages provided by LLCs. If someone in the film industry asks, "What entity should I use . . . , " you can shout, "LLC!" and be right 99% of the time without even hearing the rest of the question.

Because the importance and prevalence of LLCs, a sample form operating agreement for a California LLC is included as Form A in the appendix to this book.

POP QUIZ: (Cover the answer below.) What are the two instances where it makes sense to use a C corporation?

First, when you go public. Second, as a loan-out corporation.

4

PRIVATE OFFERINGS

IN GENERAL

Making films requires financing, and lots of it. Large companies have access to the public securities market and are also able to obtain bank loans under revolving lines of credit. Companies formed to produce one film, however, are at a significant disadvantage, as neither of these alternatives are available to them. One financing method that is available to these companies is a private offering, which entails raising financing from a relatively small group of investors.

Most private offerings are placed with investors who have a pre-existing personal or business relationship with the "promoter" (the person attempting to raise the money). Thus, the promoter's first step is to determine whether the promoter has a realistic chance of raising the necessary financing from the promoter's family, friends, and business acquaintances. If not, it is generally not worth the cost and time of preparing the documentation for a private offering, because raising film-financing money from strangers is an extremely rare occurrence.

For all film financings, a legal entity (the "issuer") must be formed to receive the funds and own the film. In most cases, the promoter and the investors will seek limited liability, which means that the legal entity will either be a corporation, a limited partnership with a corporate general partner, or a limited liability company. As discussed in Chapter 3, the entity of choice has become the limited liability company (an LLC), because it offers the simplicity and limited liability of a corporation, combined with the transparent tax treatment of a partnership.

The specific business and economic terms of a private offering are limited only by the imagination. For example, the investment can be structured as a loan or as equity. If structured as a loan, the issues to be considered include: (a) making the loan secured or unsecured, (b) making the loan recourse (with a right to sue to collect) or nonrecourse (no right to sue, but secured by property), (c) providing a guarantee by the promoter, and (d) providing for an "equity kicker," which means some form of a share of profits from the film.

If the investment is structured as equity, the issues to be considered include: Will the investors be entitled to a priority distribution, either from operations or on liquidation? What control rights or approval rights will the investors have, and what percentage of the entity will they own? In a typical private offering for films, the investment is structured as equity (instead of debt), and the promoter retains all significant control rights. The promoter is typically entitled to a below-market fee for any services rendered in connection with the film, and the investors are entitled to 100% of all other net profits until they have been repaid their investment and, often, interest on the investment as well. All remaining net profits are typically split 50/50 between the promoter and the investors.

SECURITIES LAWS

There are two primary reasons why a promoter should be concerned with complying with the securities laws: First, failure to comply effectively gives the investors a right to sell their investment back to the promoter in exchange for repayment of their full investment. Thus, failure to comply with the securities laws effectively makes the promoter personally liable for repayment of the investment. Second, intentional failure to comply with the securities laws can be punished as a criminal offense. One or both of these two consequences should be enough to get the promoter's attention.

Under the case law, the conservative approach is to assume that the definition of "security" includes *every* investment, with the following exceptions:

1. Loans from banks;

2. A general partnership interest in a partnership or a managing member interest in a limited liability company if the general partner or managing member has meaningful management and control rights; and

3. The sale of a profits interest to a single investor (for those interested, see *Marine Bank v. Weaver*, 455 U.S. 551 (1982)).

Thus, when investors are issued stock in a corporation, limited partnership interests in a limited partnership, membership interests in a limited liability company, or profits interests in a film, the transactions are almost always treated as the issuance of securities. Even a secured loan (other than from a bank) may be treated as a security. Because of the draconian consequences for failure to comply with the securities laws, the best rule of thumb is: When in doubt, comply.

REGISTRATION AND EXEMPTIONS

One requirement of the securities laws is that prior to the issuance of any securities, the proposed transaction must be registered with the Securities and Exchange Commission ("SEC"). This is a complex and expensive process that would make most private offerings impossible. Fortunately, however, there are a number of exemptions from registration, the more important of which are summarized below.

Rule 504. The issuer may raise up to $1 million without registration during any twelve-month period in reliance upon Rule 504. However, this rule contains prohibitions on both general solicitation of investors and on advertisements, but no requirements relating to the sophistication (or lack thereof) of the investors. The issuer is obligated to file Form D with the SEC not later than 15 days after the first sale pursuant to the offering.

Rule 506. Rule 506 offerings have no dollar amount limitations, but these offerings are limited to "accredited investors," which are defined as follows:

- A natural person whose net worth (together with their spouse, if any) exceeds $1,000,000.
- A natural person who had an individual income in excess of $200,000 (or $300,000 including spouse) in each of the two most recent years, and who reasonably expects an income in excess of that amount in the current year.

- An entity that has over $5 million of gross assets and that was not formed for the specific purpose of making the investment.
- An entity owned solely by one or more of the foregoing.

General solicitation as well as general advertising is strictly prohibited in a Rule 506 offering. There is no limitation on the number of accredited investors. As with a Rule 504 offering, the issuer is obligated to file Form D with the SEC not later than 15 days after the first sale. Securities issued pursuant to a Rule 506 offering must have a restrictive legend restricting resales, and the issuer is obligated to take reasonable care to limit potential resales.

Rule 147. Rule 147 is commonly known as the "intrastate exemption." Generally, the issuer must be organized and doing business in the state in which it intends to offer the investment, the offerees and investors must be strictly limited to residents of that state, and the proceeds must be used only in that state. Because it is extremely important that the issuer maintain the intrastate nature of the offering, the issuer should confirm the name and address of every potential offeree prior to any offer being made. In addition, any written materials provided to a prospective offeree should be numbered, and a precise record of who got what and where they got it should be maintained by the issuer. There is no limitation on the number of offerees or investors so long as the foregoing requirements are met. There is no limit on the amount of the offering, and there are no federal filing requirements. Interests issued pursuant to a Rule 147 offering may only be sold to other residents of the state for a period of nine months after the offer closes. The issuer is obligated to take steps to limit interstate resales, including putting an appropriate legend on the securities and otherwise disclosing the restriction.

STATE SECURITIES LAWS

Every state has securities laws, commonly referred to as "Blue Sky" laws, controlling the offer, issuance, and sale of securities in that state. Many states require some type of filing with their securities commission. Accordingly, when an issuer contemplates offering securities in a particular state pursuant to a Rule 504 or 147 exemption from federal registration, the Blue Sky laws of all states in which the offer is to be made must be consulted. However, to avoid this complication for offerings only to accredited investors, a federal statute preempts all state Blue Sky laws with respect to federal Rule 506 offerings (i.e., an offer to only accredited investors) as long as Form D is filed in each state where the securities are offered or sold and all applicable state filing fees are paid.

The exemption most commonly relied on in California arises under California Corporations Code section 25102(f). In summary, this section imposes the following requirements:

    a.   The offering is limited to a maximum of thirty-five non-accredited investors (i.e., excluding certain persons, such as "accredited investors").

    b.   The investors or their advisors must be financially sophisticated or must have a pre-existing personal or business relationship with the promoter.

    c.   No advertising is permitted. Thus, even when advertising is permitted under the federal exemption (e.g., Rule 504), use of advertising will violate California's exemption.

    d.   Form 25102f must be filed with the California Secretary of State.

DISCLOSURE

Even when an offering is exempt from federal or state registration, SEC Rule 10b-5 essentially obligates an issuer of securities to disclose all material information to offerees and investors. What information is material to a particular offering varies from transaction to transaction. As a rule of thumb, the issuer must disclose all information an investor might reasonably need to make an intelligent decision with respect to the offer. At a minimum, the private placement memorandum ("PPM") should describe the offering, including:

- The amount to be raised;
- The structure of the company;
- The relative priority of repayment of the investment, any third-party contracts;
- A description of management and their compensation packages;
- A synopsis of the film;
- A one-page budget for the picture; and
- The full text of the governing document (i.e., the operating agreement for an LLC).

Given the risky nature of investing in an independent film, certain risks should always be disclosed (e.g., films are inherently risky and most films lose money). In addition, transaction-specific risks must also be disclosed. For example, if the issuer intends to make a film utilizing a screenplay to which it does not own the rights, failure to disclose this tidbit of information would be a material omission.

As a general rule, it is unwise for the PPM to include any financial projections, because they most likely will be attached as Exhibit "A" to a complaint against the promoter for violating the securities laws. When reality does not match the projections, it is extraordinarily difficult to justify the basis for the projections in the first place. Most investors know that the film industry is risky and thus take projections with little more than a grain of salt anyway.

It is more productive to sell the "sexiness" of the industry by including color photographs or artwork showing the intended mood or look of the film, and the more risqué the better. Potential investors are far more likely to read the PPM and invest based on this approach. Best of all, no one can complain of a securities law violation based on this type of emotional sell.

SUBSCRIPTION AGREEMENT

Each investor should execute a "subscription agreement," which is a short agreement subscribing to the investment and containing certain representations and warranties relating to the offer. In particular, where the issuer is relying on the fact that all investors are accredited (i.e., Rule 506), the investors typically will represent and warrant such status to the issuer in the subscription agreement.

If the promoter is relying on California Corporations Code section 25102(f), the subscription agreement should state that the investors or their advisors are financially sophisticated or that they have a pre-existing personal or business relationship with the promoter. The subscription agreement should recite that the investor is aware of the specific risks with the offering.

The simplest procedural approach is to include a power of attorney in the subscription agreement, giving the promoter the authority to execute the actual governing agreement (e.g., the operating agreement for a limited liability company). In this manner, the investors need sign only one document to close the offering.

FINDERS

A common question that comes up is whether the promoter can pay third parties for finding or soliciting investors. The short answer is "no." Although in theory it is permissible to pay a "finder" who does *no more* than simply give phone numbers of potential investors, this limitation is rarely adhered to in practice. As soon as the "finder" makes *any* effort to describe or sell the investment, the "finder" will need to be licensed as a securities broker to receive a commission.

PUBLIC OFFERINGS

A public offering is an offering that is registered with the SEC. Because of the extraordinary transaction costs, a public offering cannot be profitably undertaken to raise less than about $5 million. Because the offering is registered, it has no investor restrictions—it can be offered to widows and orphans. Undertaking a registered public offering does not automatically mean the securities are publicly traded, although the two usually go hand in hand (as is assumed for this discussion). In some cases, a public offering is the last resort of a troubled company that must either go bankrupt or go public. The benefits of a public offering include the following:

- It aids the raising of further debt or equity financing, including by further public offerings.
- It increases name recognition and market credibility. There is a certain amount of bravado to going public.
- Typically, a given amount of equity sells for a far higher price in a public offering than in a private offering; widows and orphans are not that financially sophisticated and tend to overpay.
- It creates liquidity for shareholders (although not much for major shareholders, officers, and directors) and a readily ascertainable market value.

Public offerings, however, are mixed blessings that carry with them a number of detriments, particularly for companies that do not have the management depth and discipline to deal with the extensive ongoing reporting requirements. In these cases, a public offering is more likely to lead to disastrous shareholder litigation than to continued success. The main detriments of a public offering include the following:

- Horrendous transaction costs, including legal, accounting, and publication costs of approximately $200,000, plus commissions.
- Public disclosure of all dirty linen, both past and future, in the form of quarterly and annual reports.
- Requirement of approval of the shareholders for more transactions.
- Vastly increased exposure of management to shareholder suits, which are far more frequent than for private corporations because of the large number of shareholders and public scrutiny.

Because of all of the foregoing, management tends to hunker down, not take risks, and to focus on short-term profitability. This is the single most important detriment—I have seen management spend weeks trying to devise a transaction that would increase reported *gross* earnings (which, remarkably, analysts and public shareholders apparently care about) even though it would not increase actual *net* earnings one penny.

5

THE BUDGET

DOMINANCE OF THE BUDGET

A film's budget plays a dominant role throughout the film's life cycle—with implications going far beyond the mere cost of the film. Perhaps the most tangible aspect of a film's budget is that the amount that distributors will pay for a film is almost always calculated as a percentage of the budget (the "budget/sales corollary"), regardless of the script, the cast, or anything else. For example, if two identical films with the same script and stars were made, and one was made for $50 million and one was made for $10 million, the one made for $50 million would typically sell for five times more than the film made for $10 million. No kidding. Thus, as a film's budget increases, so do the prices distributors will pay for the film. There may be slight variations, but not much. The first question asked by all distributors is "What is the budget?" The higher the budget, the more the film sells for, so there is a perverse tendency to inflate the cost of films. Producers often increase the budget for a picture by tagging on additional inflated "producer fees" or "overhead charges" for themselves, which are nothing more than a mark-up to the true cost of the film. When all else fails, one irresistible tendency is to greatly exaggerate the true budget in order to jack-up prices.

Another impact of the budget is that many related costs rise and fall with the amount of the budget. For example, talent will charge far more on a big-budget film than they will for their identical services on a low-budget film. Similarly, premiums paid to completion guarantors and insurance companies are calculated as a percentage of the budget, not flat amounts, and every film budget includes a contingency for possible excess costs, always expressed as a percentage of the budget—usually 10%. Finally, all the guilds have fee structures that are higher for high-budget films.

The net result is that any proposed increase to a film's budget has a ripple effect that can more than double the proposed increase. As one stark example I worked on, a $20 million star was added to a $6 million film. The budget of the film did not go to $26 million—it went to over $40 million. The good news was that because of the budget/sales corollary, the pre-sales increased by more than enough to cover the increased budget. Go figure.

ITEMS INCLUDED WITHIN THE BUDGET

In general, the budget includes all costs relating to the development, production, and post-production of a film. Thus, the budget includes, for example, costs of acquiring the script, payments to talent, and production costs. There are also a number of interesting inclusions and exclusions, discussed below:

• Deferments and participations paid to talent are *not* included in the budget. For example, if talent is paid $20 million up front, that amount will be included in the budget. On the other hand, if talent foregoes the upfront payment of $20 million in exchange for a much larger, albeit contingent, deferment or participation, the budget will be reduced by $20 million. This, in turn, will have the completely crazy impact of reducing the amount that the film can be sold for because of the budget/sales corollary.

• The budget *does* include self-charged "producer fees" paid to the producer. When I first heard this, it really threw me. For example, if a film that really cost $10 million were sold for $12 million, to me, the budget was $10 million, and the producer had made a $2 million profit. Silly me. I soon learned that the budget was really $12 million, and the producer had received a "producer fee" of $2 million, which was included in the budget. Again, the tentacles of the budget/sales corollary at work. Once I got my brain around this, the rest was easy. Since most films are financed with loans to single-purpose entities, another way to view what is happening is that the producer is saying to the lender, "Please increase the loan by the amount of my producer fees, so that I can take out at least some guaranteed level of profits up front. We will increase the budget by this amount, which should increase sales necessary to repay you, the lender, because of the budget/sales corollary." Most lenders go along with this.

- The budget almost always includes an artificial mark-up referred to as "overhead," usually approximately 10-15% of the budget. For example, if the budget is really $10 million, the producer will charge and retain an additional $1.5 million to purportedly cover its overhead. As with producer fees, this is really just a disguised way of making a profit on the film. A more honest approach would be to say that the budget is $10 million, but the producer wants to make at least $1.5 million of profit. Good luck.

- There are a number of miscellaneous items that arguably should not be included as part of the budget, but are. These include all financing costs, including interest and fees, all legal fees relating to the film through delivery, and the cost of the completion guaranty. However, the cost of delivery of the film print to distributors is typically treated as a distribution cost, and is generally not included in the budget.

- Every budget includes a contingency for potential excess costs, always expressed as a percentage of the budget—usually 10%. The contingency is included in the budget for purposes of the budget/sales corollary (i.e., upping prices), even though it may never be spent.

ABOVE THE LINE, BELOW THE LINE, AND OTHER

By industry practice, the budget is divided into "above-the-line" costs, "below-the-line" costs, and "other" costs. The above-the-line costs include the costs for the rights, producer, and talent. For example, above-the-line costs include the costs of acquiring the underlying rights, script costs, producer fees, and payments to key talent (director and main actors). The below-the-line costs are basically all costs of production and post-production. Other costs include financing costs, the completion guaranty fee, and the contingency. The reason that these categories are relevant is that a number of items (such as insurance premiums and completion bond fees) are often calculated as a percentage of the budget, but excluding all or a portion of the above-the-line costs or other costs. Even the contingency itself may exclude certain above-the-line costs. Also, the below-the-line costs are used as a rough indication of the value of production going "on the screen," as opposed to payments for rights, talent, etc. Insiders are always using this lingo, so you need to know it.

WHERE DOES THE BUCK STOP?

The amount of the budget can vary widely depending on the neurosis of the director. If the director is a wild perfectionist, demanding absolutely perfect special effects and endless retakes, the budget will increase dramatically. (Witness anything done by James Cameron and Francis Ford Coppola.) Unless the person preparing the initial budget has a firm grip on the director's psychological predilections, the budget will be no more than a wild guess. Sooner or later, the budget will be handed to the lender with a request to fund the budget. The lender will, in turn, hand it to the completion guarantor with a request to guarantee that the film can be made for that budget. As you can guess, the buck stops with the completion guarantor, who is usually the first to seriously question the budget. Almost without exception, the completion guarantor demands an increase in the budget in order to give the completion guarantor more breathing room. For example, the completion guarantor may request a reduction or deferment of fees to the producer or an increase to the contingency. The completion guarantor will then make everyone sign in blood that they can live with the budget. If the budget calls for Godzilla to be played by a ten-dollar hand puppet, the director better not come whining later to the completion guarantor requesting funding for a life-size model. Completion guarantees are discussed in detail in Chapter 8.

6

GUILDS

INTRODUCTION

The primary guilds of concern to the film industry are the Writers Guild of America (WGA), Directors Guild of America (DGA), and Screen Actors Guild (SAG). As their names imply, these guilds cover writers, directors, and actors, respectively. In essence, the guilds require exclusivity—the members of the guilds may work only for companies signing with the guilds ("guild signatories"), and guild signatories may only employ guild members. Film companies are thus forced to become guild signatories in order to engage guild members as talent, and talent are forced to become guild members to work for guild signatories.

JURISDICTION

In a number of cases, the guilds do not have jurisdiction over the production of a film for various reasons. For example, if a film is produced outside of the United States by a foreign company that is not a guild signatory and is not soliciting guild members from within the United States, guild members are permitted to work on the film, in which case their services are not covered by the guild agreement.

Another example is that, by law, the guild agreements are only supposed to apply to employees, not independent contractors. However, the guilds have adopted an expansive interpretation of their authority in this area. For example, many writers, directors, and actors furnish their services through "loan-out corporations," which are corporations they wholly own to furnish their services to production companies. In these cases, the loan-out corporations are independent contractors with respect to the production companies, but the guilds assert jurisdiction over their services, and the industry has acquiesced to this position.

All subsidiaries of a guild signatory are automatically deemed signatories of the guild agreements. However, the guilds do *not* have jurisdiction with respect to the *owner* of a guild signatory or the owner's affiliates, including parent and affiliated corporations. For example, assume that company A owns companies B1 and B2, and company B1 owns company C. In this case, if company B1 signs with a guild, the guild will have jurisdiction with respect to companies B1 and C, but it will *not* have jurisdiction with respect to companies A and B2. Thus, production companies should make sure that the guild signatory is a subsidiary company, not the ultimate parent, in order to leave room for the parent to set up new subsidiaries that will not be subject to guild jurisdiction.

Many guild signatories escape guild jurisdiction by entering into production, finance, and distribution agreements ("PFD agreements") with "unrelated" production companies (typically owned by the individual producer). Pursuant to the PDA agreement, the guild signatory completely controls the production company, but the production is not subject to the guild agreements (except for residuals, discussed below) because the production company is not a guild signatory and the guild signatory does not technically own the production company.

GENERAL IMPACT

The general impact of the guilds is to increase the cost of a film in various ways. The first and most obvious way is to set minimum prices for specified work done by guild members. Typically, the minimums depend on the type of product (e.g., television or theatrical) and the budget of the film. The guilds also drastically increase the cost of a film by requiring the payment of residuals (discussed below). Other intangible benefits to their members, such as required fringe benefits and perks, also increase the cost of a film.

RESIDUALS

All the guilds require film companies to pay residuals to the guilds and their members. The majority of the payments made to guild members are contingent compensation, but some payments are also made to the guilds' health and pension benefit plans. Residuals are contingent payments based on a percentage of a film's revenue. They are calculated in the following manner:

• Residuals on theatrical films are only calculated based on video and television revenues, not on theatrical revenues.

• Residuals are always calculated based on gross revenues. Thus, they are payable regardless of whether the producer makes a profit. From the producer's perspective this is, by far, the worst aspect of residuals.

• For film companies that distribute their own videos (as opposed to sublicensing video rights), only 20% of video gross revenues are included in gross receipts.

The guild agreements are not designed to address independent film companies that use sales agents to pre-sell rights to various foreign countries. The guild agreements are negotiated between the studios and the guilds, and no one at the table is particularly thinking about how the agreements apply to independent film companies. The guilds have become increasingly aggressive in attempting to enforce the payment of residuals by independent film companies, adopting the following tactics:

• Placing a security interest on the film (giving the guilds the right to foreclose on the film if residuals are not paid).

• SAG often refuses to grant clearance to permit its members to work on a film until distributors of the film have agreed to assume residuals.

• The guilds were successful in enacting an amendment to the Copyright Act in 1998. This amendment treats distributors, in most cases, as having automatically assumed the obligation to pay residuals. However, because the Copyright Act generally does not apply outside the boundaries of the U.S., and based on the wording of the amendment, it is not clear that this provision applies to foreign distributors.

• The guilds have taken the position that residuals should be calculated "at source," i.e., based on gross receipts of the lowest level subdistributor, including foreign subdistributors.

- The guilds have taken the position that when a distributor licenses video rights to a third party (as opposed to the distributor undertaking video distribution itself), 100% of the payments received are included in gross receipts, as opposed to only 20% being included, as in the case of self-distribution. Not surprisingly, distributors have taken the position that only 20% of third-party license video royalties should be included in calculating residuals.

- When a production company receives a minimum guarantee from a distributor under a pre-sale agreement, the guilds take the position that residuals must be calculated based on the *greater of* (a) an allocable portion of the minimum guarantee (with the allocation generally being one-third theatrical, one-third video, and one-third television) or (b) the gross receipts of the distributor for the particular media. This is an obviously unfair one-way ratchet. Residuals should either be calculated based on an allocation of the minimum guarantee, or they should be calculated based on distributor's gross, but it is completely unfair for the guilds to calculate residuals based on the greater of the two numbers.

PRODUCTION DEPOSITS

SAG usually requires independent film companies to deposit with SAG an amount equal to 40% of the first $100,000 payable to talent (in order to secure the payment of the base compensation to talent) plus 13.15% of the first $200,000 payable to talent (in order to secure the payment of the pension, health, and welfare benefits to SAG equal to such amount). Additional amounts may be required to secure various fringe benefits, such as overtime, meals, etc. Critically, SAG does not use these deposits to actually make the payments in question; the payments are simply held hostage as security to make sure the film company actually makes the payments directly. If things go well, these deposits will be refunded, but in the meantime, these deposits directly increase a picture's budget, because the funds to make the deposit must come from somewhere. In addition to effectively increasing the budget, there is a risk that SAG will simply hold onto the deposit to secure residuals (which has occurred on at least one occasion), instead of refunding it to the film company. One way to reduce the deposit is to set up your own escrow, outside of SAG. The funds deposited in this escrow can be used to make the actual payments to talent or SAG. In this case, however, SAG requires the outside escrow to cover the talent's entire base compensation (not just 40% of the first $100,000).

7

LOANS AND SECURITY INTERESTS

Introduction

Terminology

Lenders and Borrowers

Interest, Fees, and Costs

Commitment Letters

Affirmative and Negative Covenants

Legal Opinions

Order of Payments

Insurance-Backed Financing

Security Interests

> Introduction
>
> Attachment and Perfection
>
> Foreclosure
>
> The Logical Extreme

Forms

"Neither a lender nor a borrower be."
William Shakespeare, *Hamlet*

INTRODUCTION

The blood in the veins of film financing is loans — far and away the major source of film financing. Most films are financed entirely with loans, and only the odd-bird film does not have a loan somewhere in sight. It thus behooves anyone interested in the film business to have a basic understanding of this important source of film financing.

TERMINOLOGY

Before proceeding, we need to define specific terminology applicable to loans. Any capitalized words in the definitions are separately defined.

Gap Financing. A single-film loan in an amount that exceeds the existing pre-sales. The "gap" is the amount by which the film's budget exceeds the existing pre-sales.

Line of Credit. A revolving loan (i.e., the borrower can repay and reborrow the amount of the loan from time to time). It is always Recourse and is usually Secured by all of the borrower's assets.

Nonrecourse. Referring to a loan that is not Recourse; i.e., in the event of default, the lender is not permitted to go after all of the borrower's assets; the lender is only permitted to proceed against the security for the loan. Thus, Nonrecourse loans are always Secured. Most film loans purport to be Recourse, but are effectively Nonrecourse because the borrower is a Single-Purpose Entity that owns only one film. Although the lender can proceed against all of the borrower's assets, since the only asset is the one film, the net result is the equivalent of a Nonrecourse loan Secured by the one film.

Perfected. To give constructive notice to the world of a security interest, typically by recording the security interest with the appropriate government agency.

Recourse. Referring to a loan that permits the lender to hang the borrower by its heels and go after every possible asset the borrower has or will have.

Secured. Referring to a loan that gives the lender a security interest in specified property of the borrower. In the event of default, this permits the lender to foreclose on the property in full or partial payment of the loan. More importantly, if the security interest is properly Perfected, the lender's claim to the property cannot be trumped by any subsequent assignments or security interests. The real benefit of a security interest is to permit the lender to retain its claim to the property in the event of a bankruptcy of the borrower.

Unsecured. Referring to a loan that is not Secured. An unsecured loan is always Recourse, or the lender would have no remedy at all.

Single-Purpose Entity. A company formed to produce one film. Lenders often require a Single-Purpose Entity to be the borrower to avoid being entangled in any potential bankruptcy of affiliates.

LENDERS AND BORROWERS

Borrowers range all the way from single-purpose entities, doing one-off low-budget films, to the large studios, financing an entire year's slate of films. Lenders range all the way from private individual lenders (a rarity) to large commercial banks that extend lines of credit for hundreds of millions of dollars to the studios.

For studios, obtaining loans is relatively easy; they can either obtain large lines of credit, or they can use negative pick-ups. Under this latter structure, the bank loans to a special-purpose entity formed to produce the film, and the studio commits to pay the cost of the film on delivery, repaying the bank.

For independent film companies, the transactions are more difficult and complex. In the absence of some other form of equity or collateral, it is generally necessary to first obtain pre-sales, whereby foreign distributors commit to pay a specified amount upon delivery, and then to obtain a loan secured by the film and the pre-sales, together with gap financing for the balance needed to produce the film. The most risky portion of the loan is the gap financing. Because gap financing is a risky endeavor that requires a thorough knowledge of the distributors, sales agents, and producers, it is a specialized niche market. At any given point in time, there are only a handful of lenders making any significant amount of gap loans, and the road is full of dead bodies.

INTEREST, FEES, AND COSTS

Interest comes in many different flavors. Long gone are the days of fixed interest at a specified rate over the term of a loan. Almost without exception, interest is specified as being a certain percentage above a floating variable rate, such as LIBOR (the London Inter Bank Offering Rate) or prime. In addition, particularly with gap financing, the lender commonly obtains some type of contingent participation in the revenues from the film, such as a specified percentage of net or gross revenues.

In addition to interest, lenders typically are paid some up-front fee, usually expressed as a percentage ("points") of the amount of the loan. For example, a two-point commitment fee equals two percent of the amount of the loan.

Lenders also want to be reimbursed their legal fees for preparation of the loan. This issue, in particular, can be remarkably unfair unless the legal fees are capped at a reasonable amount. Otherwise, the lender's lawyers are motivated to rocket into hyperspace on every issue, and the borrower has the pleasure of paying for this torture. To add to the fun, if the lender's lawyers are successful at killing the loan (which sometimes appears to be their ultimate agenda), the borrower is usually still liable for their legal fees under the terms of most commitment letters. In one extreme case I saw, a borrower was left with a tab for $400,000 for the lender's legal fees on a large loan that did not close because it was lawyered into oblivion.

COMMITMENT LETTERS

The term "commitment letter" is a misnomer. The bank commits to nothing, as all commitment letters have endless outs, caveats, exceptions, and other loopholes to let the bank out. In fact, the only legal consequence of a commitment letter is usually to make the borrower liable for the bank's legal fees, even in the case of a broken transaction. Borrowers: Dodge the commitment letter for as long as you can, and certainly don't ask for one.

AFFIRMATIVE AND NEGATIVE COVENANTS

Every loan is filled with pages and pages of affirmative and negative covenants. The affirmative covenants all start with "thou shalt," and the negative covenants all start with "thou shalt not." In most cases, the list of covenants is so long and technical that the borrower is in default on day one, giving the lender the theoretical right to accelerate the loan and foreclose on its security interest. In practice, lenders tend to ignore these covenants until the going gets tough and other problems arise, in which case all of these covenants, along with the kitchen sink, will be thrown at the borrower.

LEGAL OPINIONS

Argh! The request for legal opinions on loan transactions really gets me mad. It is standard operating procedure for banks to request a legal opinion from the borrower's counsel on various matters, the two most offensive of which are opinions stating that (a) the loan documentation is enforceable in accordance with its terms and (b) the security interest is properly perfected. In the face of much teeth gnashing by the banks and their counsel, I often refuse to give these opinions on behalf of the borrower on the grounds that (a) I didn't draft the loan documents, and they are so over-reaching that portions may in fact be unenforceable and (b) I am not the one perfecting the security interest—the bank's lawyer is. I have told banks to obtain these opinions from their own lawyers, who should be the ones properly giving these opinions. This may seem like a small, inconsequential matter, but the lawyer giving these opinions is effectively guaranteeing the loan.

ORDER OF PAYMENTS

The banks are typically not entitled to have 100% of all revenue received applied toward repayment of the loan. For starters, many foreign countries impose withholding taxes, and foreign distributors withhold these taxes and remit them to their local governments. For example, if the withholding rate is 10%, the foreign distributor will withhold 10% of every payment, reducing the net payment available to repay the bank. To avoid or minimize these withholding taxes, many film companies use intermediaries based in countries with a favorable treaty network.

Some portion of revenue will also be necessary to pay the sales agent's fees and distribution costs. Often, banks attempt to force sales agents to defer these payments until after repayment of the loan, but sales agents with clout can avoid this deferment, at least as to distribution costs and a portion of their fees.

Finally, it is often necessary to set aside a portion of the payments to pay participations (contingent payments to talent), particularly gross participations to talent, and to pay residuals to the guilds. One item that is never permitted to be deducted before loan repayment, however, is regular income taxes, and this issue can be devastating to borrowers. Even if 100% of the cash is being used to repay the bank, the borrowers may still have taxable income. This issue is discussed in more detail in Chapter 16. The net result is that the borrower may be left with an income tax liability, but no cash to pay it. Woe the borrower.

INSURANCE-BACKED FINANCING

The latest fad in film financing is insurance-backed financing, where a syndicate of insurance companies insures that a sufficient level of revenues will be reached to repay the bank after a specified number of years. In some cases, insurance companies insure a single film, but in most cases, because of the inherent riskiness of films, insurance companies will only insure a slate of films, such as eight or more, in the hope that one or two hits will make up for the inevitable flops. The insurance companies charge a premium calculated as a percentage of the amount insured, and it is often possible to reduce the premium by only insuring a portion of the loan that is repaid last (e.g., perhaps the last 30%). Even though the insurance does not cover the entire loan, the balance may be covered with pre-sales, and the portion of the loan that is repaid last is the most risky.

If film revenues do not repay the bank, the bank then looks to the insurance company for repayment. If the insurance policy is weak and contains any exceptions or exclusions, the insurance company may balk at payment and the bank may have to sue the insurance company to force payment. At the other extreme, if the insurance policy is iron clad with no outs or exceptions, it is possible to issue bonds to the public market against the policy, with the bonds given an investment grade rating by the rating agencies (e.g., Standard & Poors).

SECURITY INTERESTS

Introduction. A security interest gives the secured party a claim to specific property (the "pledged property") in order to enforce a contractual obligation of another party. Security interests are not just for loans—any contractual obligation can be secured. For example, a licensee's obligation to pay royalties under a license can be secured by the licensed rights, and a producer's contractual obligation to deliver a film and license rights to a licensee can be secured by the underlying film rights. In theory, a security interest permits the secured party to foreclose on the pledged property. In reality, a foreclosure almost never happens because borrowers typically declare bankruptcy prior to the foreclosure, which blocks it (absent bankruptcy court order). Although a foreclosure is typically blocked in a bankruptcy, the secured party is permitted to ride out the bankruptcy and retain its security interest, preventing the pledged property from being sold to a third party without the proceeds being paid to the secured party. This is the real practical impact of a security interest. In a bankruptcy, the debtor is able to void any security interest that has not been properly perfected, so every debtor hunts for reasons to throw at the secured party as to why the security interest is not perfected. Bankruptcies are discussed in more detail in a later chapter. The process is analogous to riding a bucking horse until the bell rings; the secured party rides the bucking debtor while attempting to hold on to the security interest through the bankruptcy. Success here is the acid test of the security interest.

Attachment and Perfection. A security interest gives the lender a claim to the pledged property, and with luck, this claim will survive a bankruptcy of the debtor. Any property can serve as security, and lenders typically want everything they can get their hands on. The first critical aspect of granting or receiving a security interest is to carefully identify all the various properties that will be covered. Because films are actually bundles of a multitude of rights, lenders usually obtain a security interest in each of the following separate property interests:

• The underlying literary material upon which the film is based, including the ultimate source material (e.g., a novel) and the screenplay to the extent necessary to exploit the film.

- The copyright to the film.
- The physical film elements, such as the original negative, answerprint, etc.
- Contract rights relating to the film, including, most importantly, distribution contracts.
- Accounts receivable.
- Cash.

To "attach" a security interest is relatively easy. In most cases, this simply requires a writing granting the security interest signed by the debtor and supported by adequate consideration. It is more difficult to "perfect" a security interest, which means to record the security interest in such a way so as to give notice to the world of the lender's security interest, in order to defeat subsequent claims by third parties. The common (and in most cases, sufficient) approach to perfection is to record the security interest with both (a) the secretary of state for the state where the borrower has its principal office and (b) the U.S. Copyright Office.

This double filing is caused by somewhat conflicting and ambiguous case law on the question, resulting in most lawyers adopting a belts and suspenders approach. Even this approach, however, is arguably insufficient with respect to foreign copyrights (i.e., the right to exploit the film in foreign countries). Technically, foreign copyrights should be treated as separate items of property, and the proper place to perfect should be in each local country. This approach is so impractical, however, that no one does it, and if the issue is ever raised in a U.S. court, it is possible that the court would overlook the niceties of the issue.

Foreclosure. As discussed above, foreclosure sales rarely occur. When they do, the secured party generally has two choices: First, unless the debtor objects, they can undertake a "strict" foreclosure, whereby they take the pledged property and waive any deficiency on the underlying debt. Second, they can undertake a regular foreclosure by offering to sell the property in a commercially reasonable manner through a publicized sale. In this case, the sale proceeds are first used to pay the secured party the amount owed, and any excess is paid to the debtor. That's the theory anyway. In reality, no one shows up for the sale, and the secured party bids in all or part of the amount it is owed in exchange for the pledged property and then sues the debtor if there is any deficiency.

A problem in conducting any foreclosure occurs when the obligation being foreclosed upon is not fixed. For example, if a debtor has breached its obligation to pay contingent royalties to a licensor, and has thus breached the license, a licensor foreclosing on a security interest in the licensed rights is foreclosing not upon just the actual royalties due, but upon the licensee's future royalty obligations. In this situation, the licensor should make an estimate of the value of the future royalties (or other obligation of the debtor) and should state this value as the amount of the claim for purposes of the foreclosure. Thus, the licensor can bid in the amount of this claim against the licensed rights, and if the licensor is outbid by third parties, the licensor will at least receive the full amount of its stated claim, subject to subsequent litigation with the debtor over the reasonableness of the claim.

The Logical Extreme. Because of everyone's justifiable paranoia about the consequences if the other party goes bankrupt, the industry trend has been for everyone to demand a security interest from everyone else in sight. Licensees demand security interests from licensors, and vice versa. Talent demands security interests to secure their participations, and the guilds demand security interests to secure residuals. When you add the bond company and, of course, the banks, as many as ten parties may have a security interest in one film. All these competing security interests then need to be prioritized to deal with who gets what in the case of foreclosure. In the absence of any agreement to the contrary, generally the security interests are stacked in the order of the date of perfection. However, it is typical for everyone to enter into an inter-creditor agreement, agreeing to the relevant priorities of the security interests among themselves.

FORMS

Because of the importance of loans to film financing, the appendix section of this book includes the three core documents that will be required, at a minimum, for every loan:

Form B: *Loan and Security Agreement*. Form B is a loan and security agreement, incorporating an assignment (the grant of a security interest), a draw-down notice (the borrower's periodic request for cash), a secured promissory note, and a power of attorney.

Form C: *Notice of Assignment and Distributor's Acceptance*. Form C is a notice of assignment and distributor's acceptance. This document is intended to be countersigned by distributors, whereby they confirm that they will pay all amounts owed directly to the bank upon delivery, while essentially waiving all defenses to payment.

Form D: *Inter-Party Agreement*. Form D is an inter-party agreement, which sets forth the relevant payment priority among various parties—in this case the producer, sales agent, completion guarantor, lender, and investor.

8

COMPLETION GUARANTEES

Introduction

The Document Package

Other Insurance

Role of the Completion Guarantor

Exclusions

Delivery

Takeover

INTRODUCTION

A completion guaranty is issued to guarantee that a motion picture will be completed and delivered to the distributor in accordance with the script and on schedule. In essence, the completion guaranty provides that if the motion picture runs into problems, the completion guarantor has the option to either:

- Loan money to the producer to finish the motion picture;
- Take over the motion picture itself and finish it; or
- Abandon the motion picture and repay the financier the production financing, interest, and certain other costs.

In this manner, the completion guaranty operates to protect the financier from over-budget costs created by the producer, misapplication of the production financing, and various other problems that may arise throughout the principal photography and the post-production of the motion picture. The completion guaranty ensures that either the motion picture will be completed or the financier will be repaid. A form completion guaranty agreement is included as Form E in the appendix to this book.

In motion picture production financing, the completion guaranty is a critical aspect of the financier's collateral package. The financier will often have distributors' commitments to pay on delivery of the motion picture, which serve as the collateral for the motion picture production financing. Under these circumstances, the financier will only proceed with the motion picture production financing if the producer obtains a completion guaranty to ensure the motion picture will be completed and delivered and, accordingly, that the financier will be repaid its production financing from the distributors' payments. The financier, such as a U.S. bank, must be prepared to take the credit risk of the distributors. The risk that the motion picture will be completed and delivered to the distributors is shouldered by the completion guarantor.

The completion guaranty also serves a useful purpose to studios that have a concern over their ability to control costs for directors and producers with bad reputations. The completion guarantor can permit the studio to maintain its relationship with the producer or director by putting the completion guarantor in the position of being the bad guy. Studios use outside productions to supplement their in-house productions and rely on the completion guaranty to minimize their risks for budget overruns.

The completion guarantor usually obtains reinsurance through a third-party insurance company. The completion guarantor arranges for a cut-through certificate to be issued from the reinsurer in an amount sufficient to cover the entire principal amount of the production financing, interest, and certain other costs incurred by the financier. A cut-through certificate is a statement that the reinsurer will pay claims within the specified limits in the contract between the reinsurer and the completion guarantor. The cut-through permits the financier to go after the reinsurer, and thus the financial condition of the completion guarantor is not as important, except for those items that are excluded from the reinsurance, such as claims arising as result of force majeure, amounts in excess of the reinsurance limits, or any deductible.

It is important to obtain a credible completion guaranty company even though reinsurance minimizes the need to place a big emphasis on the financial condition of the completion guarantor, since the completion guarantor may still be required to loan money to the producer to cover amounts in excess of the budget. Beyond relying on the completion guarantor to step in and deal with financial problems, the financier will often look to the completion guarantor to undertake various other items including production management and monitoring the status of the production.

THE DOCUMENT PACKAGE

The principal documentation of the various completion guaranty companies is quite similar and includes the following items:

(1) Producer's Completion Agreement (the producer agrees to behave);

(2) Completion Guaranty (the completion guarantor guarantees delivery);

(3) Production Account Takeover Letter (giving completion guarantor the right to control the payment of cash);

(4) Laboratory Letter (giving completion guarantor control of physical film material);

(5) Distributor's Notice of Irrevocable Assignment and Acknowledgment (distributor agrees to definition of "delivery");

(6) Takeover Agreement and Power of Attorney (giving completion guarantor the right to take over production); and

(7) Copyright Mortgage (giving completion guarantor a security interest).

The producer's completion agreement is the single most important document to the completion guarantor because it creates the rights of the completion guarantor against the producer and permits the completion guarantor to ensure that it will be in position to produce and deliver the motion picture in accordance with the completion guaranty that it issues to the financier. A sample producer's completion agreement is included as Form F in the appendix to this book.

OTHER INSURANCE

The completion guaranty is not a substitute for other insurance to guard against the various risks associated with the motion picture. The completion guarantor and the financier will always insist that the producer obtain E&O (errors and omissions) insurance, cast and crew insurance, negative insurance, and other customary insurance for a motion picture.

ROLE OF THE COMPLETION GUARANTOR

Production Manager. The producer's agreement permits the completion guarantor to function as a production manager. In this role, the completion guarantor attempts to minimize its financial risk by ensuring that the motion picture will be produced within the budget and delivered on time. In this regard, the completion guarantor reviews all documents associated with the motion picture, including the script, shooting schedules, budget, post-production schedules, and all agreements relating to the motion picture.

The completion guarantor is particularly concerned with the budget and carefully reviews it to ensure that a provision has been made for all expenses necessary, in the completion guarantor's opinion, to produce and deliver the film. If the completion guarantor perceives any deficiency, the completion guarantor may request that the producer increase the amount budgeted for a particular item or, if any item has been omitted, the completion guarantor may require that a provision be made for the item. The completion guarantor also will generally insist on adding a 10% contingency to the budget. If the producer and/or the director do not have a proven track record, the completion guarantor may request a larger contingency.

Beyond the thorough review of the motion picture elements and providing for the budget contingency, the completion guarantor requires the producer, the director, the production manager, and certain other key production personnel to sign off on the production schedules, the script, and the budget. The completion guarantor in this manner seeks to put the cast and crew on notice of its expectations. As noted above, the completion guarantor generally stays involved with the day-to-day production by posting a representative at the production location. The completion guarantor requires the producer to supply it with daily production reports and other related information, which is then reviewed by the completion guarantor to ensure that the production is proceeding on target.

The completion guarantor may from the outset also function as a co-signatory on the production bank account. In any case, the completion guarantor will insist that all loans from the financier be deposited into a production bank account established by the producer prior to entering into the producer's agreement. The financier's responsibility only extends to making the funds available and not to seeing that they are applied to cover the budget costs. At a minimum, the completion guarantor will insist upon receiving a schedule of all disbursements from the production bank account.

Recoupment Position. In addition to outlining the production-related rights and obligations of the completion guarantor, the producer's agreement also functions to define the completion guarantor's right to recoup any amounts it advances or loans to the producer to fund costs in excess of the budget. The recoupment position of the completion guarantor is generally nonrecourse in that it permits the completion guarantor to proceed only against revenues derived from the motion picture for recovery of its loans and not against any other assets of the producer. The recoupment position of the completion guarantor is also subordinated to the financier until the financier has been fully repaid.

Takeover. The producer's agreement also outlines in detail the rights of the completion guarantor to take over the production of the motion picture and complete it. The basis for the takeover in the producer's agreement varies from a completely subjective standard, which in essence looks to the insecurity of the completion guarantor with respect to the motion picture, to a clearly defined objective standard that only permits the completion guarantor to take over the motion picture if the budget is exceeded by a certain percentage and/or the production schedule is behind by a certain number of days.

EXCLUSIONS

The completion guaranty will specify claims from certain events and costs for which the completion guarantor is not responsible.

Chain of Title. The completion guaranty typically excludes claims that arise as a result of the producer's failure to acquire the underlying rights to the motion picture. This exclusion extends beyond claims arising from the producer's title to the underlying rights to the motion picture to include claims relating to rights of privacy and other similar areas. Given that the rights to the motion picture are part of the financier's collateral package, the completion guarantor generally does not relieve the financier from its obligation to secure and perfect the collateral package. However, the completion guarantor still reviews the chain of title documents because it may be looking to the motion picture for recovery of amounts that it advances to cover costs in excess of the budget. The completion guarantor may also do copyright and/or state security interest searches in connection with its review of the chain of title documents to confirm the producer has a clear chain of title.

MPAA Rating. The completion guarantor often excludes claims arising from failing to deliver the motion picture with a certain rating by the Motion Picture Producers' Association, such as G, PG, R, or NC-17. This exclusion often causes problems for the financier because the distribution agreement usually requires a specified rating. Under those circumstances, the financier will attempt to get the distributor to agree that the rating is not a payment condition under the distribution agreement.

Artistic Content. The completion guarantor will exclude from coverage issues relating to the artistic content of the motion picture. The completion guarantor is only responsible for the technical quality of the motion picture. The financier generally makes sure that if the completion guarantor delivers a motion picture that is in compliance with the script, the distributor will be required to make payment to the financier regardless of the artistic quality of the motion picture.

Insolvency or a Breach by the Distributor or the Financier. The completion guarantor will never provide coverage for the risks associated with the creditworthiness of the distributor; this is the financier's risk. The completion guarantor will further refuse to cover claims arising out of a contractual breach or fraud by either the distributor or the financier.

Conditions Precedent to the Completion Guarantor's Liability. The completion guarantor also conditions its liability under the completion guaranty on the financier putting all of the production financing in place. The completion guarantor's liability to the financier does not kick in until such financing is in place and available.

Beyond insuring that the financing is in place, the completion guarantor also conditions its liability upon receipt of its fee. Often, the financier will be authorized by the producer to pay the completion guarantor its fees as part of the first draw down in the production financing. The completion guarantor also will condition its liability on pre-approval of certain production-related documents, the commencement of principal photography, and certain key insurance being in place, with the completion guarantor listed as an additional insured.

DELIVERY

The completion guarantor's delivery requirements extend to delivery of all the physical elements required for the motion picture, and are generally the same requirements contained in the distribution agreement. Therefore, the completion guarantor reviews the distribution agreement in detail to make sure that it is possible to deliver the various items within the timetable anticipated by the producer. Often, it is possible to arrange with the distributor a shortened version of delivery requirements for release of payment to the financier.

The completion guarantor will also want to closely scrutinize the timetable contained in the distribution agreement to see what flexibility, if any, exists if production delays should occur. At a minimum, the completion guarantor will want to insist that it is entitled to the same extensions as are provided for in the distribution agreement.

The completion guarantor will also carefully scrutinize the distribution agreement to confirm that no artistic quality-type restrictions are placed on delivery of the film. The completion guarantor will also request the distributor to delete any other subjective-type approvals and to permit immaterial variations from the approved script. If the distributor requires a motion picture to contain certain elements, such as a particular director or actor, the completion guarantor usually attempts to get the distributor to put in place a mechanism for accepting replacement of that element if necessary.

TAKEOVER

The provisions in the producer's agreement relating to the takeover of the motion picture are often contentious.

Pre-Takeover Due Diligence of the Completion Guarantor. The completion guarantor reviews all talent-related agreements, especially the producer's and director's contracts, to ensure, except as precluded by the Director's Guild Agreement, that the completion guarantor may replace the director or producer. In the event of a takeover, the completion guarantor will have various rights and controls that will become applicable. The completion guarantor will become the sole signatory on the production bank account as well as take over the actual account through the bank so that it can use any remaining cash to complete the motion picture. The completion guarantor will also be able to draw down any remaining production financing.

In addition, in the event of takeover, the completion guarantor will eliminate any enhancements or improvements proposed by the director or producer and complete the motion picture on the basis that it is technically correct. As part of the takeover process, the completion guarantor also must ensure it has complete lab access to the physical elements of the motion picture and, at the same time, preclude the producer from such access.

Reality Of Takeovers. As a practical matter, very few motion pictures are actually taken over. In the event a motion picture runs into difficulties, the parties usually attempt to work together to resolve the problems and complete the motion picture, given that all of the parties may suffer if there is a full takeover.

If there are production problems, the completion guarantor may implement what is referred to as a "soft takeover." Under a soft takeover, the completion guarantor will exercise more administrative controls, including controls over the expenses and the bank accounts, but will leave the cast and crew in place to deal with the day-to-day production. Also, the completion guarantor will require the producer to implement its suggestions in connection with putting the motion picture back on track. The producer may be given the option to secure additional production financing to cover the over-budget costs prior to the implementation of the completion guarantor's suggestions.

Given that the reputation of the producer and director are involved and may be impacted in the event of a full takeover and that the motion picture may receive adverse publicity, which impacts the ultimate success of the motion picture, the parties generally attempt to comply with the wishes of the completion guarantor through the soft takeover mechanism rather than forcing the completion guarantor into a full takeover.

A full takeover creates a legal twilight zone. The completion guarantor does not have the right to foreclose on the motion picture in the event of a takeover. Instead, the completion guarantor must proceed as the agent of the producer pursuant to an irrevocable power of attorney.

In a takeover, the talent may assert that they have the right to quit based on a prohibited assignment of their contract to the completion guarantor. The talent should not legally have this right because the completion guarantor is functioning as the producer's agent in the event of a takeover. This argument is, however, easy to avoid by requiring the producer to include a right to assign the contracts with the talent to the completion guarantor in the event of a takeover. The right of assignment to the completion guarantor should be included by the producer in all key production-related agreements.

Another legal issue that can surface in a takeover is the completion guarantor's right to fire the talent. This issue is especially tricky in the case of a director. The completion guarantor will find it quite difficult to locate another quality director who will be prepared to take over the work of the director. The completion guarantor may enter into an agreement with the director to clarify these issues or, alternatively, the completion guarantor may insist that the producer deal with them in its agreement with the director. The single most important factor that will preclude the termination of the director will be the director's willingness to accept the completion guarantor's suggestions to avoid a full takeover and the associated negatives that attach to the director's reputation. An individual producer or director who has had a motion picture taken over may not be able to obtain another completion guaranty without significant additional fees.

9

DISTRIBUTION AGREEMENTS

Introduction

Types Of Distribution Agreements

    Production/Finance/Distribution Agreement

    Negative Pick-Up

    Pre-Sale

    Rent-A-System

    License

    Sales Agent

    Distribution Agreement

    Output Agreement

    Co-Production

Rights

    Term

    Territory

    Language

    Media

    Exclusivity

INTRODUCTION.

The monetary value of a film lies in the ability to exploit it. Since no company has the ability to exploit films in all media, much less in all territories, films must be exploited by entering into distribution agreements with third parties. The provisions of these distribution agreements are the life blood of all film companies, which live or die based on the provisions of their distribution agreements.

TYPES OF DISTRIBUTION AGREEMENTS.

Distribution agreements come in many flavors, and it is important to know what type of agreement is in question before analyzing any given issue. The various types of distribution agreements are discussed below.

Production/Finance/Distribution Agreement. In a production/finance/distribution agreement, commonly referred to as a "PFD agreement," a film company, typically a studio, hires a production company to produce a film, and the studio agrees to directly finance production of, and to distribute, the film. Under these agreements, the production company is little more than a dependent agent of the studio and is subject to the complete control of the studio on all aspects of production. The grant of distribution rights to the studio is always of all rights in perpetuity throughout the world, making the studio the complete and absolute owner of the film. The production company usually retains only a theoretical interest in net profits, if any, generated by the film.

Negative Pick-Up. A negative pick-up is similar to a PFD agreement except that the film company, again typically a studio, agrees to pay a fixed price upon delivery of the film to the studio. Because the studio does not advance the cost of production, the production company must obtain a loan to finance production, and the lender will almost always require a completion bond to guarantee completion and delivery of the film to the studio in order to trigger payment. Because of the introduction of the lender and the completion guarantor, these transactions are more complex than a PFD agreement.

Because the studio does not directly finance the cost of production, it usually does not have the same extensive controls over production as in the case of a PFD agreement. Thus, the production company typically retains more creative discretion than under a PFD agreement.

In most cases, the studio acquires worldwide rights in perpetuity upon delivery of the film to the studio. In some cases, however, the rights are limited to a specified term or territory (such as the U.S. and Canada), or there may be an exclusion of certain ancillary rights. To this extent, a negative pick-up resembles a pre-sale (discussed below), but it is common usage to refer to an acquisition of U.S. rights as a negative pick-up, instead of as a pre-sale.

Pre-Sale. A pre-sale is a limited distribution agreement for a particular country entered into prior to completion, and often even prior to commencement of production, of the film. Thus, most pre-sales involve a foreign distributor committing to pay a fixed dollar amount (referred to as an advance or a minimum guarantee) upon delivery of a film in exchange for specified rights in the film in a given country for a limited term. In most cases, no ancillary rights are acquired (e.g., merchandising, publishing, and soundtrack rights). In addition to the advance due upon delivery, the distributor commits to pay "overages," which are contingent payments based on the success of the film.

Rent-A-System. In a rent-a-system deal, a producer licenses certain film rights to a film company, typically a studio, for a limited term, but the studio is not required to pay an advance to the producer to either finance production or take delivery of the film. In fact, in some cases the producer pays all distribution expenses relating to the film. In exchange for the absence of fixed payments by the studio, the studio agrees to a very low distribution fee, and the remaining revenues are remitted to the producer. In essence, the studio avoids any risk of loss relating to the film, particularly if the studio does not pay distribution expenses, and the producer bears the full risk and reward of the success or failure of the film. Because of the absence of financial commitment by the studio, and the limited upside from the low fee, studios have little incentive to adequately market and push a rent-a-system film, so such films often flop.

License. In common usage, a license refers to any limited grant of rights to a film, with the owner retaining other rights to the film. For example, a pre-sale is merely a license entered into prior to completion of a film. Thus, licenses encompass a broad array of grants of rights, ranging all the way from a one-day pay-per-view television license to a grant of all worldwide rights for a term of twenty-five years.

Sales Agent. Under a sales agent agreement, a sales agent acts as the film owner's agent in consideration for a commission paid to the agent. Thus, there is no grant of rights from the owner to the sales agent. However, if the sales agent is exclusive and has the authority to enter into licenses for and on behalf of the owner, then the sales agent resembles a licensee. Because a sales agent does not pay an advance to the owner, and because the sales agent's distribution expenses are typically relatively low, the sales agent is usually entitled to a relatively low distribution fee.

Distribution Agreement. Many agreements are ambiguously referred to as "distribution agreements" and are unclear as to whether the intent is to grant a license of rights or to create a sales agent relationship. In most cases, these agreements contain pivotal wording referring to a "grant" of rights, resulting in such agreements being licenses, not sales agent agreements.

Output Agreement. An output agreement commits a licensee to acquire particular rights to a specified number of films produced in the future by a production company. In effect, an output agreement is a pre-sale agreement for a number of unspecified films. Typically, the output agreement governs the overall arrangment, and a separate license is entered into with respect to each film once the film is designated.

Co-Production. The term "co-production" originally designated an agreement entered into between two film companies in two different countries pursuant to a co-production treaty between the two countries. Pursuant to these treaties, if the film was produced in part in each country, the film would qualify for certain quota and subsidy benefits in each country. Each film company would own the rights within their respective country. However, the term "co-production" has mutated over time to refer to any agreement between two or more film companies relating to the production and ownership of a film. These types of arrangements resemble either a partnership (when there is a sharing of profits and losses) or a separate ownership (where there is no sharing of profits and losses).

For simplicity, the balance of this chapter will generally refer to all the types of distribution agreements list above, other than sales agents, as being licenses between licensors and licensees, regardless of the particular type of distribution agreement in question.

RIGHTS.

Every type of license must carefully define the rights it covers. Even in the case of a sales agent agreement, in which there is no grant of rights to the sales agent, this issue must be carefully dealt with in order to define the rights that the sales agent can license to third parties on behalf of the owner. The rights granted can be roughly broken down into the following subcategories: term, territory, language, media, and exclusivity.

Term.

1. *Commencement.* An increasingly contentious issue is when does the grant of rights commence—*e.g.*, upon execution of the

agreement, upon posting of a letter of credit for payment, upon delivery of the film, or upon actual payment? This issue is important because a current grant of rights typically precludes any intervening interference with the rights, such as by the subsequent grant of a security interest by, or the attachment of a judgment lien against, the licensor. In addition, the timing of the grant of rights impacts the potential remedies of the respective parties upon a breach by the other.

As a rule, licensees want the grant of rights to occur as soon as possible, preferably upon execution of the agreement. Likewise, licensees prefer that the licensor's exclusive remedy for any breach of the license by the licensee is to sue the licensee for monetary damages, as opposed to the licensor having any right either to not grant the rights in the first place or to rescind a prior grant of rights. On the other hand, licensors do not want the grant of rights to occur until full payment of any required advance, and they want the right to retain or rescind the grant of rights if there is any default by the licensee.

This tension is increased when any required advance payment is secured, such as by a letter of credit, because licensees invariably view posting a letter of credit as the equivalent of making a current payment. To add complexity, the bank financing a film's production wants to retain a security interest in the licensed rights at least until any required advance is paid, and it is loathe to permit a current grant of rights. The net result of this tension has led to ludicrous complexity, sometimes involving holding assignments in escrow and providing for the subordination of multiple interests in an inter-party agreement.

2. *Termination*. In most cases, a license has a fixed term ending on a specified date or after a specified number of years. In some cases, however, the term is automatically extended for an additional period of time if the licensee has not recouped its advance and expenses by the expiration of the initial term of the license. On the other hand, licensors often insist on provisions accelerating termination upon default of any material obligation of the licensee under the license. These provisions can be quite troubling to licensees, as they give the licensor the right to terminate a license by claiming a purported breach by the licensee.

3. *Hold-Backs*. In many cases, licenses contain specific provisions requiring the licensee to holdback the exploitation of specified media until particular time periods have expired. For example, there may be a nine-month hold-back on video exploitation, meaning that video units may not be sold prior to nine months after the initial theatrical release of the film in the territory. These hold-backs are typically to prevent overspill (inadvertant broadcast into an adjacent territory) or piracy, such as the unauthorized duplication and sale of video units outside the territory by third parties. In some cases, however, hold-backs are imposed merely so that the licensor may claim the world premiere with respect to its release of the particular media, such as a requirement that foreign licensees may not release theatrically until the U.S. theatrical release. In this case, the hold-back will be subject to some outside date, such as six months after payment of any advance by the licensee, so the licensee is not held up forever. In most cases, however, foreign licensees are more than willing to wait for the U.S. theatrical release, because the worldwide trade publicity that it generates will help propel the film in the foreign territories.

Licensees should be equally vigilant to impose similar hold-backs on licensors, to prevent licensors from releasing early in adjacent territories, resulting in overspill or piracy in the licensees' territories.

Territory. Typically, the territory is defined by reference to particular countries, including the military installations, ships, and airlines flying the flag of those countries, wherever located. Also common is the inclusion of territories, possessions, and even former colonies of the main country. In many cases, a territory includes certain areas or countries adjacent to the main country because of the use of a common language in those areas. Extra caution must be used whenever two or more language rights are granted to different parties within a particular territory. For example, licensors commonly grant German-speaking Swiss rights to one party, and French-speaking Swiss rights to another party. While this seems logical in theory, in practice it is impossible to bifurcate a Swiss theatrical release in this manner; only one party can license Swiss theatrical rights. Because of this limitation, one party needs to be licensed all language rights (*i.e.*, French, German, and Italian) for Swiss theatrical rights. In common practice, the U.S. and Canada are always combined, and most agreements define worldwide rights by the words "throughout the universe" (lawyers being cautious animals.)

New technology poses a significant impediment to the creation of territorial boundaries. For example, if someone in Germany can download a film over the Internet from a server in Pakistan, the owner of Pakistan rights effectively owns worldwide rights. Thus, it is important to impose restrictions on the use of distribution over the Internet or any similar media until technology is developed and used that restricts access to people within a given territory.

Language. Language restrictions are incredibly important, particularly within Europe where territorial restrictions have little meaning given the mobility of video units and television satellite footprints covering all of Europe. Thus, a language restriction is often the only meaningful restriction on rights. A typical language restriction requires the licensee to exploit the film only dubbed or subtitled in a particular language. Even a subtitling requirement is becoming meaningless in Europe because of its prevalence of people speaking English as a second language. Thus, for example, free television satellite transmission in the English language is commonly prohibited, even if the film is subtitled. DVDs present yet another problem: They can permit the user to choose one of several languages installed on the disk, so it is necessary to prohibit licensees from using this capability.

The licensee should insist on imposing similar language restrictions on the licensor in order to prohibit the licensor from exploiting or granting the same language rights to third parties in adjacent territories. Otherwise, the licensee will be flooded with same-language videos shipped in from adjacent territories and will be subject to same-language satellite overspill. For the same reason, the licensee should not permit the licensor access to the licensee's foreign-language version (dubbed or subtitled) of the film.

Media.

1. *Theatrical and Non-Theatrical.* Theatrical rights include all normal theaters open to the public, including drive-ins. Non-theatrical rights include quasi-public showings, such as on airlines, campuses, and military installations.

2. *Video and DVD.* Video rights are normally defined to include any type of video units, including laser disks, whether for sell-through or rental. The contract should specifically include DVD if that right is intended to be included, as DVD is typically thought of as a separate right.

3. *Television.* Television rights generally include a broad panoply of rights, including free television, pay television (both basic and premium), and pay-per-view. The contract should specifically reference video-on-demand and near-video-on-demand, which are typically thought of as separate rights. Video-on-demand allows a television viewer to order a film to commence at any time. Near-video-on-demand is similar, except that the film starts only at periodic intervals, such as every hour. To this extent, near-video-on-demand closely resembles pay-per-view, and the custom is to define near-video-on demand as a service with twelve or more simultaneous choices. Do not be fooled by the reference to "video" in the definitions of video-on-demand and near-video-on-demand; both rights should properly be included under television rights, not video rights, as they are analogous to, and competitive with, other television rights.

4. *Ancillary Rights.* Ancillary rights are such film-related rights as soundtrack rights, music publishing rights, novelization rights, stage play rights, and merchandising. Merchandising, in turn, generally includes interactive games based on the film.

5. *Future Media.* Because of rapid technological advances, distribution agreements must include a reference to all future media, whether now known or hereafter developed, with respect to all categories of rights. In the absence of such a provision, a contract that merely provides for video, for example, may not cover DVD.

6. *Derivative Rights.* Derivative rights are the rights to exploit

other works that are based on the film, such as sequels, prequels, re-makes, and television series. Most licenses exclude derivative rights, although many licenses do give the licensee a right of first negotiation or last refusal with respect to the licensing of derivative works.

Exclusivity. If a license is silent on exclusivity, it is generally presumed to be non-exclusive, meaning that the licensor can grant competing rights to a third party. For this reason, most licenses are expressly exclusive.

ADVANCE PAYMENTS.

Amount. Simply for want of a better gauge, most advances are calculated as a fixed percentage of the estimated budget for the film. The fact that advances are a function of the budget, and are not based on the inherent worth of a film, leads to absurd results, including a tendency for producers to inflate a budget or pad it with producer fees or payments to affiliates, as well as a reckless disregard for the amount of the budget in the first place. Another oddity of this approach is that the amount of the advance is generally not adjusted up for cost overruns (referred to as budget overages) or down when a film is produced for less than the budget. This latter fact has burned a number of licensees, who agreed to pay a fixed percentage of a stated estimated budget, when in fact the film was produced for far less.

Timing. Whenever a license is entered into prior to completion of a film, the timing of any advance payment is critical. Often, between 10% and 20% of the advance is paid as a deposit upon execution of the license. This is risky from the licensee's point of view, because the licensee typically has no security for repayment of the deposit, such as a security interest in the film, and licensees are typically not beneficiaries of the completion bond. Thus, if the film is never produced, they may lose their deposit.

The most contentious issue for most licenses is defining the event that triggers payment of the balance of the advance. Typically, payment is made upon "delivery" of the film to the licensee, and the battle is over what constitutes "delivery." Licensors (and particularly their banks) want delivery defined as the mere sending of a notice to the licensee that the film materials are ready and available for duplication once the licensee has paid the advance. On the other hand, licensees typically want the right not only to inspect the physical material, but also to screen the film in advance. Also, licensees want payment of the advance to be subject to such conditions as confirmation that the film conforms to the script and the accuracy of all representations and warranties made relating to the film (such as good title, no infringement, no liens, budget, cast, director, etc.).

Industry practice has resulted in a lopsided victory in favor of licensors and their banks on this issue because even if the license itself provides protections for the licensee, banks typically will not fund production of a film unless the licensee signs a notice of assignment and distributor's acceptance that waives all defenses to payment and creates direct liability from the licensee to the bank. A sample of such a notice is included as Form C in the appendix to this book. If the licensee does not sign this notice, the bank does not loan the funds, and the film does not get made. Thus, the licensee is in a Catch-22 situation. Under customary industry practice, the most that the licensee can hope for is the right to inspect and accept the technical quality of the physical material. Any disputes as to this limited issue are typically subject to expedited binding arbitration. The only other conditions are, typically, that the film must be based upon the script and that the key cast include certain actors named as "essential elements." Thus, the licensee is typically required to pay the advance even if all of the licensor's other representations and warranties are inaccurate.

Security and Letters of Credit. Often, the licensor (or its bank) insists that payment of the advance be secured in some manner. This security can take a number of forms, including a large initial deposit that is subject to forfeiture, a letter of credit, or a guarantee from a third party. The licensor's bank will typically have the licensee sign a notice of assignment and acceptance, discussed above, which effectively waives all conditions precedent to paying the advance other than availability of physical material.

In many cases, the licensor or its bank do not trust the distributor to pay the advance upon delivery, in which case they will ask the distributor for a letter of credit. A letter of credit is a direct contractual commitment requiring the distributor's bank (referred to as the "issuing bank") to pay the licensor or its bank (referred to as the "beneficiary") the amount of the advance upon delivery.

As a condition precedent to issuing the letter of credit, the issuing bank will always require the distributor to agree to reimburse the issuing bank for any payment the issuing bank makes under the letter of credit, and this reimbursement obligation is usually secured by a deposit of cash by the distributor with the issuing bank. Thus, distributors loathe letters of credit, because they view them as equivalent to the current payment of cash. On the other hand, licensors and their banks love letters of credit, because it guarantees them payment upon delivery, as most issuing banks honor their letters of credit, and if they don't, it is easier to sue and collect from a bank than from a distributor.

The mechanics of a letter of credit work as follows: All the parties agree in advance to the exact wording of the letter of credit and, critically, the documents required to be presented to trigger payment under the letter of credit, referred to as the "draw-down documents." The draw-down documents are the key to the letter of credit: At one extreme, if the draw-down documents require presentation of a notice of acceptance signed by the distributor, then the letter of credit becomes worthless because the distributor can hold up payment by not signing. At the other extreme, if the draw-down document is simply a notice of delivery from the beneficiary, the distributor risks having to make payment without the opportunity to inspect the delivery materials. In most cases, the resolution is to permit the distributor to inspect the delivery materials for technical quality only, and the draw-down documents are *either* (a) a notice of acceptance signed by the distributor *or*

(b) an arbitrator's award that delivery has occurred. The distributor should also insist that the draw-down documents include all the documentary delivery items for which the exact form of the documents can be fixed in advance. In all cases, however, the letter of credit must be payable upon presentation of pre-agreed documents; there can be no requirement that the bank confirm the existence of facts outside the written documents. For example, a letter of credit could never state that payment will be made when the bank confirms that delivery has occurred, as banks simply don't do this. The banks want only to compare the signed draw-down documents to the pre-agreed forms in order to make payment.

But what does the distributor do if the beneficiary fraudulently signs, or forges a signature on, the draw-down documents and presents them? For example, if the only draw-down document is a notice of delivery, what if the beneficiary signs and presents the notice while the film is still in production? The answer to this dilemma is that there is always a three-business-day delay between presentation of the draw-down documents and payment by the issuing bank, and this waiting period can be extended by contract. During this waiting period, the issuing bank typically notifies the distributor of presentation of the draw-down documents (and the distributor should require this notification in its contract with the issuing bank), and the distributor can run to court and seek an injunction blocking payment if the distributor has a valid complaint. In general, the only valid complaint is for outright fraud by the beneficiary; courts will not block payment under a letter of credit because of a mere good-faith dispute.

Letters of credit are of two basic types: "standby" and "payment." Under a "standby" letter of credit, the distributor is expected to pay the advance directly, and the issuing bank stands by to make the payment if the distributor defaults. Thus, one of the draw-down documents under a standby letter of credit is always a document from the beneficiary stating that the distributor has defaulted. Under a "payment" letter of credit, the distributor is not expected to pay the advance, which will be paid, in all cases, by the issuing bank under the letter of credit. One problem with a standby letter of credit is that if the distributor pays the advance directly and thereafter declares bankruptcy within ninety days of paying the advance, there is a risk that the beneficiary will be forced by the bankruptcy court to repay the advance. The beneficiary can avoid this risk of repayment if payment is made directly under a payment letter of credit. This risk can also be avoided by requiring a standby letter of credit to remain outstanding for an additional ninety days if the advance is paid directly by the distributor.

Withholding Taxes. Many countries require the licensee to withhold taxes on any license payments, including advances. Licensors typically deal with this problem with a "gross-up" clause, which means that the licensee is required to pay the distributor an additional amount sufficient to cover all withholding taxes, so the licensor receives the same net payment. These provisions can be quite unfair to licensees, particularly if the licensor obtains the benefit of a tax credit in its home country for the withholding taxes.

CONTROLS AND APPROVALS.

Licensee. A frequently contentious issue is the level of controls or approvals that the licensee will have over production of the film. Whenever the licensee has committed to pay the advance upon availability of the physical elements, the licensee's exclusive remedy for any breach of its control or approval rights will be merely an action at law for damages, as opposed to the right to withhold payment of the advance. Thus, these type of licenses rarely grant significant control or approval rights to the licensee, as the licensee's remedy would be meaningless. Instead, the licensor typically makes representations and warranties to the licensee (discussed below).

Licensor. Licensors are often wildly zealous in attempting to impose various controls and approvals over exploitation by licensees. For example, licensors may seek control or approval over (a) sublicensing, (b) packaging with other films, or (c) pricing. These restrictions are generally imposed out of the licensor's motivation to protect its right to overages, but licensees typically (and properly) object to these type of approvals and controls, as they can effectively hamstring the licensees' exploitation of the film. While they may be properly imposed on a sales agent, they are wholly inappropriate when a licensee has paid a significant advance.

REPRESENTATIONS AND WARRANTIES.

Typically, the licensor makes extensive representations and warranties to the licensee with respect to various matters relating to the film. For example, there are typically several representations relating to the validity of the grant of rights, including good title, no liens, no claims, and no infringement on the rights of third parties. There are usually representations that the film will be based on a particular script, that it will be made for a certain budget, and that it will include certain named individuals as the key actors or director. Foreign licensees often request a guarantee that the film will receive a U.S. theatrical release by a major studio, but it is typically impossible for a licensor to guaranty this, particularly a specified minimum number of theaters or a minimum prints and advertising expenditure.

The problem with all the representations and warranties is that even if the license states that their accuracy is a condition precedent to payment of the advance, they are all overridden by the standard notice of assignment and acceptance requested by the licensor's bank. Thus, the licensee will only be left with a claim for monetary damages against the licensor — often a single-purpose production company.

LICENSEE PROTECTIONS.

Chain of Title. One way for the licensee to protect its grant of rights is to carefully check the film's chain of title, including the chain of title leading from any underlying book and the screenplay. The licensee should also undertake a search of the public records available through the U.S. copyright office, a state security filing, and a litigation check to search for any voluntary or involuntary liens against the rights, and a general search of news articles, which can provide invaluable clues to potential problems. Even the most thorough search, however, will not reveal all potential problems, as it will not disclose outright plagiarism under a new title or undisclosed and unrecorded grants of rights. To protect against these type of problems, it is common to obtain (or be named as an additional insured under) an errors and omissions insurance policy, which generally insures against the risk that a film infringes on the rights of third parties.

Practical Protections. A licensee can protect its position by implementing a number of practical protections. First, it should seek to avoid making any deposits or other payments prior to delivery of the film. Not only is it difficult to obtain a refund if the film is not made for any reason, but many licensees have been snared by the age-old problem of "in for a penny, in for a pound" and find themselves throwing more and more money at a lousy film that has gone over budget. A licensee should also seek to obtain some controls or approvals over production, as well as a number of conditions precedent to payment of an advance. These protections will, however, be swept aside if the licensee signs the standard notice of acceptance and assignment to the licensor's bank.

A licensee should, of course, seek to obtain the most expansive definition possible of the term, territory, language, and media granted. The licensee should resist any clause permitting the licensor to terminate the license upon an actual or alleged breach by the licensee; in fact, the licensee should insist on an express clause stating that the license may not be terminated in such event to avoid any risk on this issue. The licensee should also obtain representations and warranties from the licensor regarding the film, although these representations and warranties are only as good as the financial solvency of the licensor.

To strengthen its rights, and to avoid any risk of losing its rights in the event of a subsequent bankruptcy of the licensor, the license should be drafted as a "purchase" or "acquisition" of rights, as opposed to a "license," and the licensee should make every effort to avoid being appointed as merely a sales agent. Similarly, licensees prefer to receive all money from exploiting the film directly, as opposed to having money paid to an escrow or collection account to secure the payment of overages to the licensor.

Modifications. Licensees generally want the unfettered discretion to edit or modify a film, including adding a logo or "presented by" credit for the licensee. Licensors are generally reluctant to permit the right to edit, and they may not be able to grant this right in any event if they have granted third parties, such as the director, discretion over any editing of the film. In addition, in some countries, such as France, droit morale rights (moral rights) of "artists" (including the director and screenwriter) may prohibit editing a film. In most cases, the end result is that the licensee has the right to edit the film only when required for purposes of censorship approval or to meet time restrictions of particular media, such as airline and television exploitation.

LICENSOR PROTECTIONS.

Licensors can undertake a number of steps to maximize their protections in the event of a default or bankruptcy by the licensee. One obvious approach is to limit the term, territory, language, or media granted to the licensee or, better yet, to appoint the licensee as the sales agent of the licensor, as opposed to granting any rights to the licensee. An alternative approach is to grant rights, but to provide an express termination right in the event of a breach by the licensee.

Generally, a clause providing for termination of a license in the event of bankruptcy of the licensee is not enforceable, but it is sometimes possible to achieve the same result by providing for termination if certain key personnel of the licensee leave, which typically occurs in bankruptcy. The safest course is to record any termination right in the U.S. copyright office, either by recording the long-form license itself or a short-form summary that incorporates the termination right.

The licensor can also use any of the normal means to secure payment of any advance, such as a letter of credit or a guaranty from a third party. The licensor will want to trigger payment of the advance by simply mailing notice of availability of the physical material and will want to eliminate any licensee approvals required to pay the advance. If substantial overages are anticipated, the licensor may want to protect its right to such overages by having the right to approve sublicenses or requiring sublicensees to make payments to an escrow account.

GOVERNING LAW, JURISDICTION, AND REMEDIES.

In most cases, the license will be expressly governed by the laws of a particular country or state. These clauses apply only for interpretation of the license and do not confer jurisdiction for litigation. Many lawyers have a knee-jerk reaction to impose exclusive jurisdiction in their home territory over any disputes, but this is an unwise approach if the other party has no assets in that jurisdiction; in most cases, it is better to provide for non-exclusive jurisdiction and venue in a particular location, leaving open the possibility of suing the other party wherever their assets are located, to avoid the time, expense, and delay of having to re-enter a judgment in the other jurisdiction.

A related question is what type of remedies will be available in the event of a breach by the other party. Typically, both parties want the right to obtain equitable relief, such as an injunction, against the other, while vociferously objecting to a similar remedy against themselves. Under most licenses, after payment of the advance by the licensee, the licensor's remedies are limited to an action at law for damages in the event of any subsequent breach by the licensee.

FORMS.

The appendix section of this book includes several types of distribution agreements;

Form G: Sales Agent Agreement. Form G is a Sales Agent Agreement that is biased in favor of the film owner, not the sales agent.

Form H: Pro-Licensor License Agreement. Form H is a Pro-Licensor License Agreement that is limited to video and television rights. It incorporates most of the licensor protections mentioned in this chapter.

Form I: Pro-Licensee Short Form Agreement. Form I is a Pro-Licensee Short Form Agreement that is intended to be used by licensees at the various film markets. As much as I detest deal memos and term sheets, the practice is so ingrained at the film markets that rather than attempt to turn the tide, we swim with it. The intent is for the licensees to whip out this Short Form Agreement (in lieu of using the licensor's short form) and to subsequently proceed to the long-form License Agreement discussed immediately below.

Form J: Pro-Licensee License Agreement. Form J is a Pro-Licensee License Agreement, intended as the long-form supplement to the Pro-Licensee Short-Form Agreement mentioned above. This form incorporates most of the licensee protections mentioned in this chapter.

CONCLUSION.

Licenses are living relationships in the context of a fast-changing industry, and there are endless opportunities for ambiguity, disagreements, and disputes. Because licenses embody an on-going relationship that typically involves the sharing of profits through the payment of overages to the licensor, they are closely analogous to partnerships. As in the case of partnerships, more important than the written agreement is the character of the parties. Each party should know and trust the other party or risk proving the proficiency of the license through litigation.

10

SPLIT-RIGHTS DEALS

INTRODUCTION

Split-rights deals are transactions that involve multiple foreign distributors forming a cooperative unit to acquire foreign film rights from a U.S. major studio. Often, the film's producer joins together with the distributors, and the producer shares in the back-end profits earned by the distributors. The agreement among the distributors and the producer is commonly called a "Co-Production Agreement" for want of a better title. Once that agreement is done, the producer and the distributors (collectively, the "Co-Producers") then jointly enter into an agreement (the "Production/Distribution Agreement") with the studio.

Under one type of split-rights deal, the distributors acquire outright all foreign rights in a film for a fixed percentage of its budget, without any sharing of profits between the studio and the distributors. More commonly, however, each party is entitled to recoup its respective investment out of revenues (net of distribution fees and expenses) from its home territory, and profits are then split pursuant to a pre-agreed formula. For example, the studio is entitled to recoup its investment from all domestic revenues, and each distributor is entitled to recoup its investment first from revenues from its own home territory and then from other foreign revenues. After all the parties have recouped, any remaining revenues from all territories are split pursuant to the pre-agreed formula. In essence, split-rights deals represent multi-level partnerships:

- A partnership among the distributors.
- A partnership between the distributors and the producer.
- A partnership between the co-producers and the studio.

The distributors typically distribute the film in all media in their home territories, but they usually must use the services of a third party to distribute the film in foreign countries outside their home territories. The most logical choice of a third party to handle this distribution is the studio, but sometimes an independent sales agent is used to pre-sell the film in other foreign territories.

There is usually at least one bank that has financed the film and that has a security interest on all the rights. The various agreements must integrate paying off the bank loan and handling the priority of any multiple security interests in the various rights.

Because of the multitude of parties and the complexity of the accountings, it is generally necessary to have a centralized collection account and a single collection agent be responsible for the collection, accounting, and payment of all revenues. The collection agent may also serve as a licensing intermediary in order to minimize and simplify tax withholding in various countries.

All parties should enter into an agreement that provides a uniform procedure for the calculation and allocation of all payments. This agreement may be entered into by the studio, the distributors, the producer, the sales agent, the collection agent, and the bank. Since each of these parties will be represented by their own legal counsel, these transactions aptly demonstrate the immutable law of quantum legal physics discussed in Chapter 2: $D = L^2$. That is, the number of *Days* required to close the transaction equals the number of *Lawyers* squared.

In a split-rights deal, distributors in a few countries can finance approximately 50% of the cost of any film, no matter how large the budget. These deals present compelling advantages to all parties:

• It has become increasingly difficult for foreign distributors to acquire quality films. Split-rights deals gives foreign distributors the opportunity to acquire big-budget studio pictures that they would not have access to if they were acting individually on a pre-sale basis.

• The producer, by becoming one of the co-producers, becomes entitled to a genuine profits interest, as opposed to being entitled to the standard contractual share of theoretical net profits from the studio.

• The studio is able to cover up to 50% of the budget from a few countries, and this money is received by the studio much more rapidly than if it were to distribute the film. Because split-rights deals drastically reduce a film's risk to the Studio, split-rights deals permit the financing of films that might otherwise not be financed. Effectively, split-rights deals permit independent films to get made within the studio structure.

CHARACTERIZATION FOR STATE LAW AND TAX PURPOSES

For a number of reasons, there is generally a tremendous reluctance to documenting any of the contractual relationships in a split-rights deal as a partnership. The studio is guaranteed to abhor partnerships for fear that partnership fiduciary obligations might inhibit the studio from engaging in its standard accounting practices. Any one or more of the distributors may be subject to a legal restriction on investing in partnerships, which is usually avoided by calling the agreement something else. There is also the general partnership paranoia that is endemic in the entertainment industry. Finally, there is the plethora of difficult tax issues that a partnership brings, including: (a) creating a taxable presence in other countries, (b) subjecting the partners to income tax and branch tax in the United States and other countries, (c) difficulty in determining the appropriate treaty rate of withholding on royalties paid to the partnership, and (d) the requirement that the partnership must withhold on certain distributions to foreign partners.

For all of these reasons, split-rights agreements are almost never cast as partnership agreements, and, in fact, the agreements almost always contain an express disclaimer of partnership status. But because the parties are acting jointly for a business purpose, the agreements may be treated as partnerships, both for state law and tax purposes if there is a cross-sharing of profits, despite the contractual denials. However, in 1995, the IRS issued regulations dealing with the tax treatment of cost-sharing arrangements between related parties for intangible assets, including films. If such cost-sharing arrangements are in place between related parties, the regulations also specify the tax treatment to any unrelated parties to the transaction. Thus, the regulations apply by direct analogy to cost-sharing arrangements between wholly unrelated parties.

Importantly, the regulations state that a "qualified cost sharing arrangement" will *not* be treated as a deemed partnership for U.S. tax purposes and that the foreign participants will *not* be treated as engaged in a U.S. trade or business.

A split-rights transaction generally meets the substantive requirements of a "qualified cost-sharing arrangement," so the regulations should apply to the tax treatment of split-rights transactions by analogy. Thus, split-rights transactions should not be treated as partnerships for U.S. tax purposes, and the foreign distributors should not be treated as engaged in a U.S. trade or business merely by reason of participation in a split rights transaction.

The regulations require a "qualified cost-sharing arrangement" to allocate the cost of a film between related parties based on the anticipated net income to each party from the film. This allocation is based on an initial projection of the net income to each party. If these projections turn out to be incorrect by 20% or more, there must be a subsequent adjusting payment from one party to the other. This adjusting payment is treated as an adjustment to the initial cost allocation, and is not treated as income subject to withholding. By direct analogy, split-rights transactions require subsequent contingent payments between the parties based on their actual net income. The net result of these subsequent payments is to bring the parties' ultimate cost allocation in line with their initial anticipated projections of net income. For example, if the parties' respective net income stays in the ratio of their stated profit percentage, there would be *no* net payment owed between the parties. If the parties' respective net income does not stay in the ratio of their stated profit percentages, then profits are not shared; rather, the party with the excess net income makes a net equalizing payment to the other party. Thus, the provisions for contingent payments based on net income can be seen as serving an identical economic function to the subsequent adjusting payments under a "qualified cost-sharing arrangement." As such, these payments should be treated as an adjustment to the initial cost allocation, and should not be treated as income subject to withholding.

THE CO-PRODUCTION AGREEMENT

The Co-Production Agreement is entered into by and among the co-producers and should specify the respective rights and obligations of the parties. Typically, this agreement should cover any representations and warranties by the producer to the distributors. One of the most difficult aspects of split-rights deals is that the producer typically takes the position that the distributors should look exclusively to the studio for any issues relating to the film, including representations and warranties. The studio, however, takes the position that the distributors should look exclusively to the producer because the distributors are effectively partners with the producer. This leaves the distributors in an awkward bind, which must be overcome by carefully parsing all obligations, representations, and warranties relating to the film between the producer in the Co-Production Agreement and the studio in the Production/ Distribution Agreement.

The Co-Production Agreement should also specify the monetary obligations of the distributors, including the amount and timing of payments they will have to make to the studio and other third parties. This issue can become highly contentious. The studio will insist that no grant of rights occurs unless it has received full payment. Thus, each distributor is at risk of losing the film and its down payment if any other distributor does not pay. Several ways to handle this problem exist, including the following:

- Require letters of credit from each distributor.
- Have a third party, such as a bank, guaranty the distributors' obligations, with the guaranty backed-up by a letter of credit from the bank to the studio. If any distributor then defaults, the bank steps into the shoes of the distributor.

• Require advance payments by the distributors, and have draconian default provisions. If a transaction must be closed fast, this is the best way to proceed, as the other methods are far more complex and time-consuming.

The Co-Production Agreement should also provide the terms and conditions of exploitation of the film by each of the distributors. The Co-Production Agreement should thus contain license provisions for each of the distributors. These license provisions must cover all the issues dealt with in a normal license agreement, including (a) the scope of rights, (b) the manner of exploitation, (c) the calculation and accounting of receipts, (d) distribution fees, (e) limitations on expenses, and (f) handling transactions with affiliates.

In most cases, the Co-Production Agreement should cross-reference to the Inter-Party Agreement for the calculation and allocation of payments by and to the distributors. If an Inter-Party Agreement is not required, these provisions should be incorporated into the Co-Production Agreement. The Co-Production Agreement should also provide for uniform accounting and auditing provisions and deal with the delicate issue of the decision-making process among the Co-Producers—some decisions may require unanimous vote, other decisions may require a majority vote. Since some distributors reply to a request for a vote only after a long delay, if at all, there should be a provision dealing with whether silence is a "yes" or "no" vote.

THE PRODUCTION/DISTRIBUTION AGREEMENT

The Production/Distribution Agreement is the agreement between the co-producers and the studio. A form Production/Distribution Agreement is included as Form K in the appendix to this book. This agreement sets out the nuclei provisions dealing with ownership and distribution of the film and the division of profits. The agreement should differentiate between ownership of distribution rights, which entitles the owner to distribution fees, and the split of net revenues from those rights—an entirely different matter. For example, one party may "own" certain distribution rights, but another party may be entitled to the net revenues (i.e., after distribution fees and expenses) attributable to those rights.

The Production/Distribution Agreement should specify in detail what constitutes "delivery" to the co-producers and the calculation and timing of the co-producers' payment obligations to the studio. If payment is based on the film's actual cost, some subsequent accounting and adjustment process with respect to the amount paid will be necessary.

The Production/Distribution Agreement should also specify the parties' respective rights and obligations with respect to production of the film. One divisive issue is control and approval rights over a film's creative and budgetary aspects, with the co-producers wanting mutual approval and the studio wanting (and being used to) unilateral control. Tied into this issue is the question of who is liable for budget overruns. The party that is ultimately liable for budget overruns (often the studio) may justifiably feel that it is entitled to control over any issues relating to the budget. In some cases, the solution is to give the co-producers the right to opt-out if the studio makes material changes from a pre-approved list of essential elements relating to the film.

The co-producers often want a joint presentation credit even in the U.S., but studios sometimes object to this. Outside the U.S., joint presentation credits are the norm, except that the distributors may have the sole presentation credit in their home territories.

The Production/Distribution Agreement should contain license provisions dealing with the terms and conditions of distribution by the studio and the distributors similar to the provisions in the Co-Production Agreement. Thus, the agreement should have license provisions dealing with (a) the scope of rights, (b) the manner of exploitation, (c) the calculation and accounting of receipts, (d) distribution fees, (e) limitations on expenses, and (f) handling transactions with affiliates.

One of the most difficult conceptual and drafting issues is the allocation of participations and residuals between the studio and the co-producers. Participations are usually contractually calculated based on the *studio*'s worldwide revenues, so it is arguable that the studio should calculate participations based only on the money the studio receives from the distributors. However, the studio is usually concerned that taking such an approach will anger key talent and generally insists on calculating participations based on aggregating the distributors with the studio. This approach requires complex accounting and audit provisions and is further complicated by the different types of participations:

- All fixed deferments may be allocated between the studio and the co-producers pursuant to some fixed pre-agreed percentage.
- All gross participations may be allocated based on the ratio of the applicable type of gross proceeds of the studio and the distributors triggering the payment.
- All net participations may be allocated based on the ratio of net proceeds of the studio and the distributors, applying the formula and calculation of net proceeds as set forth in each participation contract.

There are two approaches toward handling residuals. One approach is to aggregate the studio and the distributors, similar to the approach usually adopted for participations. Another approach is to treat the transaction as a pre-sale of foreign rights and to allocate part of the proceeds to specific media for which residuals apply. This approach will generally minimize residuals, and the distributors would then reimburse the Studio for residuals calculated in this manner.

The Production/Distribution Agreement should also deal with the order of recoupment and the allocation of net receipts between the studio and the co-producers. To enforce the provisions, the agreement should contain accounting, payment, and audit provisions.

In the Production/Distribution Agreement, the studio should make all the normal representations and warranties made by a licensor. As discussed above, however, the studio may take the position that the distributors should look to the producer if the producer is their partner.

The Production/Distribution Agreement should also deal with the ownership and exploitation of sequels and other derivative works based upon the film. Typically, the co-producers feel that they should be the joint owners of all derivative works, given that they have financed up to 50% of the film, while the studio believes that derivative works should be retained by the studio as separate from the film. The tradeoff is generally to provide the co-producers with an option on all derivative works on the same basis as in the Production/Distribution Agreement for a specified period of time.

THE INTER-PARTY AGREEMENT

The Inter-Party Agreement is entered into by and among the collection agent, the sales agent, the bank, the studio, the distributors, and the producer. This Agreement creates the central hub for the payment, allocation, and disbursement of cash. The difficulty of drafting this agreement is that each comment spurs counter-comments from every other party in an endless iterative process.

If a bank is involved, the agreement will typically acknowledge the bank's security interest and priority of repayment. Most parties will have to subordinate their right to payment to the bank with limited exceptions. It is critical, however, that the Inter-Party Agreement specify that the bank's security interest lifts as to the home territory of any distributor that has made the payment due on delivery and that if the bank forecloses on the film, it continues to be bound by the provisions of the Inter-Party Agreement, including the payment provisions.

The Inter-Party Agreement should specify the calculation and timing of the distributor's payments to the studio, generally tracking the co-production agreement. The agreement should also provide the procedures with respect to any letters of credit or guaranties of the distributors' payment obligation and the consequences of a default in those obligations. For example, if those obligations are backed-up by a bank guaranty or letter of credit, a default by a distributor will typically result in the bank stepping into the shoes of the defaulting distributor with respect to ownership of the rights, and the bank will retain an action for damages against that distributor.

The Inter-Party Agreement should specify in detail the pivotal obligations of the collection agent and the scope of and limitations on its liability. The agreement should also contain provisions applicable to the sales agent, including requiring the sales agent to direct subdistributors to deposit money to the collection account and providing for the amount and priority of the sales agent's fees. The Inter-Party Agreement should specify the calculation and timing of payments the distributors must make to the collection account attributable to profits from distribution of the film. Typically, the distributors are entitled to recoup their investment, distribution fees, and distribution expenses before remitting additional funds to the collection account.

The Inter-Party Agreement should contain detailed provisions directing the collection agent to make payments from the collection account in a specified order of priority. This provision is the essence of the Inter-Party Agreement, and it is critical to accurately integrate all the different payment instructions (often evidenced by a number of different contracts) into one coherent order of payments. To cover unexpected expenses, this agreement needs a safety valve that permits the co-producers to approve any payments to third parties that are not expressly provided for, but if a bank is involved, this provision will have to be subordinate to the bank's right of repayment. To enforce the payment order of priority, accounting and audit provisions should be provided.

MISCELLANY

All the agreements discussed above should also deal with the standard miscellaneous issues, such as any restrictions on assignment of the parties' rights under the agreements, governing law, and dispute resolution mechanisms, if any. Perhaps the most important miscellaneous provision is one that states that the agreements may be signed in counterparts and transmitted by facsimile copy. It would otherwise take months before the agreements became valid and binding.

CONCLUSION

Although complex, split-rights deals are usually beneficial for everyone. The distributors get access to large-budget studio pictures that they would not otherwise have access to, and have more clout in the process by joining together. The producer gets a *real* profits interest by joining as one of the co-producers instead of receiving a phantom share of "net profits" from the studio, and the studio benefits by being able to recover half the budget immediately from a few foreign territories. These aggregate benefits make it likely that split-rights deals will proliferate.

11

FOUR WAYS TO CALCULATE NET PROFITS (DEPENDING ON WHO'S ASKING)

INTRODUCTION

Most people assume that there is one monolithic standard for calculating "net profits" for all purposes. When they hear that a film company has reported a certain amount of net profits for one purpose, they assume that the reported net profits applies for all purposes. This assumption is the genesis of many misconceptions, such as that film companies must be lying or "cooking the books" when they report inconsistent numbers for different purposes. The truth is that film companies are permitted to calculate net profits differently for different purposes, and film companies have found a way to do the calculations differently for each purpose in a way that favors film companies for each purpose. The four different purposes for which net profits are calculated are as follows:

1. Calculating earnings based upon "generally accepted accounting principles" ("GAAP"), which is used for reporting earnings to the SEC, shareholders, and lenders.

2. Calculating income and loss for tax purposes.

3. Calculating payments to profit participants, such as writers and actors.

4. Calculating cash available to make distributions to equity holders, such as shareholders, of the film company.

Because film companies have a vested interest in making sure that net profit calculations work to their advantage, they have been active in determining how the calculations are made. This chapter briefly summarizes the major differences in the calculations for each purpose and the impact the differences have on the various calculations.

GAAP

The calculation of net profits for GAAP is discussed in some detail in the next chapter, so the rules are only briefly summarized here. These rules are generally found in Financial Accounting Standards No. 53, referred to herein as "FAS 53," published by the Financial

Accounting Standards Board. In summary, the goal of film companies in applying GAAP is to report net profits as *high* as possible in order to impress shareholders and lenders. This is achieved in a number of ways. First, and most importantly, a number of debatable items are "capitalized," which means that the costs are *not* immediately deducted but are, instead, added to the cost of films. Capitalizing costs has two salutary benefits: First, it decreases current deductions, thereby increasing reported earnings. Second, it increases film costs reported as an asset on the balance sheet. GAAP rules for film companies permit the capitalization of development costs, production costs, the cost of making physical film prints, payments of participations to third parties, a portion of the company's overhead, and even the cost of abandoned film projects.

Another way to maximize reported earnings is to accelerate the date that income is reported. Under FAS 53, this is achieved by permitting film companies to report the present value of all payments to be made under a license as income as soon as the "availability date" has occurred, which is the date that the licensee can exploit the first showing or broadcast of the film under the license. This allows film companies to report income years before it is actually received. For example, if a film company enters into a ten-year license that provides for payments of $1 million per year, the film company will report the present value of the total payments of $10 million as current income upon entering into the license. This is contrary to the rule applicable to most industries; if the same transaction had involved the lease of real property, the annual payments would be reported as income each year, instead of being all reported as income in the first year.

Another key to maximizing reported earnings is to deduct film costs as slowly as possible. Under FAS 53, this is achieved by deducting film costs based on *estimated* future income. By maximizing the estimate of future income, film companies are able to defer writing off film costs as long as possible because FAS 53 requires film companies to match, as closely as possible, the deduction of film costs with the receipt of income. For example, if a film costs $10 million, and is expected to earn $1 million per year for 20 years, for a total of $20 million, the film cost of $10 million would be deducted $500,000 per year for 20 years in order to match, as closely as possible, the deduction of the film costs with the estimated income. The estimate of future income is made by management, who are under an irresistible impulse to make the estimate as high as possible in order to defer deductions as long as possible.

TAX

For tax purposes, the goal is to report net profits as *low* as possible. This net profits calculation is relatively easy to summarize: simply do the opposite of the calculation for GAAP! For example, for tax purposes, film companies are permitted to *deduct* many of the expenses that they capitalize for GAAP, including advertising, most overhead, and abandoned film projects. Similarly, for tax purposes, film companies do *not* follow the GAAP rule of recognizing all the future income under a license on the "availability date." Rather, for tax purposes the income is reported each year when it is payable. Using the example discussed above—a ten-year license for $1 million per year—for GAAP the present value of the total payments is reported as income upon entering into the license. However, for tax purposes, the annual payments are reported each year. Further, while the goal under GAAP is to defer the deduction of film costs by *over*-estimating future income, the goal for tax purposes is to *under*-estimate future income, as this will accelerate deductions, and there is no requirement that the two estimates match. Thus, film companies have been notorious for under-estimating future income for tax purposes to accelerate the deduction of film costs. This practice was changed somewhat by the 1996 Tax Act, which required film companies to include in their estimates all income for the first ten years from the date the films are released, with a retroactive interest charge added to the film company's tax liability if the estimates prove too low in practice.

PAYING PROFIT PARTICIPANTS

As with calculating net profits for tax purposes, the goal of calculating net profits for purposes of paying profit participants is to report net profits as low as possible. Unlike the tax calculation, however, which is governed by statute, the concept of net profits for purposes of paying profit participants is entirely a contractual animal, although these contracts tend to follow a standard industry pattern. These issues are discussed in detail in a later chapter and are briefly summarized below.

With respect to gross receipts, the goal is to report as little and as late as possible. This is achieved by a number of contractual definitions permitting generous reserves, exclusions, and allocations. For example, a film company may receive a large cash advance from a television network for the right to show a film several times over a three-year period to commence in two years. Most film companies do not report the advance as gross receipts until commencement of the three-year television term after two years. For video gross receipts, it is common to partially offset gross receipts with a large reserve for potential refunds. In addition, it is common to sell or license films in packages, and it is common to allocate gross receipts away from the winning films to the turkey films, for which no participations will be payable. Further, certain sources of income, such as theme parks, are simply excluded entirely from being included in gross receipts.

The goal with respect to distribution expenses is to report as early and as much as possible. This is achieved by a number of means, including high internal fees, early accruals of expenses, payments to affiliates, overhead allocations, and deemed interest. Film companies also take a huge slice of gross receipts off the top as their distribution fee. When all else fails, contracts always permit film companies to siphon off income through affiliates.

The important point is that the definition of net profits is purely contractual. People often assume that the definition of "net profits" for paying profit participants must be grounded upon accounting, not contractual, principles. In truth, the common contractual reference to this calculation as "net profits" is a misnomer; this calculation would be more accurately referred to as "potential contingent compensation payable by contract."

DISTRIBUTIONS TO EQUITY HOLDERS

The final calculation of net profits relates to how much cash is actually distributed to equity holders, such as shareholders, in the form of dividends or similar distributions. This calculation is more complex than the others in that it is a function of three variables.

The first variable is the amount of actual cash on hand (net of reserves for expenses, debts, and the like), as most distributions are made in cash.

The next variable is contractual—namely, the provisions of the governing corporate documents, such as the articles and bylaws for a corporation, the partnership agreement for a partnership, and the operating agreement for a limited liability company. These governing documents will usually have provisions dealing with distributions, ranging all the way from requiring a minimum specified level of distributions each year all the way to granting management unbridled discretion to reinvest net profits in other businesses. Thus, the provisions of these governing documents must always be consulted to determine if a distribution can or must be made and, if so, the amount of the distribution.

Most film companies wish to retain their profits for the purpose of reinvesting in other films or in related, or even unrelated, businesses. Thus, the governing documents of most film companies, particularly the larger ones, grant management unbridled discretion to reinvest profits. The amount of net profits, if any, that are actually distributed is then left solely to the discretion of management.

The third variable is statutory: Most states have statutes that prohibit distributions while an entity is "insolvent" (defined differently by various states.) These statutes serve as a ceiling on the amount of any permissible distributions.

CONCLUSION

The consequence of all this is that, as the Red Queen said in Alice in Wonderland, "a word means what I say it means." When the words "net profits" are bantered about, ask for what purpose it is being calculated. By knowing the purpose, you will know the biases inherent in the calculation and can take the proffered number with the appropriate grain of salt.

12

GAAP ACCOUNTING PRINCIPLES FOR FILM COMPANIES

INTRODUCTION

This chapter discusses the "generally accepted accounting principles" ("GAAP") applicable to film companies. These rules are generally found in Financial Accounting Standards No. 53, referred to herein as "FAS 53," published by the Financial Accounting Standards Board. These principles are used for calculating the earnings of film companies as reported to the SEC, shareholders, and lenders. As discussed in the preceding chapter, these principles must be distinguished from other analogous calculations that serve vastly different purposes:

- Calculating "net profits" for purposes of paying net profit participants, such as writers and actors.
- Calculating income and loss for tax purposes.
- Calculating cash available to make distributions to shareholders.

The GAAP rules applicable to film companies were created by a group of people who have a vested interest in making the rules favor film companies—and they do! In fact, the rules vary so far from normal GAAP principles that it is absolutely impossible to discern any reliable financial information from reviewing the accounting statements for film companies. A film company may be reporting huge earnings and a significant positive balance sheet when, in fact, the company is running at a significant loss and is on the verge of bankruptcy. This fact has had an enormous dampening effect on financing, both of debt and equity, for film companies, because sophisticated investors know that film company accounting statements are meaningless. Thus, film financing is normally based on such tangible factors as bankable contracts or on such intangible factors as the sexiness of the industry. With a grain of salt, the GAAP principles applicable to film companies are discussed below.

CAPITALIZATION OF COSTS

If costs are "capitalized," they are *not* immediately deducted but are, instead, added to the cost of a film. For example, if a $1 million payment is "capitalized," the cost of the film goes up by $1 million instead of the $1 million payment showing up as a current loss. Thus, capitalization of costs has two salutary benefits: First, it decreases current deductions, thereby increasing reported earnings. Second, it increases film costs reported as an asset on the balance sheet. The GAAP rules for film companies permit the capitalization of more expenditures than perhaps for any other industry. For example, all of the following items are capitalized:

- All costs of acquiring stories (such as development costs and scripts), production costs, post-production costs, and interest on all of the above.

- Distribution costs that benefit future periods. This permits the capitalization of theatrical advertising costs (the most significant advertising cost) on the theory that such costs benefit video and television exploitation.

- The cost of making copies of physical film prints.

- Participations payable to third parties. These participations are initially calculated based on an estimate of a film's total revenue and expenses, and this estimate of participations is then capitalized to the cost of the film.

- A portion of the company's overhead that is allocable to produced films, including depreciation, rent, employee salaries, etc.

- Remarkably, even the cost of abandoned film projects and scripts (with abandonment presumed to occur after three years) is capitalized to current production costs.

INCOME RECOGNITION

If you own real property and lease it for ten years for $1,000 a year, you recognize $1,000 per year for ten years as income under normal GAAP. If you enter into the same transaction with film rights, however, you get to report as income the full $10,000 (albeit discounted to present value) in the first year! In other words, years before film companies have any right to receive the cash (and years before any other industry gets to report income), film companies get to report the present value of all payments to be made under a license as income. The theory for this treatment is that a license is supposedly analogous to an installment sale of property, so the license payments should be reported on the date of the "sale." Under FAS 53, the only conditions that need to be met before reporting payments under a license as income are the following:

- The amount of the payments must be known.
- The cost of the film must be known or reasonably determinable.
- Collectability of the payments must be reasonably assured (a condition that management will always find exists).
- The film must be accepted by the licensee in accordance with the conditions of the license.
- The "availability date" must have occurred, which is the date that the licensee can exploit at least the first showing or broadcast of the film under the license.

If an advance payment is received prior to the date that it can be reported as income (e.g., the availability date has not yet occurred), the advance payment is carried as a liability on the balance sheet and is reported as income at the appropriate time under the rules discussed above.

In the case of direct theatrical exhibition, contingent payments are estimated and reported as income at the time of *exhibition*, even if the actual payment is not received until a subsequent year. This, again, results in the front-loading of reported income.

FILM AMORTIZATION

The term "film amortization" refers to the calculation of the amount of the total capitalized film costs that are deducted each year. Film costs are amortized by applying a method known as "income forecast amortization." Under this method, each year the remaining unamortized film costs are multiplied by a fraction, the numerator of which is the current year's reported gross income from the film, and the denominator of which is an estimate of all future gross income from the film (including the current year's income). The formula is shown below:

$$\frac{\text{Current Year's Gross Income}}{\text{Remaining Estimated Gross Income (Including Current Year)}} \times \frac{\text{Unamortized}}{\text{Film Costs}} = \frac{\text{Current Year's}}{\text{Amortization}}$$

This calculation offers several remarkable benefits to film companies, including the following:

• As a general rule, the estimate of future gross income is *not* discounted to present value, even if the estimate is for revenues over twenty years. (The sole exception is that any estimates based on entering into future licenses must be discounted to present value as of commencement of the license under the rules discussed above.) The general rule of not discounting the estimates to present value results in a large denominator, and thus a smaller fraction and lower amortization each year. For example, if a film costs $1,000, and the company expects to exploit the film directly and receive gross income of $50 per year over twenty years (totalling $1,000), the first year's amortization is calculated as follows:

$$\frac{\$\ 50 \times \$1000}{\$1000} = \$50$$

Thus, the $50 of gross income in the first year is offset by the $50 of amortization, resulting in no profit or loss. If the estimate of future gross income had been discounted to present value, the company would have reported a loss each year from the film.

• Best of all, the estimate of future gross income is made by management. Other than a weak requirement that management's estimates be reasonable, management is given wide discretion. For example, even though a film flops theatrically, management may decide that the film will make millions when it is released on laser wrist-watch video in the year 2010. Overestimating future gross income will, once again, result in a large denominator, and thus a smaller fraction and lower amortization each year.

• There is no time limitation on estimated future gross income. In theory, the estimate could cover the next 100 years.

• The estimate of future gross income can take into account inflation, which will drastically increase the total estimate.

• The estimate of future gross income can take into account future media or markets that do not yet exist.

The result of all of the foregoing is an irresistible incentive for management to set the estimate of future gross income as high as possible in order to keep amortization as low as possible. As with capitalizing costs, reducing amortization has two wonderful effects: First, it decreases current deductions, thereby increasing reported earnings. Second, it increases film costs reported as an asset on the balance sheet.

WRITING OFF FILM COSTS

FAS 53 does, in theory, require a deduction of film costs when a film is a turkey. However, film costs are not written down below the *total* estimate of future net income from the film. For example, assume a film costs $20 million and is a theatrical flop. As long as the company estimates that it will net at least $20 million throughout the life of the film from all media, it does not have to write-down the cost of film, even if the present value of the income stream is only $10 million.

CONCLUSION

FAS 53 bends over backward to help film companies by permitting the capitalization of items that should be expensed and by minimizing amortization of film costs and write-downs. The single most important variable in the income forecast calculation—the estimate of future gross income—is left to management's discretion, and management is under an irresistible temptation to come up with the highest estimate possible in order to increase reported earnings and assets. The net result is that the financial statements for almost every film company artificially inflate film assets and earnings, making these statements practically worthless.

13

CONTINGENT PAYMENTS TO TALENT AND LICENSORS

INTRODUCTION

This chapter discusses all types of contingent compensation payable to film participants (generally talent and licensors), whether based on gross receipts, adjusted gross receipts, gross receipts after break-even, or net profits. Misunderstandings can occur with respect to each calculation, so the discussion herein is generally generic to all. As discussed in prior chapters, the calculation of contingent compensation must be distinguished from three other calculations that serve vastly different purposes:

- Calculations of earnings based upon "generally accepted accounting principles," which is used for reporting earnings to the SEC, shareholders, and lenders.
- Calculations of income and loss for tax purposes.
- Calculations of cash available to make distributions to shareholders.

GROSS RECEIPTS

Date of Reporting Gross Receipts. Unlike the calculation of expenses, in which the goal is to accelerate the calculation, a film company's goal with respect to gross receipts is to report any payment received as income as late as possible. This is achieved by a number of means. For example, advance payments, even if non-refundable, are routinely reported as income over the period to which the advance relates: If a television network pays an advance to show a film on television, the advance is commonly reported as income only upon expiration of any holdback on television exploitation.

Another approach is to offset the income with a large reserve for possible refunds. This is a common approach, for example, with video sales: A huge portion of video sales is commonly offset with a reserve for potential refunds, the amount and timing of which are unilaterally set by the film company. Yet another approach is to not report gross receipts until revenues are received in the United States in U.S. dollars, which delays the reporting of gross receipts attributable to freely remittable foreign currency already received by the film company.

Exclusions From Gross Receipts. The standard contractual definition of gross receipts contains a lengthy list of outright exclusions, with no excuses offered. For example, it is common to exclude any income from theme park exploitation of film rights and to exclude all litigation proceeds. Even where the contract is silent, film companies often find a way to avoid reporting gross receipts. For example, it is common for licensees to pay film companies fees referred to as "exclusivity fees" or "access fees," which are purportedly for the right to enter into a contract with the film company covering a number of films, so the payments are not allocated to any films at all. Another example is television barter income, which is earned when film companies license film rights to a television station or network in exchange for free television advertising time in lieu of a cash payment. Although the advertising time has the same value as cash to the film company, sometimes this value is overlooked when reporting income. These type of issues will only be picked up on a thorough audit.

Allocations. Another favorite technique to minimize gross receipts is to allocate gross receipts away from the film in question and to something else. For example, it is common to allocate a portion of gross receipts to any shorts preceding the film. In addition, films are commonly sold in a package with other films, particularly for television and foreign sales, and film companies submit to the irresistible impulse to allocate the package fee as much as possible away from the successful films, which generate participations, to the turkeys, which don't. Film companies argue strenuously to retain their right to make "appropriate" allocations, instead of making allocations by some objective formula, such as the ratio of gross theatrical receipts of the films in question.

Licensing to Affiliates. By far the most extensive problem is licensing rights to affiliates and only reporting as gross receipts the payments to the film company from the affiliates. The most common form of this practice occurs with video income, where the standard practice is to license video rights to an affiliate in exchange for a royalty equal to 20% of video sales by the affiliate. By this simple expedient, gross receipts from video sales — the single largest element of gross receipts — is reduced by 80%. The same practice is also prevalent for the exploitation of all ancillary rights, such as soundtrack and merchandising rights. Even if a film company makes millions of dollars from the sale of soundtracks or merchandise, only a small royalty will be reported as gross receipts.

DISTRIBUTION FEE

Calculation Based on Gross Receipts. Distribution fees are based on gross receipts, not net receipts. In an industry where distribution expenses (excluding distribution fees) average approximately 35% of gross receipts, the practice of calculating distribution fees on gross receipts inflates the fees. When talent with clout are able to negotiate a deal that includes video and merchandising gross income (i.e., gross receipts minus manufacturing costs), they must be careful to avoid having distribution fees based on gross receipts instead of gross income. For example, if video sales had been reported on the normal artificial royalty basis, which is analogous to a gross income calculation, the distribution fee would only apply to the royalty, not to the gross receipts.

Rate. The other extraordinary aspect of the distribution fee is the rate itself. It averages 30% and increases to 40% for television syndication and foreign exploitation. At this rate of fees, it becomes almost impossible to reach net profits.

Subdistributors. Some film companies calculate gross receipts and distribution fees at the level of any independent subdistributors that are used. Many participants assume that this approach works in their favor because the gross receipts received by subdistributors will generally be higher than the gross receipts received by the film company from the subdistributors, but the actual result may be worse depending on the particular facts (for example, when the sub-distributors *net* receipts are less than the amount of any advance paid to the film company.)

Another problem is that film companies may charge their full distribution fee even though distribution is actually handled by a subdistributor that is charging its own fee. This results in a doubling up of distribution fees, and provides a distribution fee to film companies for undertaking no work. If properly negotiated, the contract should provide that the film company's distribution fee is reduced by the fees (or retained share of income) of subdistributors, but the actual result may be worse depending on the particular facts.

DISTRIBUTION EXPENSES

In General. Every film company's list of distribution expenses begins with the mantra "all costs relating to distribution of the film including, without limitation . . ." This clause makes the subsequent list of specified costs superfluous. Before film companies even get to the list of specifically allowed costs, they deduct every imaginable cost related to the film under the quoted clause. To add insult to injury, distribution expenses are often increased in a number of ways. For example, all film companies receive discounts and rebates from service providers they use on a regular basis (such as advertising sources and print duplication labs), yet these rebates and discounts are not usually netted against distribution expenses. In addition, film companies commonly allocate expenses to more than one film, and it is not uncommon for the total allocation to exceed 100% of the expense.

Accruals. One method film companies use to accelerate distribution expenses is to accrue and deduct expenses to be incurred in the future. In accruing future expenses, film companies typically do not follow standard generally accepted accounting principles; they often effectively accrue and deduct an estimate of the expenses they expect to incur in the future. In some cases, the accrued expenses may not actually be paid for several years, as in the case of residuals paid to guilds or participations payable to third parties.

Payments to Affiliates. As with the calculation of gross receipts, film companies often deduct payments to affiliates for various actual or purported services, usually at a mark-up over actual cost. For example, payments are made to affiliates for services relating to artwork, marketing, manufacturing, publicity, etc., and in each case the price is artificially set by the film company, usually on the high side.

Trade Dues and Trade Shows. Film companies always deduct as a distribution expense a portion of their trade dues, such as dues paid to the Motion Picture Association of America, even though these trade dues do not relate directly to the distribution of any particular film. Similarly, film companies deduct all trade-show costs.

Taxes. Film companies always deduct withholding taxes as a distribution expense (or exclude withholding taxes from gross receipts, which reaches the same result). However, the withholding taxes are a dollar-for-dollar credit against the film company's U.S. tax liability, so the film company is effectively retaining the full benefit of the withholding taxes, without passing on any portion of the benefit to participants. Since withholding taxes are based on *gross* receipts, this methodology results in a windfall to film companies.

Deducting Gross Participations. The standard practice is to calculate net profits *after* deducting gross participations payable to third parties. Many participants attempt to avoid this result by providing that they will be entitled to "X% of 100% of net profits," but unless the definition of net profits specifically precludes the deduction of gross participations to third parties, the result will be the same. The net result is that gross participations make achieving net profits next to impossible.

Costs of Developing Ancillary Media. A substantial investment is often required to develop ancillary media, such as a separate interactive program based on a film. The full amount of such an investment is commonly deducted as a distribution expense, effectively putting the participants at risk with respect to exploitation of ancillary media. It is preferable if the income and expenses relating to ancillary media are not crossed against expenses and costs relating to the film itself.

PRODUCTION COSTS

In many ways, the deduction and recoupment of production costs brings with it the same issues and problems associated with distribution costs. Thus, as with distribution expenses, production costs typically include hefty payments to affiliates for various production services. Similarly, production costs rarely reflect discounts or rebates from third parties or savings to the film company from the sale of props or equipment used in the film. On top of all this, there is added the film company's "overhead fee" of approximately 15%. In addition, the cost of a film is usually artificially increased by *twice* the amount of any actual production costs over a certain level, usually 105% of the budget. While this approach may be fair as applied to the director and the producer, who may have control over the cost of the film, it is clearly unfair as applied to other participants who do not have control over costs.

Another difference between production costs and distribution expenses is that an additional interest charge is added to production costs, and this interest charge is always higher than the film company's actual cost of funds. Film companies treat participations as production costs instead of as distribution expenses because that treatment permits interest and the overhead fee to be charged on the participations.

ACCOUNTING

The periodic accounting statements sent out to participants are notable only for their brevity and opaqueness. There is usually no detailed break-out of gross receipts and expenses, and it is next to impossible to reconcile the statements with the contractual provisions. On average, the statements may be reporting income actually received by the film company six months previously, but any payments to the participants do not include interest.

Participation and license contracts almost always state that the accounting statements may not be disputed after some relatively short period of time (such as twelve months), effectively creating an extremely short statute of limitations. Worse yet, a participant may not have the resources or desire to audit the film company during the early years of a film's release, because the film company clearly may not have recouped the aggregate of its distribution and production costs by that time. By the time the film does generate net profits, the film company will state that the prior years are closed to audit, so that all that can be audited is the current year's results.

AUDITS

In many cases, the only realistic remedy for curing suspected reporting errors is a thorough audit, but the standard contracts make this all but impossible. First, film companies typically have the right to approve the auditor — unheard of in any other industry. Second, auditors are spoon-fed limited books and records of the film company (and *not* of its affiliates). For example, auditors are almost never given access to the general ledger or underlying contracts that would show unreported income or rebates. In addition, auditors are generally *not* given the right to make copies of any documents, which hamstrings a thorough review.

And what happens when an underpayment is discovered, admitted, and paid? The contracts do not provide for any interest on the payment, and the contracts rarely provide for the payment of auditors' fees, even in the case of a gross underpayment.

POSSIBLE ALTERNATIVE

A possible alternative to the current approach is to have participations tied directly to the worldwide box-office grosses as reported weekly in the trades (*Variety* or *The Hollywood Reporter*). Historically, the ratio of the worldwide box-office gross for any film compared to the worldwide revenue from all media for that film received by the studio is about 1:1.5. In other words, for every $1 million of worldwide box-office gross, a film can be expected to generate approximately a total of $1.5 million gross revenues worldwide from all media to the studio.

The other variables that are necessary to approximate net profits are (1) the final cost of the film, (2) distribution expenses, and (3) distribution fees. The final cost of the film is relatively easy to ascertain, and the parties could, in any event, simply agree up-front to an estimate of the final cost for purposes of net profits. The calculation of distribution expenses is where many disputes arise, but these disputes could be avoided by treating distribution expenses as a stated percentage of gross revenues (typically, distribution expenses run at approximately 40% of gross revenues received by the studio), with a floor of a stated dollar amount of distribution expenses equating to what the studio believes it will spend at a minimum. The final variable, distribution fees, can be simplified by roughly averaging the current multitude of different fees for different media into one uniform percentage applied to all gross revenues received by the studio. Historically, such an average would be approximately 35%.

By thus converting the variables into easily quantifiable values, the calculation of net profits becomes simple. Let's run through an example using the following assumptions:

Share of net profits:	5%
Deemed cost of film:	$30 million
Distribution fee:	35% of gross revenues
Deemed distribution expense floor:	$15 million

Deemed distribution
  expense percentage: 40% of gross revenues

Worldwide box-office gross: $200 million

Based on these assumptions, the studio would be deemed to receive gross revenues worldwide from all media of $300 million (equal to 150% of the worldwide box office). The calculation of net profits would thus be as follows:

> $300 million deemed gross revenues
> $ 30 million cost of film
> $105 million distribution fee (35% of $300 million)
> $120 million distribution expenses (40% of $300 million)
> $ 45 million net profits.

The payee would thus be entitled to a net profits payment of $2,250,000 (5% of $45 million).

For this approach to be embraced, the studios will have to appreciate the following advantages that will accrue to them:

• First and foremost, significantly lower costs for making films. If payees know that the calculation and payment of net profits will be meaningful, they will be willing to accept significantly lower up-front payments as compensation.

• Shifting of risk. If a film performs poorly, the studio will have less invested in it, and if the film performs well, the studio will be able to afford the payments of net profits.

• Reduction of legal fees attributable to drafting and negotiating long, arcane net profits definitions.

• No audits!

• Far less, if any, litigation relating to net profits.

• Perhaps a lower percentage of net profits to the payees as a trade-off for the certainty of calculation and payment.

Similarly, payees will have to appreciate the following advantages that will accrue to them:

• Short and understandable net profits definitions.

- The amount owed is easy to monitor by simply reading the trades.
- Faster payments, because they depend only on domestic box-office gross.
- Reduction of legal fees attributable to drafting and negotiating long, arcane net-profits definitions.
- No audits!

Yes, there is a trade-off. The proposal is designed to render an approximation, not an exactitude. Particular films may vary from the statistical average, either on the ratio of worldwide gross revenue to the U.S. box office or on the ratio of distribution expenses to gross revenues. Thus, the formula may be imbalanced toward either party on such films. What can be said with some assurance, however, is that the proposal will always be better than the current lunacy.

Forms

The world's shortest definition of net profits is included as Form L in the appendix to this book. Longer definitions, in the context of various license agreements, appear in Forms H (Pro-Licensor License Agreement), I (Pro-Licensee Short Form Agreement), J (Pro-Licensee License Agreement), and K (Split-Rights Production/Distribution Agreement).

CONCLUSION

The amusing aspect of the participations process is that film companies, by gradually making the concept of contingent compensation almost meaningless, have shot themselves in the foot. What used to be a valid and necessary means for spreading risk in a risky industry is now discounted as a joke. The result is that talent demands money up-front or a *gross* participation, resulting in top star salaries reaching the astronomical figure of $20 million per film.

Film companies would be far better served if they return to a realistic and fair approach to contingent compensation, which would result in a drastic reduction in fixed film costs and the spreading of risk. Participations would be paid on successful films, where it can be afforded, and unsuccessful films would not be the devastating blow that they are today.

14

LAW OF IDEAS

INTRODUCTION

Who cares about the law of ideas: Aren't ideas "free as air"? And hasn't the law of ideas been supplanted by the Copyright Act? Wrong on both counts. As discussed in this chapter, ideas are not at all "free as air," and the Copyright Act does not supplant state law in many cases. Let's start with the Copyright Act.

COPYRIGHT ACT PREEMPTION

Section 301 of the United States Copyright Act provides that the Copyright Act preempts all state laws or legal rights that are equivalent to any of the exclusive rights granted to the owner of a copyright. When this section applies, it trumps all state statutory or common-law rights that would otherwise provide protection similar to that afforded under the Copyright Act. The analysis basically breaks down like this:

1. The Copyright Act preempts state laws only if the claim involves a "copyright work." For this purpose, a "copyright work" means any tangible work of authorship, even if it is not entitled to protection under the Copyright Act (e.g., the copyright work is in the public domain, the copyright term has expired, it is an unauthorized derivative work, or it is not original). For example, if you orally tell someone an idea, and he or she "steals" the idea without reducing it to a tangible medium of expression, there is no Copyright Act preemption.

2. There is *no* Copyright Act preemption unless the plaintiff is the author or owner of the copyright work. For example, if you tell someone an idea, and he or she "steals" the idea by writing it down (and thus recording it in a tangible medium of expression), there is *no* Copyright Act preemption, because you (the plaintiff) were not the one who wrote it down. As another example, if someone takes your picture without your permission and puts your picture on soup cans, you will be able to sue for violation of your right of publicity even though the photographer owns the copyright to the picture.

3. There is *no* Copyright Act preemption if the action in question could still be brought even if the copyright work did not exist. For example, if someone breaks into your house at night and steals a script you wrote, you can sue them for trespass even if the script did not exist.

4. There is *no* Copyright Act preemption if the act complained of does not come within the exclusive rights granted under the Copyright Act. For example, if someone takes your script and burns it, you can sue them for theft under state law, because burning a work is not one of the exclusive rights granted under the Copyright Act.

5. There is *no* Copyright Act preemption if the action is based on contract (whether expressed or implied-in-fact). For example, if you submit a script to a Hollywood producer, there is generally an implied-in-fact contract that you are entitled to fair consideration if your script is used.

The analysis set forth above is an over simplification; the case law is still a bit rough around the edges on these issues. Nonetheless, in a broad spectrum of situations, there is no Copyright Act preemption. That is not to say, however, that the plaintiff will win (that issue is discussed below); it only means that the plaintiff will be entitled to sue on a state law cause of action, in addition to any action under the Copyright Act that the plaintiff may also have. In many cases, this threshold issue determines the outcome of the case; the plaintiff may lose under the Copyright Act for any number of reasons, but may prevail on a state law cause of action.

LIABILITY

So, when do the courts find liability when one person uses another's idea? Well, judges are no different than you and I, and if they think that the act was "wrong," they will generally rule in the plaintiff's favor. From there on, it is simply a matter of finding a legal rationale to justify the decision. Some of these rationales include: misappropriation, conversion, unfair competition, quasi contract, unjust enrichment, breach of fiduciary duty, express contract, and implied-in-fact contract. Here are the facts from some sample cases:

- One news service copied and sold news stories prepared by a competing news service. Held: misappropriation.
- A radio station had someone sit at high school ball games and broadcast a running commentary. Held: misappropriation.
- A director of a company used certain ideas owned by the company. Held: breach of fiduciary duty.
- An individual bought software (containing the standard shrink-wrap license prohibiting any further dissemination) and distributed the software for free over the internet. Held: Theft.
- A number of cases involve submission of ideas for television shows or movies to producers. Most cases hold that these submissions create an implied-in-fact contract. California courts, however, generally require the idea submitted to be "novel" before they impose liability.

FILM COMPANY RESPONSE

In response to the fact that ideas are *not* "free as air," the response of most film companies is to reject unsolicited submissions and to only accept submissions from known sources, such as agents or lawyers. Even then, many film companies require an executed "submission contract" as a condition to their review of any submission. Although these contracts differ, at the extreme they basically state that the film company already owns similar ideas, so no compensation will be owed if they use the one being submitted. In fact, one of these submission contracts was held so egregious as to be unenforceable on public policy grounds (in a case dealing with submission of a toy idea to a toy manufacturer).

15

COPYRIGHT

INTRODUCTION

The film industry revolves around copyright, because almost every film company asset relates to the ownership or exploitation of copyrights, including film and television rights, film libraries, and licenses. Thus, an understanding of the basic issues relating to copyright is critical for understanding almost any film transaction.

COUNTRY-BY-COUNTRY DETERMINATION

A common misconception is the assumption that there is one worldwide copyright, furthered by the misconception in the U.S. that somehow the U.S. Copyright Act applies to this worldwide copyright. Both premises are absolutely incorrect. Copyright exists on a country-by-country basis, and the rights and remedies of the copyright holder vary from country to country. The owner of a film actually owns separate copyrights in each country. Under treaties entered into between most countries (e.g., the Berne Convention), publication in one country will trigger copyright protection in the other signatory countries, based on the law of each of those countries. The Berne Convention does *not* supply a uniform copyright law. As a metaphor, assume that each country's copyright law were represented by a different colored light bulb. The Berne Convention provides that if the light bulb goes on in any signatory country, the light bulbs in all the other signatory countries are automatically switched on. However, the Berne Convention does not mandate that all the light bulbs have the same color.

I want to emphasize this point because this chapter discusses the U.S. Copyright Act, and the reader should not assume that the same rules apply outside the U.S. Some foreign countries do follow the U.S. model, but most foreign countries have different models. It is important to consult each country's laws to determine the rules applicable to exploitation of a film in that country.

PROTECTED WORKS

The Copyright Act gives the copyright owner the exclusive right to exploit the copyrighted work. The Copyright Act protects "original works of authorship" that are "fixed in any tangible medium of expression, now known or later developed, from which they can be perceived, reproduced, or otherwise communicated, either directly or with the aid of a machine or device." Thus, an original screenplay is deemed to be a copyrighted work from the moment it is "fixed" in writing. Copyright protection for a motion picture arises as each frame is shot and therefore becomes fixed in a tangible medium, whether on film or videotape. A motion picture is a separate work, although it incorporates such other copyrighted works as the screenplay and the music soundtrack.

DERIVATIVE WORKS

Copyright protection also extends to "derivative works," which are defined as works of authorship that are "based upon" a copyrighted work. The single most litigated issue under the Copyright Act is whether a given work is an infringing derivative work "based upon" a copyrighted work owned by another person. On the one hand, copyright protection does *not* extend to the underlying ideas contained within a copyrighted work; copyright protection is only intended to extend to the particular expression of the underlying idea. On the other hand, copyright protection extends far beyond verbatim copies of the original work. Ultimately, it is a matter of degree, and the courts have found infringement whenever the new work is "substantially similar" to the copyrighted work. As an example, assume the following chain of works, each one of which is based upon the preceding work:

Novel - Treatment - Screenplay - Film - Sequel - Television Series

On these assumed facts, each work is (a) a separate copyrighted work and (b) a work that is a derivative work based upon all of the preceding works. Thus, to have the right to make the television series, you may need the express authorization of every owner of every other work in the chain. These authorizations are referred to as the "chain of title," and obtaining a good chain of title can be a daunting task. I have never yet seen a 100% clean chain of title. There are almost always undocumented links, unexercised options, ambiguous grants of rights, or multiple owners. Going back to the example, you may be able to obtain good chain of title back to the original film, but it may be unclear who owns television series rights, and it may be impossible to obtain clearance from the owners of the preceding works, in which case you may have to drop the project.

TERM OF COPYRIGHT

For individuals, the copyright term is the individual's life plus seventy years. If the individual licenses the work to a third party, the individual automatically retains the non-waivable right to terminate the license after thirty-five years. However, this termination right does not apply with respect to any derivative works created by the licensee under the license. For example, if the owner of a novel licenses the film rights to a film company, which makes a film in reliance on the license, the individual cannot terminate the film company's right to exploit the film after thirty-five years.

In the case of a "work made for hire," the copyright term is ninety-five years from the date of publication. A "work made for hire" is either of the following:

1. A work made by an employee for an employer, whether or not pursuant to a written contract.

2. For certain types of works (including films), any work (including the treatment or screenplay) that is created pursuant to a written contract that expressly provides that it is created as a "work made for hire" for another party.

In both of these cases, the work will be owned by the employer or the party the work is made for, respectively, and the individual creating the work will have no ownership rights to the work.

TRANSFERS

With very little effort, a copyright can be splintered into thousands of microscopic pieces. Critically, under the Copyright Act the owner of the *exclusive* right to any or these pieces is treated as the *owner* of an interest in the copyright. For example, the owner of the exclusive right to show a film right now in the room you are reading in is treated as the owner of an interest in the copyright to the extent of these rights. This fact is referred to as the "bologna theory" of copyright; the overall copyright is treated as the bologna, which can be carved up into endless smaller pieces of bologna.

To grant *exclusive* rights, the grant must be in writing, must expressly grant exclusive rights, and must be signed by the transferor. Any grant not meeting all three of these requirements is automatically treated as the grant of *non-exclusive* rights. In Copyright Act parlance, any grant of exclusive rights is referred to as a "transfer," even if the document is titled a "license."

As bologna is carved up with a knife, a copyright is carved up with words. Thus, the precise drafting of all copyright-related documents is critical. It is important to carefully delineate who owns derivative rights, such as sequels as spin-offs, and who owns the right to exploit a work in future media that are not yet invented.

The word "copyright" is also used as a shorthand to refer to "everything else." For example, if I grant you exclusive theatrical rights, but I retain the copyright, you will have exclusive theatrical rights to the original work, but I will retain the exclusive right to exploit the original work in all other media and to exploit all derivative works in all media. Some people rather myopically focus on ownership of the copyright as though it has some independent significance. Assume that you own the copyright, but I am granted the exclusive right to exploit the work and all derivative works in all media in perpetuity. What do you own? (Not much.)

COMPETING TRANSFERS

Who prevails if the copyright owner transfers the same exclusive rights to two different parties? The Copyright Act provides for a registration and recording system to answer this question. To use Copyright Act terminology, a work itself is "registered" for copyright, and transfers of exclusive rights in the work are "recorded." As long as the underlying work is registered, the first transferee to record its transfer with the Copyright Office prevails (unless this transferee knew of a prior conflicting transfer at the time of its transfer). This recording system is similar to a real property race-notice statute, such as exists in California. The moral of the story is that before you pay for a license of rights, *first* undertake a search of the Copyright Office to make sure that the underlying work is registered and that all prior links in your chain of title are properly recorded, and *then* pay and promptly record your transfer.

FAIR USE DEFENSE

The Copyright Act permits a "fair use" defense to what would otherwise be copyright infringement. The basic theory is that certain uses of a work should not be actionable if they are "fair," and the cases are all over the board as to what qualifies as "fair." Rather than attempt to rationalize the holdings (which is impossible anyway), it is easier to simply summarize some relevant case holdings:

- Fuzzy background use of photographs in the film "Seven" was held fair use.
- Use of school charts and decorations in the background of the "Barney" set was held fair use.
- A twenty-second use of a quilt with a church picnic story on the television show "ROC" was held *not* fair use.
- Use of mobiles for a total of ninety-six seconds in a film was held fair use.

- Books about *Seinfeld* and *Star Trek* were held *not* fair use.
- A half-time skit (at football games) parodying Barney, the dinosaur, was held fair use.

The problem with copyright disputes is that merely to be sued is to lose, because legal defense costs are so high, and these suits generally cannot be thrown out at the summary judgment stage. Therefore, the industry practice - unfortunately - is to have armies of people that do nothing but obtain clearances on everything. The practice has become so pervasive as to be absurd. I routinely advise clients to rely on the fair use defense, but even when my clients are brave, their insurance companies are not. With no insurance, there is no loan. With no loan . . . . You get the picture.

16

RIGHT OF PUBLICITY

INTRODUCTION

The right of publicity protects people from the unauthorized exploitation of their name, likeness, or voice by other persons. All states recognize the right of publicity as a common-law right. Many states have statutes dealing with the right of publicity, but these statutes are generally *in addition to*, and not in replacement of, the common-law right. Thus, plaintiffs usually get the benefit of the broader of the two rights (statutory or common-law). The laws in various states have different nuances, and this chapter discusses the general rules applicable in most states.

The right of publicity has become so expansive that the easiest way to think of the action is that there is a potential case for liability *any time anybody uses anyone's name, likeness, or voice (or imitation thereof) for any reason.* Beyond that, it is just a matter of what defenses, if any, might apply.

Note the breadth of the action: anyone can be a plaintiff, not just celebrities. Also, the right applies to any use, not just a commercial use. It does not even require use of the plaintiff's actual name, likeness, or voice; liability can be based on use of the plaintiff's nickname or a "look-like" or voice imitation.

POTENTIAL DEFENSES

Fair Use. For want of a better name, I group a number of cases under a "fair-use" defense, analogous to the fair-use defense to a copyright claim. Basically, this category is just to permit any use that a court does not find to be "wrong." As an example, one court held that James Brown could not sue based on a scene where actors were watching a twenty-seven second clip of his singing performance on television in the movie "The Commitments." Similarly, a brief discussion of someone in a book has been held not actionable. The California right of publicity statute contains its own incidental use concept, permitting use of any photograph, videotape, etc., of a person as part of a "definable group," such as a crowd or audience, as long as the individual is not singled out in some manner.

Idea/Expression Defense. A number of defendants have attempted to have the courts accept a defense based on use only of items that trigger recognition of the idea of the plaintiff, without actual or imitated use of plaintiff's name, likeness, or voice. To date, however, the courts have rejected this defense and have permitted liability when, at best, only the idea of the plaintiff was being used. For example:

• Vanna White won a claim against Sumsung for using a robot wearing an evening gown spinning the *Wheel of Fortune* in an advertisement.

• Johnny Carson won against a company selling "Here's Johnny" portable toilets.

• A race-car driver won against a tobacco company using a highly-modified photograph of his race car in an advertisement, even though the driver was not visible.

In the author's opinion, the courts should accept this defense to protect the free flow of ideas. For better or worse, celebrities are woven into our social fabric, and ideas that allude to them are part of our cultural language.

First Amendment. As an initial comment, the First Amendment can be a valid defense to a right of publicity action, and the Supreme Court has held that commercial speech qualifies for protection under the First Amendment.

The First Amendment provides an absolute defense for reports on matters of public interest, unless the reports are knowingly or recklessly false. This protection applies to a broad range of expression, including magazines, books, and movies. The definition of "public interest" sweeps up any report regarding public figures and celebrities, as well as reports regarding private citizens who become associated with some issue that has caught the public eye. This is almost always the defense argued by the tabloids when celebrities sue based on some scandalous article.

The Supreme Court has held that a parody, even a highly-offensive one, of a public figure is also protected by the First Amendment. Although the Vanna White/Sumsung case dealt with an action for intentional infliction of emotional distress, the result should be the same for a right of publicity action, or the decision would be toothless. However, for reasons that escape the author, the Ninth Circuit rejected this defense in permitting Vanna White to prevail against Samsung for use of a robot in an evening gown spinning the *Wheel of Fortune* in an advertisement. As discussed above, commercial speech is entitled to First Amendment protection, so the parody defense should have applied.

Some courts have held that there is First Amendment protection for works of fiction based on real characters. For example, one case held that a fictional story based around Valentino's life was not actionable.

Express or Implied Consent. Another defense to a right of publicity action is that the plaintiff has given his or her express or implied consent to the publication. Express consent is straightforward, but implied consent should be interpreted broadly based on the expectations of a reasonable person in the circumstances. For example, actors in a movie should be held to implicitly consent to use of photographs of them in advertisements for the movie. Similarly, athletes in a game that they know is being televised should be held to implicitly consent to the televised broadcast.

Publication of Public Facts. In general, another defense is that the act complained of was merely the publication of public facts, such as publication of a photograph or video of the plaintiff taken in public. A classic example of this was a case that upheld this defense to a right of publicity claim brought by a surfer who appeared in a surfing documentary without his consent. This defense should not, however, be expanded to include such pictures or videos on advertisements for products, because it creates a false implied association between the plaintiff and the product.

RESULT

The real problem with right of publicity cases is that merely to be sued is to lose, even if the defendant ultimately wins the case, because of the legal fees incurred to defend the case and the threat of almost limitless liability. Because of the muddy law in this area and the fact-based nature of the defenses, these cases are almost never resolved at the summary judgment stage. The mantra of all film companies has thus become "When in doubt, leave it out," resulting in a real hit to the First Amendment.

TRADEMARK

INTRODUCTION

In analyzing a trademark issue, it is tempting to analogize to copyright or right of publicity. However, trademark law serves a vastly different purpose, and the three areas of law are not comparable. The purpose of trademark law is consumer protection: Consumers who have identified a quality good with a particular trademark, and thus wish to acquire that or other goods from the same manufacturer, are not to be led astray by confusingly similar trademarks used by unrelated manufacturers. No formal registration is required to have trademark protection, just actual use in commerce. However, a filing in the U.S. Patent and Trademarks Office gives constructive notice to third parties and provides various procedural advantages.

As with any product, the title of a movie can be protected by trademark in order to avoid consumers confusing one movie with another. To avoid stepping on each other's toes, the studios have a system of registration of film titles, with arbitration of competing claims.

FAIR USE DEFENSE

If an audience watches an actor drink Perrier in a movie, hopefully no one in the audience will think Perrier made the movie. Stated otherwise, no reasonable member of the audience would be confused as to the source of the movie, notwithstanding the use of the Perrier trademark in the movie. If Perrier were to sue the producer, Perrier would lose. Because reasonable consumers did not believe that Perrier made the movie, the case should be resolved by holding that there was simply no trademark infringement. Most courts reach the same result but call it the "fair use" defense. That is, it is "fair use" to use another person's trademark if the use does not mislead or confuse consumers as to the source of the goods. For example, a parody of Barney, the dinosaur, was held not actionable because the public was not misled as to the source of the parody—they certainly did not think that

Barney's creator sponsored the parody. Thus, in general, film companies are free to blatantly use third-party trademarks in their movies, such as on billboards in a city scene or on products that appear in the movie, as long as the film does not imply nasty things about the trademarked product (in which case they may be sued for trade libel.) The flip side of the coin is that if the product is being shown in a good light, why not charge the trademark owner for the publicity—thus the booming business of product placements.

COMMERCIAL USE OF FAMOUS TRADEMARKS

Until 1996, this chapter would have gone no further, and the law would have remained relatively clear. In 1996, however, trademark owners successfully convinced Congress (probably with donations to PACs) to bar the "commercial use" of a "famous trademark" in a manner that would "dilute" the trademark. Each of these terms is discussed below, and the net result is to give certain trademarks protection analogous to copyright or right of publicity; i.e., it no longer matters whether the use of a trademark confuses consumers.

The term "commercial use" is probably limited to commercial advertisements and actual use to identify a product. It probably does not apply to use of a trademark in a news article, book, or movie. A "famous trademark" is a trademark that is widely known, as opposed to a trademark known only within a limited geographic area. A trademark is "diluted" if the use of the trademark tends to "tarnish or blur" the trademark. Almost any use of a trademark arguably tarnishes or blurs the trademark, so this provision basically stops any commercial use of a famous trademark. However, some courts have read into the statute a requirement that the use must cause some economic harm to the trademark in question. For example, Barnum & Bailey Circus sued Idaho over the use of the phrase, "The Greatest Snow on Earth" in advertising for Idaho's skiing. Although all the statutory requirements for liability were met, the court ruled for Idaho on the basis that there was no economic harm to Barnum & Bailey's famous trademark, "The Greatest Show on Earth." In fact, people that had seen the ad were more aware of Barnum & Bailey and its trademark than people who had not seen the ad. Another court held that a parody of Barney, the dinosaur, in a public skit was not actionable under this section, because the public was no less likely to love Barney. With luck, this approach might graft the consumer confusion requirement onto this cause of action in order to show economic harm. However, the influential Second Circuit has expressly disagreed with this line of cases, so it may take the Supreme Court to sort it out.

RESULTS

Unfortunately, in the mind of film companies, trademarks rank right next to copyrights and rights of publicity, so the general refrain of "when in doubt, leave it out" applies in full force. Film companies are just too gun shy of litigation. Film companies now have legions of lawyers who do nothing but scan scripts and movie sets for potential problems (copyright, right of publicity, *and* trademarks), and all problems must be deleted or waivers must be obtained from the owners.

18

CREDITS

INTRODUCTION

Friendships end over it, partnerships dissolve, and battles rage. More acrimonious fights are fought over who gets what credit, and in what order, than over any other issue in the film industry. Let's look at what the fuss is all about.

TYPES OF CREDIT

- *Logo*. The logo is the animated artwork (usually moving) that appears at the very front of a film. For example, Universal has the globe, MGM the lion, Paramount the mountain, etc. The film's distributor always puts its logo up front, but there may be a second logo for the production company.

- *Presentation Credit*. The next credit to appear on a film is usually the presentation credit, which again usually goes to the distributor of the film. The credit usually reads "Presented by [Distributor]" or "[Distributor] Presents." Sometimes, other parties get into the act, and the credit might also read "In Association With [someone else]," usually the production company or financier.

- *Film By Credit*. Frequently, but not always, there will be a credit, referred to as a possessory credit, reading "A Film By [director]." Don't ask me why the director needs this credit in addition to the standard "Directed By" credit, except that you can never have too many credits.

- *Executive Producer Credit*. The "Executive Producer" credit usually goes to the person that found (or supplied) the money to the producer. Usually, the executive producer merely acts as a broker, or finder, hooking the producer up with one or more distributors or financiers to arrange financing for the film.

- *Produced By Credit*. The "Produced By" credit goes to the producers of the film. Usually, these are people who found or liked the script, and were able to "attach" such talent as the director or stars, and then shopped the concept to a distributor (often with the help of an executive producer). The producers are the individuals who get to stand on stage and accept an Oscar for "Best Picture" (everyone's dream), so this is a highly coveted credit.

- *Associate Producer Credit.* When you can't think of what other credit to give someone, they get an "Associate Producer" credit, usually with a litany of others. For example, the credit often goes to girlfriends, boyfriends, assistants, and hangers-on.

- *Story By Credit.* The "Story By" credit goes to the writer of the underlying story, if any, such as the writer of the underlying novel or article upon which the script was based.

- *Written By Credit.* The "Written By" credit goes to the screenplay writer. Whenever the writer is a member of the WGA, the WGA Basic Agreement sets out the requirements for the credit, and any disputes (such as between competing writers) is subject to binding WGA arbitration.

- *Directed By Credit.* Guess who this goes to.

PLACEMENT

- *On-Screen.* An "on-screen" credit is a credit that appears on the movie itself. These credits are always divided into "main title" credits, which appear with the first credits that appear (usually in the beginning of a film) and "end credits," which is the small print at the end of a film that only die-hards read. When a main title credit is to appear on a "separate card," it means that the credit in question appears on the screen alone, and does not appear together with other credits. A "shared card" credit is a credit that appears on the screen simultaneously with one or more other credits.

- *Advertising.* A "key art" credit will appear on the marketing poster created for the picture, which typically appears in theater lobbies, video stores, etc. A "paid ad" credit means that the credit will appear in all advertising for the picture, other than a standard list of "excluded ads," which include teaser campaigns, trailers, radio ads, television ads, and award ads.

- *Position.* It is always important to designate the precise location where the credit will appear. Top stars will insist that their credit appear "above" (before) the title of the picture, while everyone else is generally "below title." The contractual credit provision will usually state that the credit must be a certain size compared to the title of the picture, such as 100% of title, 50% of title, etc. When more than one person is to be given a certain credit, it is important to specify who is in first position, second position, etc., and the on-screen credit must specify whether the credits are to appear on a separate or shared card. The contract can also specify such minute details as the type size, color, width, and duration of the credit, and this issue is often dealt with by simply saying the credit will be handled the same as the credit given to some other person who, it is hoped, will get some respect. In some cases, a credit will state that it has "favored nations" status, which simply means that the credit is to be handled no worse than anyone else's credit. The best way to deal with all of these issues is to do a "credit bible," which is a pictorial chart of every credit, with the exact title, order, and size.

Talent with clout often have the right to approve certain of the credits, such as other credits that appear above the title of the picture and even unrelated credits, in order to prevent being outdone by other credits.

ENFORCEMENT

In order to enforce a contractual credit requirement, it is important for the contract to state that the distributor will require all subdistributors to comply with the credit, with the credit recipient as an intended third-party beneficiary of the undertaking. Similarly, if there are credit approval rights, these credit approval rights must also be complied with by the subdistributors, which can drive them crazy.

Almost always, the contractual credit provision contains significant limitations on the liability of the distributor (or subdistributor) for breach of credit obligations. Typically the contract states that in the event of a breach of any credit obligation: (a) there can be no injunction blocking distribution of the picture, (b) the distributor's only obligation is to cure the breach prospectively on new prints (without any obligation to destroy old prints), and (c) there are no damages in the event of a "casual or inadvertent failure" to provide the credit.

19

TALENT

Writers

Fixed Compensation

Credit

Derivative Works

Turnaround

Contingent Compensation

IN GENERAL

You already know many of the issues of concern to talent. For example, credits and contingent compensation are discussed in prior chapters. This Chapter discusses the other main issues that get talent excited. To some extent, this chapter may be used as a checklist when negotiating a deal.

ACTORS

The main issues for actors are set forth below:

Start Date/Stop Date. One difficult issue is coordinating the availability dates for the various actors on a picture, to make sure that they are free from the scheduled start date through the stop date. Some pictures are postponed for one or more years because of the difficulty of lining everyone up.

Pay or Play. Actors will always want to be "pay-or-play," which means that they get paid whether or not the movie is made. Since there is always a risk that a movie will not be made, and film companies are not keen on incurring substantial pay-or-play commitments, two games have evolved to deal with this problem. Many pay-or-play commitments expressly state that they are "subject to final approved bonded budget," which effectively neuters the commitments, because if the film is never made, there will never be a final approved bonded budget. Studios usually get away with this approach. Another approach is to have the pay-or-play commitments come from a shell company that is intended to be the production service subsidiary. Again, if the film is not made, the liability is meaningless since the shell company has no assets. Independent film companies usually try this approach. If the actors are playing hardball, they will insist on a deposit or escrow to cover the pay-or-play commitments.

Approvals. Actors like to have approval over a plethora of issues, including the script, co-stars, and director. Major stars may require approval over other credits, the marketing campaign, and paid product placements in the picture.

Tax Indemnity. If a film is being shot outside the United States, an actor should always insist on a tax indemnity from the film company, to cover the risk that foreign taxes will exceed U.S. taxes. Many film companies blithely set production for some exotic location, without realizing the devastating tax impact involved. Many films have ground to a halt over this issue, because the actors insisted on a tax indemnity that the film companies had not budgeted and were not prepared to pay.

Entourage. Major stars will insist on bringing along (at the film company's expense) an entire entourage, including their own hair stylist, makeup person, wardrobe person, assistant, secretary, etc. It is in part due to the cost of this entourage that the cost of a picture increases by at least 150% (not 100%) of a major star's salary.

Transportation. Of course stars want first-class airfare and limousines. In one case, we had to rent the star's jet—from the star!

Accommodations. Stars want first-class hotel accommodations, but even on the set, they want their own forty-foot trailer, with full living accommodations, including kitchen, bar, and entertainment center.

Premieres. Any attendance at premieres (often with full entourage in tow) will be at the film company's expense.

Video Cassettes. My personal favorite. Almost all contracts, including for a $20-million star, will require the film company to purchase the star a video cassette of the picture when it is released on video.

Contingent Compensation and Credit. See Chapters 13 and 18.

DIRECTORS

For most issues, a director's concerns are identical to an actor's. For example, the following issues discussed above for actors apply with equal force to directors: start date/stop date (but with a longer window), pay-or-play, approvals, tax indemnity, transportation, accommodations, video cassette, contingent compensation, and credit. In addition, directors have a few unique issues of their own, including the following:

Pay and Play. Major directors may insist on being pay *and* play, which means that they have the absolute right to direct and cannot be removed, even if they are paid in full.

Final Cut. Major directors will want "final cut" of the picture, which means they have the complete creative freedom and discretion to make the film the way they want to, even if the distributor or financier disagrees. When they do get final cut, it is usually subject to some minimum requirements, such as the film tracking the script, time limitations, and a rating no more restrictive than "R".

Editing/Dubbing. Many directors want at least the first opportunity to make any edits required for television or airline versions and to create any dubbed versions of the film for the foreign markets.

Marketing. Many directors like to be involved in the marketing of the film, including creation of the key-art, trailer, and commercials, and want to be consulted on the release schedule and pattern.

Derivative Works. Many directors want at least a right of first negotiation to direct any derivative works, such as remakes, sequels, or television spin-offs.

WRITERS

And, finally, writers have their own unique concerns:

Fixed Compensation. Writers are usually paid their fixed compensation in installments, based on a first draft, subsequent drafts, and polish of the script. Sometimes this fixed compensation will be subject to a retroactive increase based on the actual budget of the picture. For example, a writer may receive $200,000 up front, against a final payment equal to 2% of the budget upon commencement of principal photography.

Credit. Writers usually run the risk that the script may be modified or rewritten by other writers, so the "written by" credit may go to someone else. Top writers can prevent this by prohibiting the film company from using any other writers to make any modifications to the script.

Derivative Works. In addition to the right of first negotiation to write derivative works, such as sequels, remakes, or television spin-offs, writers will usually be entitled to a royalty on derivative works, even if they do not write them. The WGA Basic Agreement provides for minimum royalties, which may or may not be increased by contract.

Turnaround. Most contracts provide that if the film company that purchased the script does not produce a picture based on the script by a certain date, the script will "turn around," which means that ownership of the screenplay will revert from the film company to the writer. In this case, however, if any other film company ever commences principal photography of a film based on the screenplay, the original film company that failed to film the script will be entitled to be repaid at that time an amount equal to all the costs it incurred in acquiring or developing the screenplay, and this liability will be secured by a security interest in the screenplay.

Contingent Compensation. The customary practice is to give writers, at most, 5% of the net profits from the picture. Sony, however, has agreed to pay certain top writers 2% of "adjusted gross receipts" (defined in this case as gross receipts less all distribution costs), and it is yet to be seen whether this practice will spread to other studios or other writers.

20

LITIGATION

INTRODUCTION

One word of advice on litigation: DON'T! Or at least think long and hard before you do. Here are some reasons why not to litigate:

- Within days after you thump your chest and file your claim, you will be subject to a counterclaim. People do not like being sued, even plaintiffs. In one case, PBS sued a video licensee over chump change and was promptly subject to a counterclaim that resulted in a $47-million verdict against PBS. Ouch.

- Yes, I know it's the principle of the thing, expenses be damned, but that only holds until the first legal bill arrives. After the second or third bill, the enthusiasm is long gone.

- There is an extraordinary aggravation factor; it is not a pure monetary analysis. There are depositions, interrogatories, and motions, and even putting aside going to court, the stress can eat you alive.

- Ninety percent or more of the time, the cases settle. Very few go through a court trial. Why not just settle up front without all the fuss and muss of litigation?

- Lawyers should be aware that there are always two sides to every story. After you have used up a box or two of Kleenex, crying over your client's sob story, and have filed the action, you will quickly receive the counterclaim, outlining all the scumbag things your client did.

STRATEGY

If you do find yourself in the unfortunate circumstance of litigation, you might want to try one strategy I often use—tennis. In this game, the goal is simply to get the ball back over the net with the least effort. Let the other side run around the court with motions, demurrers, interrogatories, etc., until their legal fees sink them (or at least dampen their spirits).

ARBITRATION

Is arbitration the answer? No way. In many cases, the only thing worse than litigation is arbitration. Consider these issues:

- Statistically, 50% of the time you (or your client) will be the party being sued. Rather than wanting a supposedly quick and efficient dispute resolution mechanism, you may want a long, drawn-out process where you can wear down the other side.

- In arbitration, there is very little, if any, discovery. You basically have to argue your case cold, without being able to find out all the relevant facts.

- In arbitration, what do you do when the arbitrator has just ruled against your 100% correct sure-fire case? You suck wind. At least in litigation, you can say, "Don't worry; we will appeal." In arbitration, you are stuck with whatever lunatic decision the arbitrator renders.

ATTORNEY FEES

The American rule is that the prevailing party in litigation does not recover their attorney fees from the other party. Thus, from the plaintiff's point of view, there is almost no risk of bringing almost any litigation against anybody, so the system has become one of legalized extortion. For example, I once had a client who was accused, among other things, of leaving his body at night and having out-of-body sex with the plaintiff/employee. Because the case was not thrown out at the summary judgment stage, our client was forced to settle for what would have been the cost of his defense (approximately $200,000).

FOREIGN DEFENDANTS

Most lawyers have a knee-jerk reaction to draft contracts imposing exclusive jurisdiction for litigation in the lawyer's home forum. This is usually a bad idea. Even if the lawyer is careful enough to also have the other party consent to personal jurisdiction in the home forum and agree to a local agent for service of process (good luck serving a foreign defendant under the Hague Convention!), what good is a United States judgment if the defendant has no assets in the United States? I know you are supposed to be able to enforce a United States judgment under enforcement-of-judgment treaties with many foreign countries, but there is always local judicial review, both procedural and substantive, before enforcement, so don't bet on automatic enforcement. It is far better to provide for non-exclusive jurisdiction and venue wherever you want, so you at least maintain the flexibility to sue in the defendant's home country if you need to.

AVOIDANCE

The real solution to litigation is to avoid it. Some suggestions discussed in this book include:

- Learn to spot and avoid schemers and dreamers.
- Keep the structure simple.
- Use clear, concise contracts.
- Do not take any act in reliance on oral agreements, including commencing production, making pay-or-play commitments, or issuing press releases. It ain't over 'til it's over, and it ain't over until a binding contract is signed.
- Do not use letters of intent, term sheets, or deal memos. Instead, use complete, concise contracts.

21

BANKRUPTCY

Introduction

Executory Contracts

Determining Ownership of Film Rights

Summary of Protection for Licensors and Licensees

Voidable Preferences

Fraudulent Conveyance

INTRODUCTION

Have I mentioned that most films lose money? One consequence is that a great number of independent film companies (and, unfortunately, many of my former clients) have gone bankrupt. But that is the least of the reasons to understand bankruptcy; far more important are the draconian results from a bankruptcy of the other party to a transaction. The United States Bankruptcy Code is written so perversely in favor of the bankrupt party (usually referred to as the "debtor") that a bankruptcy upsets all reasonable expectations of anyone doing business with the debtor. Film rights can be lost, payment obligations can be canceled, and other contractual obligations can be left in limbo for years. The havoc is so great that it is absolutely necessary to plan in advance for the tragic event: "What if the other side goes bankrupt?"

EXECUTORY CONTRACTS

One of the first things you will hear about in any bankruptcy is the dreaded threat that whatever contract you have with the debtor is an "executory contract." If such it is, the debtor is given the option of either (a) behaving and performing, (b) breaching almost with impunity (you will be left with an unsecured claim in the bankruptcy), or (c) dragging the matter out while it leisurely decides what to do. All of this is obviously maddening to the non-debtor, who is thus guaranteed to argue that the contract is *not* "executory."

So what is an "executory contract"? Unfortunately, the law is in complete chaos on this question. A majority of courts require both parties to have remaining material obligations under a contract in order for the contract to be executory, but these courts apply this test inconsistently. A minority of courts have rejected that test and have held that a contract is an executory contract if the *debtor* has *any* remaining contractual obligations that it is permitted or required to perform as of the bankruptcy filing date.

To add to the confusion, the courts consistently confuse the executory contract analysis with the issue of who owns the underlying rights (e.g., who owns the licensed rights as between a licensee and a licensor). In fact, these two issues are completely separate: a finding that a contract (such as a film license) is or is not executory is irrelevant to determining who owns the underlying rights. The election to assume or breach an executory contract (including a license) in bankruptcy only relates to the *contractual provisions* of the contract. If there are property rights relating to the contract (e.g., an exclusive license of film rights), the determination of ownership of the property rights is a separate, independent question. The determination does *not* flow automatically from the decision of whether to assume or breach the contract or even from the determination of whether or not the contract is executory at all. For example, a debtor may reject an executory contract, but the debtor may be entitled to retain any property (such as film rights) relating to the contract. Conversely, a contract may not be executory, but the debtor may not be entitled to retain property relating to the contract.

DETERMINING OWNERSHIP OF FILM RIGHTS

In bankruptcy, the determination of the ownership of property relating to a contract (such as film rights) is determined under general legal principles, including the Copyright Act. If the licensee of film rights has gone bankrupt and has ceased making payments under the license, the licensor is out of luck unless the license contains an express provision permitting the licensor to terminate the license in the event of such a breach. Otherwise, the licensee can keep the licensed rights, and the licensor's only remedy is to file an unsecured claim for damages in the bankruptcy. If the license does permit the licensor to terminate, the licensor generally may do so subject to obtaining advance permission from the bankruptcy court.

If a licensor declares bankruptcy and attempts to regain ownership of the licensed rights, section 365(n) of the Bankruptcy Code permits the licensee to retain the licensed rights. Although there are several anomalies in the wording of this section, it more or less does the job.

Because of chaotic case law and ambiguities in the Bankruptcy Code, most licensors and licensees are not willing to rely solely on the terms of the license for their protection, and it is common practice for each party to request the other party's obligations to be secured by a security interest in the underlying film rights.

SUMMARY OF PROTECTION FOR LICENSORS AND LICENSEES

This section sets forth a brief summary of the protections that can be adopted by licensors and licensees to protect against a potential bankruptcy of the other.

1. *Licensors*

To protect themselves against a potential bankruptcy of a licensee, licensors should consider adopting all or some of the following protective strategies:

a. Instead of making the other party a licensee, and entering into a license, attempt to appoint the other party as a sales agent performing services for a commission, and have the licenses come directly from the licensor to the next level in the distribution chain. Have revenues paid directly to the licensor or placed in a segregated trust account, with the sales agent taking a commission with the balance remitted to the licensor.

b. Put a "key-man" clause in the license, terminating the license if certain key employees of the licensee leave. This type of clause should be enforceable in a bankruptcy of the licensee, and key personnel often leave in a bankruptcy.

c. Make sure the license contains an express right to terminate if the licensee breaches.

d. Structure the transaction as a "license," not as a "sale" in perpetuity. This is a cosmetic difference only, but it may influence a court to permit termination.

e. Obtain a protective security interest in the licensed rights.

2. *Licensees*

To protect themselves against a potential bankruptcy of a licensor, licensees should consider adopting all or some of the following protective strategies:

a. Do not accept appointment as a sales agent; insist on receiving a grant of rights.

b. Make sure that the license expressly states that it is exclusive.

c. Have the license expressly state that it will not terminate for any reason.

d. Record the license (or a short-form assignment that refers to the license) in the U.S. Copyright Office and in the major foreign countries that have a recording system.

e. Structure the transaction as a "sale" of the rights in perpetuity, instead of as a license for a limited term.

VOIDABLE PREFERENCES

In certain cases, a debtor can rescind as a "voidable preference" any "transfer" made by the debtor within ninety days before the bankruptcy to repay or secure a pre-existing debt. A "transfer" includes not only a payment of cash, but also the perfection of a security interest in the debtor's assets. In the film industry, it is quite common for a security interest to be perfected for a pre-existing debt for several reasons. The most common situation arises when a loan is used to produce a film, but the film's registration does not occur until the film is completed many months later. Under the Copyright Act, it is impossible to perfect a security interest in a film until the film itself is registered with the Copyright Office. Thus, while it may be possible to obtain a security interest in the underlying rights, such as the script, it is impossible to perfect an interest in the copyright to a film until the film itself is completed and registered with the Copyright Office. Another situation arises when perfection of a security interest secures a revolving line of credit that has been fully used up. In both cases, perfection of the security interest may be voidable.

FRAUDULENT CONVEYANCE

The debtor is also able to rescind any transfers that occur generally within four years (depending on state law) of the bankruptcy if one of the following two conditions is met:

1. The transfer was made for less than adequate consideration at a time when the debtor was insolvent; or

2. The transfer was made with the intent to hinder or delay creditors.

These transfers are referred to as "fraudulent transfers." The intent of this provision is to protect the debtor from selling assets at a fire-sale price due to financial pressures.

POP QUIZ: On the day before filing bankruptcy, a film company sells its entire film library for its fair market value of $100 million. Can the sale be rescinded?

ANSWER: No. The transaction is not a voidable preference because it was not a transfer made on account of a pre-existing debt. The transaction is also not a fraudulent conveyance because the transfer was made for full value consideration, and the transfer will not hinder or delay creditors, as they now have liquid assets to proceed against.

22

INTERNET DISTRIBUTION OF FILMS

INTRODUCTION

It's here! That is, distribution of films on the Internet, and it will have the same revolutionary impact on the film industry as the introduction of video in the '70s. It will require a complete rethinking of the film business, and the streets will be lined with dead bodies and lottery winners.

THE HOW

Already, films that are shot on celluloid can be subsequently transferred to a digital file that is stored on a computer server located anywhere in the world. In time, films will be shot digitally in the first instance, which will make this process easier. It will also expedite digital transmission of films to theaters. (Ah, but that is another story. . .) The server can hold many films, and anyone with a personal computer will be able to access the server and download a film (for a reasonable fee, of course). There are several barriers to making this practical, but these barriers are rapidly falling:

Speed. Using a normal modem, a full day is required to download a two-hour movie. There is currently available high-speed download technology, but it is relatively expensive. In a short time, however, the cost will drop and the technology will become widely affordable. The next widely anticipated development is the implementation of broadband cable technology (the equivalent of unwinding a string into its separate strands), which will permit the rapid transmission of massive amounts of data, permitting the rapid download of films.

Quality. Currently, downloaded films are viewed on a computer screen, which causes a serious degradation of quality compared to theaters or even video. Two recent developments are changing this. The first is that Microsoft recently introduced software that permits playback of downloaded films at thirty frames per second, comparable to VCR tapes played on TV sets. The second development is technology permitting downloaded films to be replayed directly on television sets, rather than on computer screens.

Piracy. Fear abounds that once a film is in the digital world, where perfect copies can be made over and over, rampant piracy will occur. There are two answers to this problem: The first is, so what? The studios long ago accepted piracy as an unfortunate but acceptable cost of doing business. They crossed this bridge with video, they crossed this bridge with DVD, and they will cross it with Internet distribution. The second answer is that technology has been and will be developed that prevents downloaded films from being re-transmitted to third parties.

A dream? Hardly. Several companies are distributing films over the Internet. The first for-pay distribution was in April, 1999, when Sightsound.com distributed Artisan's film "Pi" over the Internet for $2.95. With the use of high-speed download technology, the film could be downloaded in about twenty minutes. Using Microsoft's software, the film could be played back at almost VCR quality. Sightsound claims to have patented technology that prevents the piracy of downloaded films. Other companies have entered the fray, including Reel.com, Broadcast.com, Global Media, Inc., and Reel Networks.

BUSINESS MODEL

Distribution. The most likely scenario is that studios will distribute their own films through their own servers, rather than licensing their films to third-party servers. This model seems likely for several reasons: First, it will permit the studios to maintain control over their film libraries, rather than risk losing control, particularly in the easily pirated digital format. Second, distribution costs will be relatively low (other than advertising, which the studios already know how to do); it will not require an extensive staff of employees, such as is required to service theatrical or video distribution. Finally, it gives the studios direct contact with the consumers, giving the studios the opportunity to cross-sell other films or media. The main benefit of the Internet is to give companies direct access to consumers, and the studios will not relinquish this benefit lightly.

It also seems likely that several of the studios may combine resources in a joint venture, analogous to UIP (for theatrical distribution) or CIC (for video). In this manner, consumers could hook up with one server to obtain the vast majority of potential films.

Window. Initially, the Internet release window will probably come after the video and pay-TV window, and before the free-TV window. Those two windows are too well entrenched to permit being preempted lightly. In time, however, the Internet window should cannibalize both pay-TV and video, effectively moving forward the Internet window to shortly after the theatrical release, analogous to the current video window.

It is highly unlikely, however, that Internet distribution will ever replace the primacy of the theatrical release. Just as video, pay-TV, television, DVD, etc., have not spelled the demise of theatrical, neither will Internet distribution. People—particularly teenagers—like to get out of the house, and it is difficult for any home system to compete with theaters' large screen and multi-channel sound system.

Pricing. The per-film pricing for Internet distribution must drop compared to the video and DVD rental business. This is because there are no manufacturing costs associated with Internet distribution, and the distribution costs are far less. This substantial drop in costs can only correlate to lower pricing. It is also likely that in addition to, or in lieu of, a per/film fee, consumers could pay a monthly fee to obtain a specified number of films per month. The film-distribution server should also be able to earn ad revenues through advertising, banners, and links to other Internet sites.

ISSUES

Who Owns It? The immediate issue will be, who owns Internet rights? The disputes will include issues such as whether or not the producers granted the studios Internet rights in the first place and whether the studios have licensed those rights to third parties. The answers will depend on the terms of each contract, and this issue will be endlessly litigated. Since Internet rights will cannibalize both video and pay-TV, one can expect the argument to be made that Internet rights come within the definition of one or both of those rights. In the author's opinion, it is inappropriate to do so; it just cannot be said to be within anyone's reasonable expectations that "video" or "pay television" would include a media as novel and different as Internet rights. A more problematic issue is whether Internet rights fall within the definition of "video on demand" or "near video on demand" —definitions that have been used for some time in contemplation of unlimited at-will access to films. The difficulty is that it was generally contemplated that such access would be via cable or satellite, so it really will depend on the precise definitional language used. The simplest case is a future media clause, covering distribution by "all media, whether now known or hereafter devised." Whoever owns these rights should certainly own Internet rights.

Territoriality. Territoriality will be the single most problematic aspect of licensing Internet rights. Under current distribution models, most distribution rights are ultimately handled by different distributors on a territory-by-territory basis. For example, a German distributor may be licensed certain rights within Germany, and a French distributor may be licensed certain rights within France. Each distributor then distributes the film within its own country, and there are elaborate restrictions on inadvertent distribution outside of the prescribed territory, including terrestrial and satellite broadcast restrictions. All of this suffers the fate of the stone axe under Internet distribution because consumers in any part of the world can hook-up to a server located anywhere else. Unless caution is used, a licensee of Zimbabwe rights could set up a server permitting worldwide access to the film. Because of this risk, one solution is for both the licensor and licensee to "freeze" Internet rights until technology that limits Internet access to a prescribed country or territory is developed and used. For example, technology may be developed to limit access to phone numbers starting with a certain prefix (although call forwarding may defeat this). The most likely solution is that Internet rights will be left with the licensor (typically a studio), and perhaps the licensor will be required to pay the licensee for revenues attributable to Internet access within the licensed territory. For example, it may become possible to source revenues within that territory based on phone number prefixes, or perhaps some specified percentage of worldwide revenues can be used.

Another approach is to license Internet rights, but to require the Internet version used by the licensee to be dubbed into the home language. This is similar to what is currently done for satellite broadcasts (unless they are encrypted for reception within the home territory). It is unlikely that requiring only subtitling will be sufficient if the film is still in English, as subtitling in a foreign language would not be an effective block against consumers who speak or understand English and are willing to ignore the subtitles.

Holdbacks. The resolution of determining the appropriate holdback for Internet rights will depend on where the Internet release window falls, discussed above. As discussed there, one might expect Internet rights to initially be subject to a holdback until after the video and pay-TV window, with this holdback subsequently moving up to replace the video and pay-TV windows entirely.

Calculating Contingent Payments to Talent and Licensors. One of the wonderful battles will be over the calculation of participations owed to talent and overages owed to licensors. The resolution of this issue will depend on the business model used for Internet distribution. As discussed above, it is likely that the studios will undertake

Internet distribution directly or through a multi-studio joint venture. In this case, the immediate question is what revenues constitute "gross receipts" as the starting point for calculating contingent payments? Talent and other payees will obviously take the position that revenues received by the server from consumers should constitute gross receipts. It can be predicted with absolute certainty that the studios will take the position that these revenues must be excluded, and that gross receipts must start with a deemed royalty paid by the server to the studio. For example, the studios still generally get away with including in gross receipts a deemed royalty as low as 20% on video revenues, and video revenues never include payments by the consumers, even if the studio owns the retailer (e.g., Blockbuster, which is related to Paramount.) Similarly, when Disney licenses films to ABC, its wholly owned network, only the revenues received by Disney, not ABC, are included in gross receipts.

If the studios prevail in adopting a similar inter-company deemed royalty model for Internet distribution, the remaining question is what the inter-company price will be. Presumably, it will be stated as a percentage of server revenues, and one can expect the studios' opening bid to be 20% (after all, they generally get away with this on video). In lieu of a percentage of gross receipts to the server, another model may be an arbitrary price, to some extent based on theatrical receipts, which is basically how inter-company sales to television networks are done.

Another issue will be what distribution fee, if any, applies to Internet gross receipts. If gross receipts are calculated at the server level, then it seems fair to have a distribution fee, albeit a low one, because distribution activities should be relatively modest. If, however, gross receipts are calculated based on a deemed royalty to the studio, then there should be no distribution fee, just as there should be no distribution fee on a deemed video royalty (unless the contract is really piggish).

The next issue will be what, if any, distribution costs are deductible. Again, if gross receipts are based on gross receipts to the server, then it is appropriate to deduct all actual costs incurred in connection with Internet distribution. If, however, gross receipts are calculated based on a deemed royalty to the studio, then no distribution costs should be deductible on the grounds that the royalty percentage is in lieu of all costs. For example, this is how video is typically handled. On this point, someone should argue that a large portion of theatrical advertising costs are intended to benefit Internet distribution, and so should not be deductible. (However, this same issue applies to the current calculation of video net receipts, and the author is not aware of anyone winning this argument . . . yet.)

A further complication will be how to allocate revenues among pictures, particularly if consumers pay a monthly subscription price in lieu of a per/film price. This same issue currently applies to any package sale of film rights, and the best that can typically be achieved is vague "fair and reasonable" allocation language in the contract.

Finally, you can be sure that, one way or another, ad revenue received by the server will not be included in gross receipts. If server income is included in gross receipts, there will most likely be a blanket exclusion for ad revenue. Alternatively, the very existence of ad revenue will be an argument for why gross receipts must be calculated based on a deemed royalty to the studio, as in the case of an affiliated television network.

All of these issues will be particularly fun in the context of contracts that do not contemplate Internet distribution. The studios will most likely resort to self-help in the form of forming the server as a separate company and entering into a formal inter-company license. The interesting issue will be if the contract in question picks up revenues received by affiliates or refers to "at-source" accounting.

Guild Residuals. Another problematic issue will be determining how to calculate guild residuals on Internet revenue. Similar to the question of calculating contingent payments owed to talent and licensors, the question under the guild agreements is what will be the starting point for calculating gross receipts. Until the guild agreements are amended to expressly deal with this question, the same battles discussed above in connection with calculating participations and other contingent payments owed to third parties will apply in calculating guild residuals. But just where do Internet revenues fall under the current guild agreements, which currently divide film revenues into theatrical, video, pay-TV, and free-TV? Perhaps the answer is "Nowhere."

CONCLUSION

The ability of consumers to pay to see a film of their choice at any time will have profound implications on the film industry. At a minimum, the value of film libraries should skyrocket, just as they did with the introduction of video. It will take years to sort out the business and legal implications of the new distribution pattern, and lawyers will have their hands full negotiating and drafting contracts that properly deal with the issues—or litigating those that don't.

23

TAXATION

Tangible v. Intangible Property

Ownership

Rents v. Royalties

Licensee v. Agent

Royalties v. Compensation

Inventory

Partnership

Foreign Production And Distribution

Depreciation/Amortization of Films

At-Risk Rules

Advances

Personal Holding Company Tax

Financing Film Production And Distribution

    Domestic Tax Shelters

    Co-Productions

    Loans

    Foreign Tax Shelters

Tax Planning For Talent

Withholding

    Wage Withholding

    Payments to Foreign Persons

California Taxation

This chapter summarizes and provides a general overview of the significant tax issues that often arise in the entertainment industry, offering the reader a general issue-spotting checklist. If you are a real tax junkie, you can get my other book, *Taxation of the Entertainment Industry*, from Panel Publishers (800 234-1660) or through Amazon.com.

TANGIBLE V. INTANGIBLE PROPERTY

One tax issue that comes up repeatedly in the film industry is whether films are tangible or intangible property. It is somewhat amazing that, after more than seventy years, this is still an unresolved tax issue. The issue of tangible versus intangible property finds its way into many areas of taxation, including depreciation, investment tax credit, Subchapter S, passive activity losses, and Subpart F, to name a few. It is also relevant for state sales tax and unitary taxation. As a broad generalization, the case law has held that films are tangible property, and the IRS has consistently argued and ruled that films are intangible property.

Congress has passed many statutes that effectively treat films as intangible property for certain purposes and as tangible property for other purposes. One of the areas where Congress has effectively treated films as intangible property is depreciation. By statute, films are prohibited from using accelerated depreciation, which applies to tangible property under Internal Revenue Code (the "Code") Sec. 168. Thus, under current law, films are relegated to the use of the income forecast method of amortization or straight-line depreciation. Outside of the express statutory provisions, taxpayers have the best of both worlds; if they want to treat films as tangible property, they can rely on the case law, and if they want to treat films as intangible property, they can rely on IRS pronouncements.

OWNERSHIP

Notwithstanding the tax characterization of films as tangible or intangible, in the real world the value of a film lies in the intangible right under copyright law to exploit the film (*i.e.*, a film print is not worth much if you cannot exhibit it). This intangible right can be splintered into numerous pieces, based on the medium of exhibition, territory, and time. This ability to splinter film rights does not fit well with general tax principles, which seek to find one person who is the "owner" of the film. The "deal makers" in the film industry are generally not concerned with the niceties of tax law, and the tax law grew out of concepts and principles that apply to tangible property, and which do not apply well to intangible property, such as films.

The result is that it is not always clear who is the "owner" of a film for tax purposes, which has implications that run throughout the Code. For example, it is often critical to determine whether a transaction is a sale, lease, or license. This issue is important in determining the calculation of gain, amortization of costs, accrual of income, and character of income, to name a few issues. For example, if all film rights to Canada are "sold" in perpetuity for a contingent price, is the transaction a sale or a license? What if the parties call the transaction a "license"? What if the payment were a fixed sum instead of contingent?

RENTS V. ROYALTIES

Another area of uncertainty, which tends to overlap with the tangible versus intangible distinction, is whether income from exploitation of a film is "rents" or "royalties." This distinction is extremely important in applying many tax provisions, such as the personal holding company rules, the foreign personal holding company rules, Subchapter S, the passive activity rules, and treaty provisions. In general, it appears that theatrical film income is characterized as rent, and film income from other sources is characterized as royalties. This generalization gives way to the rules applicable to each specific statutory provision, which rules are sometimes found only in the legislative history.

LICENSEE V. AGENT

Another common issue is determining whether a person is a licensee or a sales agent. The terms are often used interchangeably, but the distinction can have important tax implications, including determining who is entitled to the foreign tax credit for any withheld taxes. The distinction depends on whether there has been a grant of rights to the person in question. If so, the person is a licensee. If not, the person is a sales agent.

ROYALTIES V. COMPENSATION

It is often necessary to determine whether payments should be characterized as royalties or as compensation in order to determine the timing and characterization of the income and the appropriate level of withholding. In general, payments are characterized as royalties or sale proceeds (and not compensation) if the property (*e.g.*, film or screenplay) was completed on "spec" and not pursuant to any contract with a third party. In addition, payments for a name and likeness license are characterized as royalties, while payments for product endorsement are characterized as service income.

INVENTORY

Determining whether particular film rights constitute either inventory, on the one hand, or Code Sec. 1231 property or a capital asset, on the other, is critical to the determination of the timing, character, and amount of gain recognized on a sale. For example, inventory does not qualify for capital gain treatment on sale. In general, film rights will be characterized as inventory if they are frequently sold or are created pursuant to a pre-existing contract of disposition.

PARTNERSHIP

If two or more parties undertake a transaction together, they may find themselves with unintended tax consequences and liabilities if the transaction is recharacterized as a partnership for tax purposes. For example, foreign corporations in a partnership doing business in the U.S. may be taxed in the U.S., and their U.S. partners may be liable for the foreign corporation's U.S. tax.

In general, the characterization of an entity as a partnership for U.S. tax purposes does not depend on the labels applied by the parties, but on the intent of the parties and whether there is a sharing in profits or losses and a joint contribution of property or services.

FOREIGN PRODUCTION AND DISTRIBUTION

Over the years, foreign-source income has increased as a percentage of worldwide income from the exploitation of films. U.S. taxation on foreign revenues can often be deferred with appropriate tax planning. Foreign production has also become more common because of cheaper foreign labor costs. Proper advance tax planning can save substantial taxes for any entity engaged in foreign production or distribution.

In the case of foreign distribution, the U.S. tax laws have a number of obstacles that must be avoided to defer U.S. tax on foreign-source income. The first obstacle is a set of tax provisions that impose a toll charge whenever tangible or intangible assets are transferred to a foreign corporation. The purpose of these provisions is to require the U.S. transferor to pay tax on gain with respect to assets that are transferred outside of the U.S. taxing jurisdiction. These tax provisions include Code Secs. 367 and 1491 (which apply to otherwise tax-free transactions) and Code Sec. 482 (which imposes an arm's-length pricing rule for taxable sales or licenses). Avoiding these provisions is usually possible by having the assets acquired or produced directly by the foreign corporation, instead of having a U.S. taxpayer transfer the assets to the foreign corporation.

Once the assets are owned by a foreign corporation, a number of U.S. tax provisions seek to tax the U.S. shareholders on their share of certain types of the foreign corporation's income. These tax provisions include Subpart F, the foreign personal holding company rules, and the passive foreign investment company rules. In addition, other U.S. tax provisions tax the foreign corporation directly on certain types of income that it earns. These tax provisions include rules relating to foreign income that is attributable to a U.S. office, the personal holding company rules, and the accumulated earnings tax.

Even if U.S. taxation is avoided, the foreign corporation will have to avoid or minimize taxation in foreign countries. This will require an understanding of foreign tax systems and any applicable tax treaties. If foreign taxes are imposed, the United States may allow a portion of the foreign taxes to be credited against any U.S. taxes.

DEPRECIATION/AMORTIZATION OF FILMS

The costs incurred in producing a film or in acquiring film rights can be depreciated or amortized. The most common approach is the use of the income forecast method, which allows the cost of the film to be amortized based on the ratio of the net revenues received each year to the net revenues expected over the life of the film. In projecting ultimate income, the taxpayer must include all income estimated to be generated by the property within the first ten years after the property has been placed in service, including income from all ancillary markets, merchandising, and expected licensing of characters, etc. At the end of the third and tenth year after the property is placed in service, a recomputation of amortization is made using actual income. If actual income differs from estimated income by more than 10%, the taxpayer is subject to a retroactive interest charge or refund based on a corrected recalculation of income forecast amortization. The only other depreciation method allowed is straight-line depreciation over the useful life of the film, with an allowance for the salvage value of the film at the end of that useful life.

If an entire film library is acquired, the purchase price must be amortized straight-line over fifteen years (instead of using the income forecast method) if the purchaser acquires the goodwill (such as trademarks, employees, or customer lists) of the seller.

AT-RISK RULES

The ability of the producer or distributor to deduct amortization of their film costs will depend, in part, on the application of the at-risk rules. In general, the at-risk rules limit the ability of individuals and closely held C corporations to deduct losses in excess of their amount "at risk." In general, a taxpayer's amount at risk will include any money and the fair market value of property the taxpayer has contributed to the activity, as well as any debts for which the taxpayer is personally liable if the lender does not have a prohibited interest in the activity.

ADVANCES

Producers often receive "advances" to fund production. They view these advances as loans and generally do not recognize the income for accounting purposes until the film is completed. For tax purposes, however, such advance payments are generally fully taxable upon receipt, regardless of the method of accounting used by the taxpayer. There are ways to avoid this result, such as by structuring the transaction as a loan or as a contractual commitment backed up by a letter of credit against which amounts can be borrowed.

PERSONAL HOLDING COMPANY TAX

A film production or distribution entity that operates through a closely held C corporation must be careful to avoid the personal holding company tax, which is a penalty tax imposed on certain types of income, such as investment income or service income if the principal shareholder is named in the contract. In general, this tax can be avoided if the income qualifies as "produced film rents," which requires an interest in the film to be acquired prior to substantial completion of the film. The personal holding company tax also may be avoided if the income is royalty income so long as certain expense tests are met. If a company is a personal holding company, a penalty tax is imposed on the corporation's undistributed personal holding company income.

FINANCING FILM PRODUCTION AND DISTRIBUTION

The common denominator among all film production and distribution entities is the need for financing. Film production and distribution is extremely expensive, and raising the required capital requires the use of many innovative and creative techniques.

Domestic Tax Shelters. One form of financing is the use of tax shelters. In broad terms, investors contribute money for use in film production or distribution in exchange for an allocation of tax deductions as well as a share of potential profits from a film. Over the years, U.S. tax shelters have been curtailed as a result of successive tax legislation and case law that cut back on the benefits of tax shelters. First, any allocations of taxable income or loss must have "substantial economic effect" under Code Sec. 704(b). Next, the taxpayers must be able to demonstrate that they have a profit motive with respect to their investment, and they must be able to prove that the substance of the transaction is not a loan or a purchase of a mere profits interest. The passive loss rules also substantially limit the ability of individuals to deduct losses allocated to them if such losses constitute "passive activity losses." This restriction has resulted in the tax shelter industry turning to corporate investors, because corporations are not subject to the passive loss rules (except in the case of certain closely held and personal service corporations).

Co-Productions. A common form of financing film production and distribution is a co-production between two separate entities, at least one of which is foreign and can take advantage of its country's subsidies or quota requirements. For example, co-productions are commonly done within the European Community countries, Canada, and Australia pursuant to co-production treaties among those countries. These transactions may be treated as partnerships for tax purposes, raising all the tax issues applicable to partnerships.

Loans. Loans are also often used for financing film production or distribution. The lender often receives fixed interest plus contingent interest based on the profits from a film. The initial inquiry is whether the "loan" is, in fact, an equity investment. Next, the timing of the accrual of the interest income or deduction must be determined under the imputed interest and original issue discount rules. In general, this rule requires both the lender and borrower to accrue interest using the accrual method of accounting, regardless of when payments are received.

Foreign Tax Shelters. One common financing technique is to take advantage of foreign tax systems that permit or encourage film tax shelters. A typical transaction involves a sale-leaseback whereby a film is "sold" to a foreign partnership, which then "licenses" the film back to the seller. These transactions are fairly complex and involve many U.S. and foreign tax issues. The most pervasive issue is whether taxpayers are bound by the form of the transactions; if so, the "sale" may be immediately taxable, and the "license" payments may be subject to withholding. If taxpayers can disregard the form of their transactions and treat the transactions as financings based on the substance of the transactions, these issues disappear. In general, most courts hold taxpayers to the form of their transactions, but the IRS has been surprisingly liberal on the issue, at least in advance rulings.

TAX PLANNING FOR TALENT.

Tax planning for talent involves special tax considerations that differ from the tax considerations for film production and distribution. Several tax benefits are obtained if the services are performed through a corporation owned by the talent (a "loan-out corporation"). However, if a loan-out corporation is used, care must be taken to avoid certain tax traps, including the personal holding company rules and the foreign tax credit rules. In addition, every now and then the IRS attacks loan-out corporations, arguing that they should be disregarded on the basis of substance over form. Of late, however, the IRS has dropped this issue without explanation.

Whenever services are performed in a foreign country, the talent or the loan-out corporation may end up being taxed in that foreign country. These foreign taxes can be avoided or minimized by careful attention to tax treaties, the structure under which the services are performed, and the terms of any tax indemnity with the film producer. If foreign taxes are imposed, it will be critical to structure the transaction in a manner that will allow the foreign tax credit to be taken against U.S. taxes that are also imposed on the income. This usually requires the services to be rendered directly by the individual or through an S corporation (where the credits can pass through to the individual).

WITHHOLDING.

In many cases, payments in the film entertainment industry are subject to withholding — either wage withholding imposed on payments to employees or withholding on payments to foreign persons. The payor's liability for failure to withhold can far exceed the payor's own tax liability.

Wage Withholding. Wage withholding is imposed on all payments to "employees." In general, the determination of employee status depends on whether the employer has the right to control the manner and means of accomplishing the desired results. The federal and state tax authorities have been very aggressive in attempting to treat everyone in the entertainment industry as employees and subjecting all payments to wage withholding, including payments to free-lancers and writers. In addition, withholding can be imposed in some situations on expense reimbursements, contingent compensation, and compensation for services rendered outside the United States.

Payments to Foreign Persons. Payments of U.S. source income to foreign persons are generally subject to 30% withholding, unless (1) the income is effectively connected with a U.S. trade or business, (2) the payments are subject to wage withholding, or (3) a treaty lowers or eliminates withholding. In some cases, it is possible to avoid U.S. withholding by structuring the transaction as a sale instead of a license. Even if withholding is avoided, the foreign person may be subject to U.S. tax: "effectively connected income" may be subject to regular taxation plus a branch tax, while "noneffectively connected income" may be subject to a flat 30% tax.

CALIFORNIA TAXATION.

Many film transactions have some California nexus, either because the film was produced in California, the distribution contract was entered into in California, or the film generates California revenue. In such cases, it is critical to consider the California tax consequences of the transaction. For example, if the taxpayer is doing business in California, it (and all affiliates that are part of a "unitary group") will be subject to the California franchise tax. Even if the taxpayer is not doing business in California, it will be subject to the California income tax on California source income, and such income may be subject to withholding. In addition, the sale of film rights is subject to the state sales tax, unless one of several exemptions apply.

APPENDIX

FORMS

FORM A

LIMITED LIABILITY COMPANY OPERATING AGREEMENT

1. Definitions

2. Purpose of the Company

3. Principal Office

4. Term.

5. Capitalization

6. Management

7. Voting Procedures

8. Admission of New Members

9. Compensation to Managing Member

10. Distributions

11. Tax Allocation

12. Tax Withholding

13. Annual Reporting

14. Competition Allowed

15. Special Power of Attorney

16. Waiver of Certain Judicial Remedies

17. Transfers

18. Dissolution and Liquidation

1.   <u>Definitions</u>. All capitalized terms used herein shall have the meanings as set forth below:

a.   "Act" means the California-Beverly-Killea Limited Liability Company Act.

b.   "Agreement" means this Operating Agreement for the Company.

c.   "Available Cash" means cash funds, both from operations and on liquidation, in excess of a reasonable reserve for expenses and liabilities of the Company (and excluding all fixed, deferred or contingent compensation payable to the Managing Member for services rendered).

d.   "Capital Contributions" means the capital contributions of the Members as set forth on Exhibit "A".

e.   "Code" means the United States Internal Revenue Code, as amended.

f.   "Company" means this limited liability company, which shall be named _____, LLC.

g.   "Majority Vote" means the affirmative vote of the Members in question owning in the aggregate more than 50% of the Percentage Interests owned by such Members.

h.   "Managing Member" means _____, who shall remain as the sole Managing Member of the Company for so long as he is a Member of the Company.

i.   "Members" means all members of the Company, including the Managing Member and any subsequently admitted members. Attached hereto as Exhibit "A" is a list of current Members, with their respective addresses, tax identification numbers, Capital Contributions, and Percentage Interests.

      j.   "Membership Interest" means all of a Member's rights in the Company, collectively, including the Member's right to distributions, any right to vote or participate in management, and any right to information concerning the business and affairs of the Company.

      k.   "Percentage Interests" means the percentages set forth on Exhibit "A" with respect to each Member.

    2.   <u>Purpose of the Company</u>. The purpose of the Company is to engage in any legal activity permitted by the Act.

    3.   <u>Principal Office</u>. Unless and until another principal office is selected by the Managing Member, the principal office of the Company shall be located at _____.

    4.   <u>Term</u>. The Company shall have a term ending on _____ unless sooner terminated as provided for in Paragraph 18.

    5.   <u>Capitalization</u>. Each Member has made Capital Contributions to the Company in the amount set forth next to their name on Exhibit "A". If the Company needs additional funds, the Managing Member may, but need not, make demand loans to the Company at an interest rate equal to two percentage points over the prime rate prevailing from time to time.

    6.   <u>Management</u>. The Managing Member shall have the sole authority to manage, control, vote on, and approve all of the affairs of the Company and to make all tax elections for the Company. The other Members expressly waive their right to vote on or approve any matters that they would otherwise be entitled to vote on or approve pursuant to the Act, except (a) to the extent such vote or approval rights may not be waived by the Act or (b) any amendment of this Operating Agreement other than as provided in Paragraph 8. Any amendment to this Operating Agreement other than as provided in Paragraph 8 shall be binding only upon the affirmative written vote of the Managing Member and a Majority Vote of the other Members.

    7.   <u>Voting Procedures</u>. All voting shall be evidenced by the written vote of those Members necessary to take the action. No formal meetings of the Members shall be required to take any action, and the Company shall

not be required to have periodic meetings of the Members. If a written request for a vote is circulated, failure to reply within ten business days shall be deemed to be a written "yes" vote on the matter.

8. <u>Admission of New Members.</u> The Managing Member may permit the admission of new Members to the Company from time to time, and the Managing Member shall have the exclusive right to make and execute any amendments to this Agreement in connection with the admission of such new Members.

9. <u>Compensation to Managing Member.</u> In consideration for services rendered, the Managing Member shall be entitled to reasonable and customary fixed, deferred or contingent compensation, whether paid directly to the Managing Member from third parties or from the Company.

10. <u>Distributions.</u> Available Cash shall be distributed to the Members as follows:

a. First, to the Members in an amount equal to 50% of the income allocated to them under Paragraph 11(d). All distributions under this Paragraph 10(a) shall be treated as an advance against, and shall be deducted from, distributions under Paragraphs 10(b) and (c).

b. Next, to the Members until they have received an amount equal to their Capital Contributions, payable pro rata in the ratio of such Capital Contributions.

c. All remaining Available Cash shall be distributed to the Members pro rata in the ratio of their Percentage Interests.

11. <u>Tax Allocation.</u> For tax purposes, the taxable profits and loss of the Company shall be allocated to the Members as follows:

a. All losses shall first be allocated to the Members until they have been allocated losses under this Paragraph 11(a) in an amount equal to their Capital Contributions.

b. All additional losses shall be allocated to the Members pro rata in the ratio of their Percentage Interests.

c. All profits shall be first allocated to charge-back losses allocated pursuant to Paragraphs 11(b) and (a), in that order.

d. All profits shall thereafter be allocated to the Members pro rata in the ratio of their Percentage Interests.

12. <u>Tax Withholding</u>. In the event that the Company is required to pay or withhold any federal or state tax attributable to distributions or allocations to any Member, such withholding shall come solely out of the distributions due to such Member (but shall be treated as an actual distribution to such Member). If the required withholding exceeds such distributions, such Member shall be obligated immediately to contribute to the Company cash in an amount equal to such excess plus interest at 10% until paid.

13. <u>Annual Reporting</u>. Annually, the Company shall send each Member a copy of the Company's annual federal, state, and local tax and information returns, as well as any other information necessary for the Members to prepare their own tax returns.

14. <u>Competition Allowed</u>. The Managing Member and its affiliates shall be permitted to engage in other activities for profit whether or not competitive with the business of the Company, including the organization and management of entities for acquiring and investing in motion pictures.

15. <u>Special Power of Attorney</u>. Any members that are or become non-residents of California hereby grant the Managing Member an irrevocable power of attorney, coupled with an interest, to execute any and all consents or documents required for such members to agree to file California tax returns, to make timely payment of all taxes imposed on such members by California with respect to the income of the Company, and to be subject to personal jurisdiction in California for purposes of the collection of income taxes, interest, and penalties imposed on such members by California with respect to income of the Company.

16. <u>Waiver of Certain Judicial Remedies</u>. The Members hereby waive their right to initiate or assert (a) class actions on behalf of the Members, (b) derivative actions on behalf of the Company, (c) judicial dissolution of the Company, or (d) dissenter's rights.

17. <u>Transfers</u>. No Member may sell, assign, mortgage, dispose of, or transfer any portion of their Membership Interest without the written consent of the Managing Member, which consent may be withheld arbitrarily, even if such refusal would appear to be unreasonable. The Managing Member may condition its consent on the transferee's payment of costs to the Company related to the transfer and the transferee's signing such documents

and making such representations as are required by the Managing Member. The Managing Member may not transfer any of its management rights in the Company without the Majority Vote of the other Members.

18.　Dissolution and Liquidation. The Company shall be dissolved and its affairs shall be wound up upon the happening of the first to occur of the following:

　　　　a.　The affirmative vote of the Managing Member and a Majority Vote of the other Members.

　　　　b.　The expiration of the stated term of the Company;

　　　　c.　Upon the death, retirement, resignation, or bankruptcy of the Managing Member, unless the business of the Company is continued by a Majority Vote of the other Members.

Upon dissolution of the Company for any reason, the Managing Member shall act as the liquidator of the Company, and all of the Company's assets shall be sold in a commercially reasonable manner. After payment of all liabilities of the Company, and a set aside of a reasonable reserve, any remaining cash shall be distributed to the Members in accordance with the provisions of Paragraph 10.

19.　Jurisdiction and Venue. All the Members hereby agree that, unless the Managing Member consents to or chooses another forum, the state with jurisdiction over any disputes relating to this Agreement shall be California, and the sole location for proper venue shall be in Los Angeles, California.

20.　Indemnification. The Company shall indemnify and hold harmless the Managing Member and its affiliates from and against any loss, cost, or expense (including attorneys' fees) relating to the Company, including the defense of, or a judgment resulting from, any action brought by a Member, unless a court determines that the action or omission in question constituted willful fraud.

21.　Entire Contract. This Agreement constitutes the sole and entire agreement between the Members relating to the subject matter hereof. Any prior agreements, promises, and negotiations not expressly set forth in this Agreement are of no force and effect whatsoever.

22.　Execution. This Agreement may be executed in counterparts and transmitted by facsimile copy, each of which shall constitute an original.

IN WITNESS WHEREOF, the Members have executed this Agreement effective as of the __ day of _____, ____.

MANAGING MEMBER:

_____

_____

OTHER MEMBERS:

_____

_____

EXHIBIT A

Members	Capital Contributions	Percentage Interest

FORM B

"SAMPLE FILM" LOAN AND SECURITY AGREEMENT

1. Definitions

2. Conditions Precedent to Loan

3. The Loan

    a.   Commitment to Lend

    b.   Advances

    c.   Interest

    d.   Interest Reserve

    e.   Lender's Fees

    f.   Repayment

    g.   Promissory Note

    h.   Costs

4. Grant of Security Interest

5. Events of Default

    a.   Occurrence

    b.   Consequence

6. Covenants

7. Right to Inspect

8. Power of Attorney

9. Credit

    a.   Lender

    b.   John Doe

10. Miscellaneous

    a.   Lender's Representatives

    b.   Waivers

    c.   Rights or Remedies

    d.   Entire Agreement

    e.   Modification

    f.   Notices

    g.   Applicable Law

    h.   Jurisdiction

    i.   Assignability

    j.   Counterparts

EXHIBITS:

A   Assignment

B   Draw Down Notice

C   Secured Promissory Note

D   Power of Attorney

This "Sample Film" Loan and Security Agreement is entered into by and between Producer and Lender.

1.   <u>DEFINITIONS</u>. All capitalized words used herein shall have the meanings as set forth below:

a.   "Advance" means each separate advance of funds by Lender under the Loan.

b.   "Agreement" means this "Sample Film" Loan and Security Agreement.

c.   "Approved" means approved in writing by Producer, Lender, and Completion Guarantor.

d.   "Assignment" means the Assignment attached hereto as Exhibit "A" evidencing the Security Interest.

e.   "Budget" means the final Approved budget for the Picture.

f.   "Cash Flow Schedule" means the final Approved cash flow schedule for the Picture.

g.   "Collateral" means Producer's property that is subject to the Security Interest as set forth in the Assignment.

h.   "Commitment Amount" means $_____. However, pursuant to Paragraph 3(a), the Commitment Amount is not a cap or ceiling on the amount of the Loan.

i.   "Completion Guarantee" means the completion guarantee for the Picture.

j.   "Completion Guarantor" means _____.

k.   "Draw Down Notice" means the Draw Down Notice attached hereto as Exhibit "B".

l.   "Event of Default" has the meaning set forth in Paragraph 5(a).

m.   "Inter-Party Agreement" means the "Sample Film" Inter-Party Agreement entered into by and among Producer, Completion Guarantor, Lender, and the Sales Agent.

n.   "Investor Contract" means the Approved contract with a third party investor providing for an equity investment in the Picture of at least $___ million, to be placed in escrow upon execution thereof.

o.   "Laboratory Pledgeholder Agreement" means the "Sample

Film" Laboratory Pledgeholder Agreement for the Physical Film Elements entered into by and among Producer, Completion Guarantor, Lender, and [laboratory].

p.   "Lender" means _____.

q.   "Lender's Approval" means written approval by Lender, which shall be subject to Lender's good faith sole discretion.

r.   "LIBOR" means the average London interbank rate for one-year loans as published in The Wall Street Journal on the first business day of each calendar month, for purposes of calculating interest on the portion of the Loan outstanding at the beginning of such calendar month. For Advances made during a calendar month, "LIBOR" shall be the same rate as published on the first business day preceding the date the Advance is made, for purposes of calculating interest on that Advance for the balance of that calendar month.

s.   "Loan" means the aggregate amount that is owed by Producer to Lender hereunder, including, without limitation, all actual or constructive Advances and all interest, fees, and costs hereunder.

t.   "Loan Documents" means this Agreement, all Exhibits attached hereto, and all ancillary documentation relating to the attachment or perfection of the Security Interest.

u.   "Maturity Date" means _____, subject to acceleration as provided herein.

v.   "Physical Film Elements" means all tangible personal property embodying any visual or audio aspects of the Picture, such as film negatives and sound tracks.

w.   "Picture" means the motion picture to be produced tentatively titled "Sample Film."

x.   "Prime Rate" means the prime rate as published in The Wall Street Journal on the first business day of each calendar month, for purposes of calculating interest on the portion of the Loan outstanding at the beginning of such calendar month. For Advances made during a calendar month, "Prime Rate" shall be the same rate as published on the first business day preceding the date the Advance is made, for purposes of calculating interest on that Advance for the balance of that calendar month.

y.   "Producer" means _____ [borrower].

z.   "Production Bank Account" means the following bank account, into which all Advances shall be wire transferred except as otherwise provided herein:

_____

_____

_____

Account No. _____
ABA No. _____
Account Name: _____

aa.   "Production Schedule" means the Approved production schedule for the Picture.

bb.   "Relevant Documents" means the Budget, the Cash Flow Schedule, the Production Schedule, the Screenplay, the Loan Documents, the Completion Guarantee and cut-through endorsement, the Inter-Party Agreement, the Investor Contract, and all other contracts relating to the Picture, collectively.

cc.   "Sales Agent" means _____.

dd.   "Screenplay" means the final Approved screenplay for the Picture.

ee.   "Security Interest" means a continuing first priority security interest in the Collateral granted to Lender pursuant to the Assignment.

2.   <u>CONDITIONS PRECEDENT TO LOAN</u>. Lender's obligation to make each and every Advance shall be subject to the continuing conditions precedent of:

a.   The complete execution, and Lender's approval, of all of the Relevant Documents on or before _____.

b.   At least $_____ million of the investment under the Investment Contract being spent in accordance with the Cash Flow Schedule.

c.   Lender's receipt of a Draw Down Notice for the Advance in conformity with the Cash Flow Schedule.

d.   The attachment and perfection of the Security Interest.

e.   The receipt of any documents reasonably requested by Lender.

f.   There having been no Event of Default.

g.   The Completion Guarantor not having elected to abandon the Picture pursuant to the Completion Guarantee.

3.   <u>THE LOAN</u>

a.   <u>Commitment to Lend</u>. Subject to the conditions precedent of Paragraph 2, Lender hereby agrees to make the Loan, in an amount not to exceed the Commitment Amount inclusive of all fees, reserves, and costs referred to in this Agreement. Notwithstanding the forgoing, if Lender does make Advances in excess of the Commitment Amount, such Advances shall be added to the Loan.

b.   <u>Advances</u>. Subject to satisfaction of the conditions precedent of Paragraph 2, not less than four business days after receipt of a Draw Down Notice, Lender shall make the requested Advance to the Production Bank Account. However, upon an Event of Default, Lender may make all further Advances directly to Completion Guarantor if Completion Guarantor has taken over production of the Picture, or to other third parties in connection with production of the Picture, all of which Advances shall be included as part of the Loan.

c.   <u>Interest</u>. The unpaid balance of the Loan shall bear interest at ___ percentage points over [the Prime Rate or LIBOR]. Interest shall be compounded at the end of each calendar month and shall be calculated on the basis of a 360 day year. Commencing upon an Event of Default, the interest rate on the unpaid balance of the Loan shall be increased to the lesser of (1) the maximum legal rate of interest permitted by applicable law (2) ____ percentage points over [the Prime Rate or LIBOR], and shall continue until the earlier of repayment of the Loan in full, or the date that such Event of Default is cured.

d.   <u>Interest Reserve</u>. At the time of the first Advance, Lender shall establish an interest reserve of $_____ to cover anticipated interest under the Loan. Lender shall have the right to make withdrawals monthly in arrears from the reserve to make payments of interest under the Loan, which withdrawals shall be treated as Advances at the time made.

e.   <u>Lender's Fees</u>. In consideration for its obligations hereunder, Lender shall be paid a financing fee of $_____ at the time of the first Advance. This fee shall be paid out of the Loan proceeds and shall be treated as an Advance under the Loan.

f.   <u>Repayment</u>. The Loan shall be due and payable in full by Producer on the Maturity Date. Producer shall have the right to pre-pay the Loan in full or in part from time to time, without premium or penalty. Producer shall be required to pre-pay the Loan to the extent of:

        i.   Any remaining balance in the Production Bank Account upon completion and delivery of the Picture, subject to a reasonable reserve (the amount of which shall be subject to Lender's Approval) for anticipated remaining expenses. Producer may provide for total deferments payable out of the unspent contingency of $_____.

        ii.   All amounts paid to Producer attributable to the Picture.

        iii.   Any insurance proceeds paid to Producer attributable to the Picture.

All payments shall be made in such manner and to such accounts as Lender shall designate from time to time.

g.   <u>Promissory Note</u>. In order to evidence the Loan, upon execution of this Agreement, Producer shall execute and deliver to Lender the Secured Promissory Note attached hereto as Exhibit "C".

h.   <u>Costs</u>. Any and all costs (including legal fees) paid by Lender in connection with (i) the preparation and negotiation of the Loan Documents, (ii) the attachment and perfection of the Security Interest, (iii) enforcement of the Loan Documents (including exercise of its inspection rights under Paragraph 7 hereof), (iv) confirming delivery of the Picture pursuant to the Inter-Party Agreement, or (v) collection of the Loan shall be treated as additional Advances under the Loan.

4.   <u>GRANT OF SECURITY INTEREST</u>. In order to secure all of Producer's obligations under the Loan Documents, upon execution of this Agreement, Producer shall execute and deliver to Lender the Assignment attached hereto as Exhibit "A".

5.   <u>EVENTS OF DEFAULT</u>

a.   <u>Occurrence</u>. An "Event of Default" hereunder shall be caused by the occurrence of any of the following:

        i.   The failure by Producer to produce the Picture in conformance with the Relevant Documents or any material breach by Producer of any pro-vision of the Relevant Documents.

ii.   Any event or claim which, in Lender's good-faith judgment, results in, or may with the passage of time result in, any material impair-ment to (1) the existence, attachment, priority, or perfection of the Security Interest, (2) the value of the Collateral, (3) the effectiveness of any of the Loan Documents, or (4) Producer's ability to perform its obligations under the Relevant Documents.

iii.   Subject to Lender's Approval (hereby granted with respect to subordinated guild liens), the creation or attachment of any security in-terest, lien, or charge against the Collateral (other than the Security Inter-est).

iv.   Any amendments to the Relevant Documents without Lender's Approval.

v.   Any lawsuit being filed against Producer for more than $25,000 that is not dismissed within 30 days.

vi.   The placement of any Physical Film Elements in any labo-ratory that is not approved by Lender.

vii.   Any actual or pending consolidation, merger, or dissolution of, or sale of Collateral by, Producer.

viii.   Any insolvency or bankruptcy filing or material adverse change with respect to Completion Guarantor, Producer, the Sales Agent, or any insurance companies insuring any aspect of the Picture.

ix.   Producer giving Lender false or misleading information or representations or not disclosing all material facts that might be relevant to Lender.

x.   Any insurance company that is insuring any aspect of the Picture denying or failing to affirm any of its obligations.

xi.   Completion Guarantor taking over production of the Picture.

xii.   Failure of the Sales Agent to make and document sales in form and substance meeting Lender's Approval (a) of at least $_____ within thirty days after the end of the 1999 American Film Market or (b) covering the entire Loan by June 30, 1999.

b.   Consequence. Upon the occurrence of any Event of Default, the following consequences shall occur:

i.   Lender may terminate making all further Advances hereunder, the Maturity Date shall be accelerated, and the Loan shall become immediately due and payable.

ii.   Lender may immediately commence enforcement of the Loan, including by foreclosing on the Security Interest, and Lender may exercise all of the rights and remedies of a secured creditor under applicable law.

iii.   Lender shall automatically hold all of the Collateral for Producer, and may take any action, including taking possession of, licensing, or disposing of the Collateral, as Lender in its good-faith discretion deems appropriate, including the settlement or compromise of any claims relating to the Collateral. Any costs paid by Lender in connection with such actions shall be deemed to be Advances under the Loan. Producer does hereby waive any claim for damages it might otherwise have against any third parties (as express third party beneficiaries) who handle, acquire, license, or dispose of the Collateral in accordance with the instructions of Lender operating pursuant to the provisions of this subparagraph.

iv.   Lender shall have the right to take over production of the Picture as the agent of Producer.

v.   Lender shall be entitled to the appointment of a receiver to take immediate possession of the Collateral.

vi.   Lender shall have the right to apply any cash or deposits held by Producer against the Loan.

vii.   The Loan shall bear interest at the default rate set forth in Paragraph 3(c).

6.   COVENANTS. Producer covenants to Lender as follows:

a.   Producer shall produce the Picture in accordance with the Relevant Documents.

b.   Producer shall at all times own all rights in and to the Screenplay and the Picture.

c.   There are no existing Events of Default.

d.   Producer shall promptly notify Lender of any of the following: (a) any actual or pending Event of Default, (b) any change to the location of Producer's chief executive office, (c) any change to the name or trade name of Producer, (d) any change in the location of any laboratory holding any Physical Film Elements, or (e) any change to the name of the Picture.

e.   All Physical Film Elements shall be kept in laboratories approved by Lender.

f.   Producer shall promptly register the Picture with the United States Copyright Office upon completion of the Picture.

g.   For so long as the Loan is outstanding, Producer shall maintain all policies of insurance covering the Picture as shall be required by Lender.

h.   Producer shall execute such further documents, and take such further actions, as shall be reasonably requested by Lender to implement the provisions of the Loan Documents or to evidence, attach, perfect, or enforce the Security Interest.

i.   Producer shall not enter into any sales agent agreement, license, or other form of distribution agreement relating to the Picture without the advance written consent of Lender.

7.   RIGHT TO INSPECT. Producer shall maintain complete and accurate books and records relating to the Collateral, and Lender shall have the un-limited right to inspect and copy such books and records, including access to all computer hardware or software necessary to inspect any books and records kept on computers. Lender shall also have the right to inspect any of the Collateral at any time. Upon request of Lender, Producer shall furnish Lender with any information as Lender may request from time to time. Pro-ducer shall supply Lender with copies of all production reports (e.g., bud-get, shooting schedule, and cost to complete) for the Picture. Lender shall have the right to visit the set and talk to production personnel regarding the progress of the Picture.

8.   POWER OF ATTORNEY. Upon execution of this Agreement, Producer shall execute and deliver to Lender the Power of Attorney attached hereto as Exhibit "D".

9.   CREDIT

a.   Lender. Lender will have a main title "Produced In Association With" credit in a position to be determined by Producer. The same credit will also appear on all key art and in all paid ads whenever the "Produced by" credit appears.

b.   John Doe. John Doe will have a first-position, shared card (with one other second position credit), main title Executive Producer credit. The same credit will appear on all key art and in all paid ads whenever the "Produced by" credit appears. All aspects of such credit shall be on a favored-nations basis with all other credits provided to any other individuals.

10.   MISCELLANEOUS

a.   Lender's Representatives. Any action that may be undertaken by Lender hereunder may be undertaken by any of Lender's agents or representatives.

b.   Waivers. No waiver by Lender of any of the conditions precedent in Paragraph 2, any Event of Default, or any of the obligations or covenants of Producer shall act as a subsequent waiver of the same matter or as a waiver of any other matter.

c.   Rights or Remedies. All the rights and remedies of Lender under the Loan Documents or by operation of law shall be cumulative, and not exclusive of any other rights or remedies available.

d.   Entire Agreement. The Loan Documents constitute the entire agreement between Lender and Producer with respect to the subject matter hereof, and supersede all prior term sheets, correspondence, and negotiations. The Loan Documents are an integrated agreement.

e.   Modification. Any modifications to the Loan Documents shall only be valid if evidenced by a writing executed by both parties hereto.

f.   Notices. All notices under the Loan Documents shall be given in writing by registered mail, return receipt requested, or by facsimile and shall be sent to the respective addresses for notices listed below, or to such other addresses as each party may notify to the other from time to time. A notice sent by registered mail shall be deemed received on the date inscribed in the official return receipt. A notice sent by facsimile shall be received on the next business day.

Addresses for Notice:
Producer:

Lender:

Copy to:
Schuyler M. Moore
Stroock & Stroock & Lavan
2029 Century Park East, Suite 1800
Los Angeles, CA 90067-3086
Fax No. 310-556-5959

    g.   Applicable Law. The Loan Documents shall be governed by and construed in accordance with the internal laws of the State of _____ (i.e., without regard to its conflict of law principles).

    h.   Jurisdiction. Lender and Producer hereby consent to _____, as a non-exclusive location for jurisdiction and venue of any legal actions brought relating to the Loan Documents and waive any objection they might otherwise have to such jurisdiction and venue, including for non-convenient forum.

    i.   Assignability. Lender may assign or delegate any or all of its rights and obligations under the Loan Documents at any time. Producer may not assign or delegate any of its rights or obligations hereunder without Lender's Approval.

    j.   Counterparts. The Loan Documents may be executed in counterparts and transmitted by facsimile copy, each of which shall constitute an original.

    IN WITNESS WHEREOF, the parties hereto have executed this Agreement effective as of _____.

             [PRODUCER]
             By: _____
             Title: _____

[LENDER]

By: _____

Title: _____

EXHIBIT "A"

ASSIGNMENT

This Assignment is executed by _____ ("Producer") pursuant to the "Sample Film" Loan and Security Agreement (the "Agreement") entered into by and between Producer and _____ ("Lender"). Unless otherwise defined herein, all capitalized words used herein shall have the same meaning as set forth in the Agreement. In order to secure all of Producer's obligations under the Loan Documents, Producer hereby grants to Lender a first priority security interest in all of Producer's right, title, and interest in and to all personal property of every kind and nature, tangible or intangible, whether now owned or hereafter acquired or created, including all products and proceeds thereof and specifically including, without limitation, the following:

a.   The Screenplay, the play upon which it is based (to the extent required to exploit the Picture), the Picture, the sound track and music for the Picture, all marketing material relating to the Picture, and all copyrights and ancillary and derivative rights relating to any of the foregoing.

b.   All tangible personal property embodying any visual or audio aspects of the Picture.

c..   All contracts, rights, and claims against third parties.

d.   All insurance policies.

e.   All accounts receivable.

f.   All cash, deposits, or bank accounts.

g.   All books and records.

h.   All tangible property used in connection with the production or exploitation of the Picture.

i.   All trademarks and servicemarks.

j.   All permits and licenses.

IN WITNESS WHEREOF, this Assignment has been executed by Producer effective as of _____.

[PRODUCER]

By: _____

Title: _____

EXHIBIT "B"

DRAW DOWN NOTICE

Unless otherwise defined herein, all capitalized words used herein shall have the same meanings as set forth in the "Sample Film" Loan and Security Agreement (the "Agreement") entered into by and between _____ ("Producer") and _____ ("Lender"). The undersigned hereby requests the Advance set forth below and certifies as of the date hereof that:

A.   I am the sole manager of Producer;

B.   I have reviewed the terms of the Loan Documents, and I have made a detailed review of the transactions and conditions of Producer as of the date hereof;

C.   All conditions precedent set forth in Paragraph 2 of the Agreement have been, and continue to be, met;

D.   The requested date and amount of the Advance, which conforms to the date and amount specified therefor in the Cash Flow Schedule, are _____, 1998, and $_____, respectively. The purpose of the requested Advance is to pay production costs included in the Budget and to pay accrued but unpaid interest or other charges under the Agreement;

E.   After giving effect to the Advance requested hereby, the aggregate amount of all Advances outstanding will not exceed the Commitment Amount; and

F.   Producer hereby requests that the Advance be paid directly into the Production Bank Account or as otherwise provided in the Agreement.

IN WITNESS WHEREOF, Producer has caused this Draw Down Notice to be executed as of _____.

Signature:_____

PrintName:_____

Title: _____

THE UNDERSIGNED HEREBY CONSENTS
TO THE FOREGOING REQUESTED ADVANCE:

[BOND COMPANY]

By: _____

Title: _____

EXHIBIT "C"

SECURED PROMISSORY NOTE

US $_____   As of _____ _____

FOR VALUE RECEIVED, _____ ("Producer") hereby promises to pay to _____ or order ("Holder") the amount of $_____ , or so much or more as may be borrowed under the "Sample Film" Loan and Security Agreement (the "Agreement") entered into by and between Producer and Holder, together with interest thereon as provided in the Agreement. Except as otherwise defined herein, all capitalized words used in this Secured Promissory Note (the "Note") shall have the same meaning as set forth in the Agreement. The Loan shall be payable upon the Maturity Date or earlier as provided in the Agreement. All interest shall be paid monthly in arrears or as otherwise provided in the Agreement. This Note is subject to certain voluntary and mandatory prepayment provisions, as set forth in the

Agreement. This Note is secured by a Security Interest in the Collateral, as described in the Agreement. All payments under this Note shall be payable in lawful money of the United States of America and shall be paid in such manner and to such accounts as Holder may designate from time to time. For the avoidance of doubt, the stated amount of this Note is not a ceiling or cap on the amount of the Loan payable pursuant to this Note.

Upon the occurrence of any Event of Default, the Loan shall become immediately due and payable. In the absence of manifest error, Holder's calculation of the outstanding amount of the Loan shall be conclusively binding on Producer. Producer shall pay all expenses of Holder incurred in connection with the preparation and enforcement of this Note and the Agreement and collection of the Loan, including attorneys' fees and costs.

This Note shall be governed by and construed in accordance with the internal laws of the State of _____ (i.e., without regard to its conflict of law principles).

IN WITNESS WHEREOF, this Note has been executed and delivered in _____, ___ ____, on the date set forth above.

[PRODUCER]

By: _____

Title: _____

EXHIBIT "D"

POWER OF ATTORNEY

This Power of Attorney is entered into by and between _____ ("Producer") and _____ ("Lender") pursuant to that certain "Sample Film" Loan and Security Agreement (the "Agreement") entered into by and between Lender and Producer. Unless otherwise defined herein, all capitalized words used herein have the same meanings as set forth in the Agreement. Producer hereby irrevocably designates, constitutes and appoints Lender as its true and lawful attorney-in-fact with full power of substitution and with full and irrevocable power of attorney (which power shall be coupled with an interest), on behalf of Producer, at any time or from time to time and in Lender's sole and absolute discretion to execute any and all documents and to take any actions reasonably necessary in Lender's good faith sole discretion to evidence, attach, perfect, or enforce Lender's Security Interest, and, upon an Event of Default, to take any of the following actions:

a.   Execute any and all documents (including the endorsement of checks) or take any actions reasonably necessary in Lender's good faith sole discretion to enforce any of the provisions of the Agreement.

b.   Take any action, including taking possession of, licensing, or disposing of any property of Producer, as lender in its good-faith judgment deems appropriate, including the settlement or compromise of any claims relating to such property.

c.   Lease, license, sell or otherwise dispose of that certain feature-length motion picture currently entitled "Sample Film" (the "Picture") and any and all distribution rights in and to the Picture in any and all media, markets and territories (or to engage others to do so on Lender's or Producer's behalf).

d.   Demand, collect, receive, settle, adjust, or compromise any and all monies payable to the Producer.

e.   File any claims and proofs of claim or to commence, maintain or discontinue any actions, suits or other proceedings deemed by Lender advisable for the purposes of collecting or enforcing payment of any monies owed to Producer.

f.   Endorse any checks, drafts or other orders or instruments for the payment of monies to or by Producer.

g.   Execute any and all such instruments, agreements or documents as may be necessary or desirable in connection with the foregoing.

Producer does hereby waive any claim for damages it might otherwise have against any third parties (as express third party beneficiaries) who handle, acquire, license, or dispose of Producer's property in accordance with the instructions of Lender operating pursuant to the provisions of this Power of Attorney.

Lender may, at any time and from time to time, without notice to Producer, sell, transfer or assign any or all of its rights hereunder.

This Power of Attorney shall be governed by and construed in accordance with and be governed by the internal laws of the State of _____ (i.e., without regard to its conflict of law principles).

IN WITNESS WHEREOF, Producer has executed this Power of Attorney as of _____.

[PRODUCER]

By: _____

Title: _____

STATE OF   )
) ss.
COUNTY OF)

On this ___ day of _____, ____, before me, the undersigned officer, personally appeared _____, to me known to be the person who executed the foregoing instrument, and who, being by me duly sworn, did depose and say that (s)he is [a] Member of _____, a _____ limited liability Producer, and that (s)he executed the foregoing instrument in the name of said limited liability Producer, and that (s)he had authority to sign the same, and (s)he acknowledged to me that (s)he executed the same as the act and deed of said limited liability Producer for the uses and purposes therein mentioned by signing the name of the limited liability Producer by himself/herself in his/her authorized capacity as such officer as his/her free and voluntary act and deed and the free and voluntary act and deed of said limited liability Producer.

_____
Notary Public

[Notarial Seal]

My Commission Expires:

_____

FORM C

NOTICE OF ASSIGNMENT AND DISTRIBUTOR'S ACCEPTANCE

1. Definitions

2. Notice of Assignment

3. Payment of Lender Assigned Receipts

4. Miscellaneous

This Notice of Assignment and Distributor's Acceptance (the "Notice of Assignment") is made and entered into as of _____, by and among _____ ("Producer"), _____ ("Distributor"), _____ ("Lender") and _____ ("Agent").

1.   Definitions. All capitalized words used herein shall have the meanings set forth in the opening paragraph hereof or as specified below:

a.   "Distribution Agreement" means that certain Distribution Agreement as it may be amended or modified, dated as of _____, ____, by and between Agent, as agent for Producer, and Distributor relating to the exploitation of the Picture.

b.   "Lender Assigned Receipts" means all amounts payable by Distributor pursuant to the Distribution Agreement, including the Minimum Guarantee and all other payments due thereunder.

c.   "Minimum Guarantee" means all minimum guarantee or advance amounts payable by Distributor to Producer pursuant to the Distribution Agreement as modified by this Notice of Assignment.

d.   "Notice of Availability" shall mean the notice attached hereto as Schedule 1.

e.   "Picture" means the full length-theatrical motion picture tentatively entitled "Sample Film," or whatever title under which this picture may be exploited.

f.   "Rules" has the meaning set forth in Paragraph 4(g).

2.   <u>Notice of Assignment</u>. Producer and Agent hereby notify Distributor that, notwithstanding anything to the contrary in the Distribution Agreement, all Lender Assigned Receipts are hereby irrevocably assigned to Lender until written notification from Lender to the contrary.

3.   <u>Payment of Lender Assigned Receipts</u>. Notwithstanding anything to the contrary in the Distribution Agreement, Distributor agrees to pay the Lender Assigned Receipts, including the Minimum Guarantee, exclusively to Lender in accordance with Schedule 2 attached hereto. Distributor hereby agrees that notwithstanding anything to the contrary contained in the Distribution Agreement, the balance of the Minimum Guarantee shall be payable upon receipt of the Notice of Availability. Distributor acknowledges and agrees that it shall immediately pay all Lender Assigned Receipts (without offset, set-off, deduction or withholding of any kind or nature) to Lender via wire transfer to the following account (or such other account as Lender may notify to Distributor in writing):

_____

_____

_____

Account Name _____

Account No. _____

ABA No. _____

4.   <u>Miscellaneous</u>

a.   <u>No Amendment</u>. Producer, Agent and Distributor acknowledge and agree that the Distribution Agreement is in full force and effect enforceable against the parties thereto in accordance with its terms, and that the

Distribution Agreement shall not be amended, modified or terminated absent the prior written consent of Lender.

      b.   Inspection. Distributor shall afford Lender all rights of audit and inspection with respect to Distributor's books and records pertaining to the Picture that are granted to Producer under the Distribution Agreement.

      c.   Notices. Distributor shall furnish Lender duplicates of all notices and statements from Distributor to Producer or Agent.

      d.   Condition Precedent. The timely payment of all Lender's Assigned Receipts, including the Minimum Guarantee, in accordance with the terms and conditions of this Notice of Assignment, constitutes an express continuing condition precedent to the grant of rights to Distributor pursuant to the Distribution Agreement.

      e.   No Refund. Once the Lender Assigned Receipts have been paid to Lender, the same shall not be subject to refund or return to Distributor by Lender for any reason whatsoever.

      f.   No Assumption. Lender has taken assignment only of the Lender Assigned Receipts, and Lender has not assumed any obligations or liabilities of Producer or Agent under the Distribution Agreement. Distributor shall look solely to Producer for the performance and discharge of such obligation and liabilities.

      g.   Arbitration. Each of the parties hereto agrees that any dispute under the Distribution Agreement or this Notice of Assignment shall be resolved by mandatory binding arbitration under the American Film Marketing Association Rules of International Arbitration (the "Rules") in effect as of the date the request for arbitration is filed. The arbitration will be held in Los Angeles, California. Each of the parties hereto submits to the exclusive jurisdiction of the courts of the state and country of such forum as an appropriate place for compelling arbitration or giving legal confirmation of any arbitration award. Each of the parties agrees to accept service of process for all arbitral proceedings in accordance with the Rules and to accept service of process for any judicial or other proceedings by registered mail. The prevailing party and Lender in any such actions shall be entitled to prompt payment of costs and fees, including reasonable attorneys fees.

h.   Override. For the avoidance of doubt, in the event of any inconsistency between this Notice of Assignment and the Distribution Agreement, the provisions of this Notice of Assignment shall control.

i.   Counterparts. This Notice of Assignment may be executed in counterparts and transmitted by facsimile copy, each of which shall constitute an original but, when taken together, shall constitute one instrument.

j.   Governing Law. This Notice of Assignment and the rights and obligations of the parties hereunder shall be construed in accordance and governed by the laws of the State of California (without regard to its conflict of law principles).

IN WITNESS WHEREOF, the parties have executed this Notice of Assignment to be effective as of the date first above written.

[SALES AGENT]   [PRODUCER]

By: _____   By: _____
Its: _____   Its: _____

[DISTRIBUTOR]   [LENDER]

By: _____   By: _____
Its: _____   Its: _____

FORM D

"SAMPLE FILM" INTER-PARTY AGREEMENT

EXHIBITS:

A: Mandatory Delivery Items

B: Notice of Assignment and Distributor's Acceptance

1.   <u>Definitions</u>. All capitalized terms used herein shall have the meaning specified in the opening paragraph hereof or as defined below (or, if not defined below, as defined in the Loan and Security Agreement).

a.   "Acceptance Notice" shall have the meaning specified in Paragraph 8(a)(i) hereof.

b.   "Agent" means _____.

c.   "Arbitration Notice" shall have the meaning specified in Paragraph 8(b)(ii) hereof.

d.   "Collateral" shall have the meaning ascribed to such term in the Loan and Security Agreement.

e.   "Collection Account" shall have the meaning specified in Paragraph 13, and the details of the Collection Account are as follows:.

_____

_____

_____

Account No. _____

ABA No. _____

Account Name: _____

f.   "Collection Agent" means _____.

g.   "Completion Agreement" means that certain Completion Agreement relating to the Picture by and between Producer and Guarantor pursuant to which Guarantor has agreed to issue the Guaranty to Lender.

h.   "Cure Notice" shall have the meaning specified in Paragraph 8(b)(i) hereof.

i.   "Delivery" shall have the meaning specified in Paragraph 7(a) hereof.

j.   "Delivery Date" shall be _____, subject to automatic extension for (a) Force Majeure (for a period not to exceed ninety days) and (b) the period of notice and cure described in Paragraph 8.

k.   "Distributors" means all licensees and sub-distributors that enter into agreements with Agent (on behalf of Producer) relating to the exploitation of the Picture.

l.   "Element" means any and all elements relating to the Picture, including cast (including principal and secondary actors), crew (including all above and below the line personnel), the writer or writers, the budget, shooting schedules and the script (as it may be amended or modified).

m.   "Force Majeure" means any event beyond the control of Producer or Guarantor that causes an interruption or suspension of, or materially hampers, interferes with, or delays, the production or delivery of the Picture.

n.   "Guarantor" means _____.

o.   "Guaranty" means that certain Completion Guaranty relating to the Picture issued by Guarantor in favor of Lender.

p.   "Investor" means _____.

q.   "Investor Agreement" means that certain Investor Agreement relating to the Picture by and between Producer and Investor.

r.   "Lender" means _____.

s.   "Loan" shall have the meaning ascribed to such term in the Loan and Security Agreement.

t.   "Loan and Security Agreement" means that certain "Sample Film" Loan and Security Agreement relating to the Picture by and between Producer and Lender.

u.   "Mandatory Delivery Items" shall mean those delivery items set forth on Exhibit "A" hereto and incorporated herein by this reference.

v.   "Non-Cured Item" shall have the meaning specified in Paragraph 8(b)(i) hereof.

w.   "Objection Notice" shall have the meaning specified in Paragraph 8(a)(ii) hereof.

x.   "Picture" means the full length theatrical motion picture presently and tentatively entitled "Sample Film."

y.   "Producer" means _____.

z.   "Producer's Agreement" means the "Sample Film" Producer's Completion Agreement entered into by and between Guarantor and Producer.

aa.   "Receipts" means any and all amounts payable or which become payable to Agent or Producer pursuant to the distribution agreements entered into pursuant to the Sales Agency Agreement.

bb.   "Response" shall have the meaning specified in Paragraph 8(b)(i) hereof.

cc.   "Sales Agency Agreement" means that certain sales agreement by and between Agent and Producer relating to the sale of the Picture.

2.   <u>Sales Agent and Investor Acknowledgment</u>

a.   Agent and Investor acknowledge and agree that, notwithstanding anything to the contrary set forth in the Sales Agency Agreement or the Investor Agreement, no Element is essential, and to the extent any such Element must be modified, replaced or changed for any reason whatsoever, Agent and Investor hereby consent to and approve of such modification, replacement or change.

b.   The delivery date for all purposes of the Sales Agency Agreement, the Investor Agreement, and hereof shall be the Delivery Date.

c.   Notwithstanding anything to the contrary set forth in the Sales Agency Agreement, Agent acknowledges and agrees that all of the rights granted to Agent under the Sales Agency Agreement are subject to and overridden by the provisions of this Inter-Party Agreement. Notwithstanding anything to the contrary set forth in the Investor Agreement, Investor acknowledges and agrees that all rights granted to Investor under the Investor Agreement are subject to and overridden by the provisions of this Inter-Party Agreement.

d.   Agent represents and warrants that, as of the date of execution of this Inter-Party Agreement, no default exists under the Sales Agency Agreement and that the Sales Agency Agreement is in full force and effect. Producer and Agent acknowledge and agree that, without the prior written consent of Lender and Guarantor, they will not modify, alter, terminate or amend the Sales Agency Agreement. Investor represents and warrants that, as of the date of execution of this Inter-Party Agreement, no default exists under the Investor Agreement and that the Investor Agreement is in full force and effect. Producer and Investor acknowledge and agree that, without the prior written consent of Lender and Guarantor, they will not modify, alter, terminate or amend the Investor Agreement.

e.   Investor acknowledges that Lender may exercise any of its rights under the Loan and Security Agreement (including foreclosing on the Picture or exercising a right of sale) in a manner that may reduce or eliminate entirely any payments to Investor under the Investor Agreement or this Agreement. Investor's sole remedy in such event is to buy out the Loan in full pursuant to the Investor Agreement.

3.   <u>Producer Covenants</u>. Producer hereby:

a.   Authorizes, directs and instructs Agent to obligate all Distributors to pay the Receipts, without set-off, offset, counterclaim, deduction, withholding, defense or reserve, when and as owning, by wire transfer of immediately available funds directly to the Collection Account (or such other address and account as Lender may designate in writing); and

b.   Acknowledges that Lender and Guarantor each may exercise all rights of examination and audit of Agent's books and records pertaining to the Picture permitted to Producer pursuant to the Sales Agency Agreement, and may share such information with each other and instructs Agent to furnish to Lender and Guarantor duplicates of all notices and statements from Agent to Producer under the Sales Agency Agreement.

4.   <u>Sales Agent Covenants</u>. Agent hereby acknowledges, covenants and agrees:

a.   To insure that all Distributors make payment of the Receipts to Lender and to require such Distributors to execute and deliver Notices of Assignment and Distributor's Acceptance in form and substance attached hereto as Exhibit "B" (any modification to such form being subject to the prior written approval of Lender);

b.   To send to Lender and Guarantor duplicates of all notices furnished by Agent to Producer under the Sales Agency Agreement and to permit Lender and/or Guarantor or their respective representatives all rights to audit and examine and copy all books and records of Agent pertaining to the Picture;

c.   That, notwithstanding anything to the contrary set forth in the Sales Agency Agreement, Agent shall remit as trustee for Lender all Receipts to the Collection Account, without set-off, offset, counterclaim, deduction, withholding, defense or reserve which Agent may have or claim under the Sales Agency Agreement or otherwise;

d.   That Agent does not have a present grant of rights, security interest or other lien against the Receipts, the Collateral or the Picture; and

e.   That Lender shall have the right to replace Agent at any time if Agent does not make and document minimum sales in form and substance acceptable to Lender (a) of at least $_____ within thirty days after the end of the 1999 American Film Market or (b) covering the entire Loan by June 30, 1999, and that upon such replacement, Agent's rights under the Sales Agency Agreements (including the right to receive any further payments thereunder) shall thereupon immediately terminate, and Agent's rights, if any, in and to the Receipts, the Picture, and the Collateral shall be solely owned and controlled by Lender.

5.   Acknowledgment of Priorities

a.   Guarantor hereby acknowledges and confirms that (i) its security interest and rights in the Receipts, the Picture and Collateral, are subject and subordinate to the rights of Lender under the Loan and Security Agreement and this Inter-Party Agreement, and (ii) until Lender notifies Guarantor in writing of Producer's release of its security interest in the Receipts, the Picture and the Collateral, Guarantor agrees not to exercise its rights as a secured party in the Receipts, Picture or Collateral. Guarantor shall execute and deliver to Lender immediately upon Lender's request, any and all documents creating or evidencing such subordination for filing by Lender when and where Lender deems appropriate.

b.   Investor hereby acknowledges and confirms that (i) its security interest and rights, if any, in the Receipts, the Picture and Collateral, are subject and subordinate to the rights of Lender under the Loan and

Security Agreement and Lender and Guarantor under this Inter-Party Agreement, and (ii) until Lender and Guarantor notify Investor in writing of Lender's and Guarantor's release of their respective security interests in the Receipts, the Picture and the Collateral, Investor agrees not to exercise its rights, if any, as a secured party in the Receipts, Picture or Collateral. Investor shall execute and deliver to Lender any and all documents creating or evidencing such subordination for filing by Lender when and where Lender and/or Guarantor deem appropriate.

6.   Completion Agreement. Producer and Guarantor each represents and warrants that, as of the date of execution of this Inter-Party Agreement, no default exists under the Completion Agreement and that the Completion Agreement is in full force and effect, binding upon the parties thereto and enforceable in accordance with its terms. Furthermore, Producer and Guarantor agree that, without the prior written consent of Lender, they will not modify, alter, terminate or amend the Completion Agreement or any other agreements executed pursuant thereto.

7.   Delivery. It is acknowledged and agreed between the parties hereto as follows:

a.   Producer and/or Guarantor shall make delivery, no later than the Delivery Date, of the Mandatory Delivery Items to Lender by providing Lender with the Mandatory Delivery Items. All Mandatory Delivery Items, and the determination of whether or not Delivery has occurred, shall be subject to the inspection and cure periods specified in Paragraph 8 hereof, and shall comply with the following specifications: the Picture shall be in color on 35mm virgin film stock, with Dolby SR and SRD stereo soundtrack, in the English language, with an aspect ratio of either 1.85:1 or 2.35:1, not less than 90 minutes and not more than 120 minutes (inclusive of main and end titles), shall be based upon the shooting script dated _____, written by _____ and shall be of a first class technical quality. Satisfaction of all of the foregoing requirements shall be referred to herein as "Delivery."

b.   Guarantor covenants and agrees that, when the Picture is delivered to Lender, to the extent that certain costs attributable to the production of the Picture as set forth in the budget have not been paid by Producer, all such costs and expenses related to the production, completion and Delivery of the Picture to Lender, in accordance with and satisfying the requirements of Delivery, will have either been paid, or in the case of costs which are either (i) not then due and payable, (ii) are being contested in good faith or (iii) are subject to payment by insurance, Producer or Guarantor, as the case may be, will secure the payment thereof in a manner acceptable to Lender in its sole and absolute discretion.

8.   Delivery Procedure; Inspection; Cure; Payment

   a.   Lender shall have twenty business days from and after its receipt of the Notice of Availability together with access to the Mandatory Delivery Items, within which to verify that Delivery has been so effected and to notify Producer and Guarantor in writing that either:

   i.   Delivery has been made ("Acceptance Notice"); or

   ii.   Delivery has not been made ("Objection Notice"), which notice shall specify (with particularity and in detail) the purported defect in delivery and all items that must be delivered, corrected or otherwise modified in order to complete same; provided, however, that if within three business days after receiving such Objection Notice, Producer or Guarantor requests additional information which it believes in good faith is necessary in order to determine whether Delivery has been effected notwithstanding such Objection Notice, or how any defect in delivery can be cured, Lender shall have five business days after its receipt of such request to respond in good faith thereto.

   iii.   Notwithstanding the foregoing, Lender shall have the right (but not the obligation) to create or correct outstanding delivery materials and to add any costs associated with such correction or creation to the Loan, but in no event shall Guarantor be responsible for such costs.

   b.   If Lender fails to give either an Acceptance Notice or an Objection Notice within the time periods set forth in subparagraph (a) above, or if, after giving an Objection Notice, Lender fails to respond to a request for additional information made by Producer or Guarantor as aforesaid, then Lender shall be deemed to have given an Acceptance Notice for all purposes hereof. If Lender gives an Objection Notice as aforesaid and is not thereafter deemed to have given an Acceptance Notice hereunder, then Producer and/or Guarantor shall either:

       i.   Effect delivery in accordance with the specifications of the Objection Notice and (if applicable) Lender's response (the "Response") to a request for additional information made by Producer or Guarantor as aforesaid as soon as shall be reasonably possible, but in no event later than twenty business days after receiving the Objection Notice or (if applicable) the Response, and give Lender notice thereof ("Cure Notice"). Nothing herein shall be deemed to require Guarantor to cure all objections identified by Lender in the Objection Notice if Guarantor does not agree that such items require cure (each such item a "Non-Cured Item"), and in such event, Guarantor shall have the right to claim during any later arbitration that such Non-Cured Items were not defective when originally tendered to Lender; or

       ii.   Give Lender notice ("Arbitration Notice") within three business days after receiving the Objection Notice or (if applicable) the Response that, notwithstanding the Objection Notice, Delivery has been made and that Producer and/or Guarantor, have elected to submit the issue of whether Delivery has been made for expedited arbitration in accordance with Paragraph 9 below.

       c.   If a Cure Notice is given as aforesaid, then Lender shall have five business days from and after its receipt of same within which to verify that Delivery has been effected so as to cure the deficiencies specified in the Objection Notice and (if applicable) the Response and to notify Producer and Guarantor that either:

       i.   Delivery has been made as aforesaid, which notice shall constitute the Acceptance Notice for all purposes hereof; or

       ii.   Delivery has not been made and Lender has elected to submit the issue of whether Delivery has been made hereunder for expedited arbitration in accordance with Paragraph 9 below.

       d.   If Lender fails to give either of the notices described in clauses (i) and (ii) subparagraph (c) above as aforesaid within the applicable time period, then Lender shall be deemed to have given the notice described in clause (i) of said subparagraph (c) for all purposes hereof, and Delivery shall be deemed to have been made, and Lender shall be deemed to have issued the Acceptance Notice.

9. <u>Arbitration</u>. Notwithstanding anything to the contrary in any other agreement to which the parties hereto are a party, the parties hereto agree that in the event any dispute arises between any of the parties hereto as to whether Delivery has been made, such dispute shall be submitted to binding arbitration as hereinafter provided:

a. The arbitration shall be submitted to an arbitrator who shall be selected in accordance with the Rules for International Arbitration of the American Film Marketing Association in effect at the time the arbitration is initiated hereunder.

b. The arbitration shall commence in Los Angeles, California within five business days after the arbitrator has been selected as aforesaid, and such arbitration shall continue on each consecutive business day therefrom until fully concluded, unless continued by the arbitrator for good cause shown.

c. There shall be made available to the arbitrator all relevant documents and materials and the parties shall participate in an exchange of relevant information before the hearing. In this regard, the parties to the arbitration shall be entitled to reasonable discovery for the purposes of such arbitration, including, without limitation, document production and the taking of depositions. If any such discovery is not voluntarily exchanged among the parties, the party desiring such discovery may apply to the arbitrator at the outset of the arbitration for particular discovery requests. The arbitrator may deny only such discovery as is unreasonable or is intended to unduly delay the prompt conclusion of the arbitration.

d. The arbitration must result (inter alia) in either a finding that Delivery has been effected or a finding that Delivery has not been effected and the arbitrator shall promptly notify the parties hereto in writing of the finding made. If it is found that Delivery has been effected, the arbitrator shall issue a final award against Lender indicating that Delivery has been made. If, on the other hand, it is found that Delivery has not been effected, the arbitrator shall promptly notify the parties of such finding and shall issue a final arbitration award against Guarantor requiring Guarantor immediately to pay to Lender an amount equal to Guarantor's liabilities to Lender under the Guaranty together with interest, costs and expenses provided for in Paragraph 10 below. The arbitrator's award shall provide for payment by the losing party of the arbitrator's and any court reporter's fees.

  e.   The parties hereto may also proceed to arbitration as herein provided in the event that Guarantor acknowledges that Delivery has not been made and/or payment of all sums owed to Lender under the Guaranty or hereunder are not timely made.

  10.   Obligation to Pay Interest Pending Notice and Cure or Arbitration. Notwithstanding anything to the contrary in the Guaranty, the Sales Agency Agreement or the Loan and Security Agreement, if it is determined that Guarantor is obligated to make payment to Lender pursuant to the procedures herein provided, Guarantor shall be obligated to pay any additional interest (at the non-default rate) accruing under the Loan and Security Agreement as a result of Guarantor's failure to effect timely Delivery hereunder, and the Arbitrator shall so provide in his (or her) award. The provisions of this Paragraph 10 shall be enforceable by Lender by compelling an arbitration under Paragraph 9 hereof.

  11.   Notices. All notices required to be given hereunder must be in writing and delivered by hand, by air courier, by mail, or by telecopy (with a confirming copy by mail), and shall be deemed to have been given when received by the party to which the notice is sent or five business days after deposit in the U.S. mail by certified or registered mail, return receipt requested, with postage prepaid. The address for notices to Agent, Producer, Guarantor, Investor and Lender shall be as follows:

To Agent:

To Producer:

To Guarantor:

To Investor:

To Lender:

With a copy to: Stroock & Stroock & Lavan, LLP
                    2029 Century Park East, Suite 1800
                    Los Angeles, CA 90067
                    Attn: Schuyler M. Moore
                    Facsimile: (310) 556-5813

12.   Insurance Recoveries. Notwithstanding any provisions of this Inter-Party Agreement, the Loan and Security Agreement, the Sales Agency Agreement, the Investor Agreement, the Guaranty, or the Completion Agreement to the contrary, if any claim should arise under any of the policies of insurance to be provided under said agreements, with respect to which the insurer is to make a payment to Producer (as distinguished from a case in which payment is to be made to a third party), such payments shall be made to the Production Bank Account of the Picture and shall be disbursed as follows: (i) first, in case the Picture has been abandoned, such proceeds shall be paid to Lender under the Loan and Security Agreement and applied to the repayment of all amounts outstanding thereunder or in connection therewith, and the excess, if any, shall be paid to Guarantor as reimbursement of any funds advanced by Guarantor under the Guaranty; and (ii) second, if the Picture has not been abandoned, such proceeds, to the extent necessary, shall be used to pay production costs of the Picture; provided, however, and notwithstanding anything herein contained to the contrary, if directly as a result of an insured event Guarantor has advanced funds for the production of the Picture prior to the recovery of said insurance loss, the proceeds of such insurance for such loss shall be paid first to Guarantor up to the amount of said advance(s) directly related to such insurance loss and thereafter in accordance with the first part of this clause (ii) irrespective of when the insurance recovery is paid. Any balance remaining after the payments called for in clauses (i) and (ii) above shall be paid to Lender until the amounts specified in sub-clause (i) above have been

repaid to Lender in full, then to Guarantor until the funds advanced by Guarantor under the Guaranty, if any, have been reimbursed in full, then to the other parties to this Inter-Party Agreement as their respective interests under such policies may appear.

13. <u>Collection Account</u>. All gross receipts (including, without limitation, deposits, minimum guarantees, and overages) payable by any Distributors attributable to exploitation of the Picture shall be irrevocably assigned and paid directly into a segregated escrow account (the "Collection Account") maintained by Collection Agent for the purpose of the receipt and disbursement of such gross receipts. All gross receipts deposited in the Collection Account shall be distributed by Collection Agent within 30 days after the end of each calendar month in the following order of priority:

a. First, the "Fee" and "Distribution Expenses" (as defined in, and subject to the limits of, the Sales Agency Agreement) to Agent.

b. Next, to Lender until the Loan has been repaid in full.

c. Next, the payment of any residuals then owed to the guilds.

d. Next, payments to third parties (i.e., other than Producer) of participations that are payable prior to the Picture achieving "actual breakeven" (as that term is commonly understood in the motion picture industry).

e. Next, repayment of any funds that any person (including Producer) has advanced that, but for such advance, Guarantor would have been required to advance under the Completion Guaranty, provided that Guarantor has pre-approved such advances in writing.

f. Next, to Guarantor until Guarantor has been paid in full all amounts owed to Guarantor pursuant to the Producer's Agreement.

g. Next, payment of all other participations (i.e., other than those payable under Paragraph 13(d) above).

h. The remainder to Producer.

Each disbursement from the Collection Account shall be accompanied by a written statement setting forth the calculation of payments from the Collection Account.

14. <u>Governing Law; Consent to Jurisdiction</u>. This Inter-Party Agreement shall be governed by and construed and enforced in accordance with the internal laws of the State of California, excluding any laws regarding the conflict or choice of laws. Each of the parties hereto hereby agrees that, except as otherwise provided in Paragraph 9 above, any legal action or proceeding arising under or with respect to this Inter-Party Agreement or any action or proceeding to execute or otherwise enforce any judgment obtained against any party hereto or any of their respective properties may be brought in the courts of the State of California, or in the Federal courts of the United States for the Southern District of California, provided always that suit also may be brought in the courts of any country or place where any party or any of its assets may be found, and, by execution and delivery of this Inter-Party Agreement, irrevocably waives any objection which such party may now or hereafter have to the venue of any such action or proceedings brought in the courts of the State of California or in Federal courts of the United States for the Southern District of California, and hereby further irrevocably waives any claim that any such suit, action or proceeding brought in any such court has been brought in an inconvenient forum. Service of writs, processes and summonses in any action, suite or proceeding instituted by any party in any of the courts of the State of California or of the United States of America may be made upon any party by any means permitted by law, and to the extent permitted by law, by the mailing of copies of the same to such party, enclosed in registered or certified mail cover, at the address designated for each party in this Inter-Party Agreement.

15. <u>Amendment</u>. No amendment to this Inter-Party Agreement shall be effective unless in writing and signed by each party hereto.

16. <u>Counterparts</u>. This Inter-Party Agreement may be in one or more counterparts and transmitted by facsimile copy, each of which when taken together will constitute one and the same agreement, and all of which shall constitute an original copy of this Inter-Party Agreement.

IN WITNESS WHEREOF, the parties hereto have executed this agreement as of the day and year first above written.

[PRODUCER]

By: _____

Title: _____

[SALES AGENT]

By: _____

Title: _____

[COMPLETION GUARANTOR]

By: _____

Title: _____

[LENDER]

By: _____

Title: _____

_____

[INVESTOR]

EXHIBIT A

DELIVERY SCHEDULE

All capitalized words used herein shall have the same meanings as set forth in the Inter-Party Agreement for "Advice From A Caterpillar." The Mandatory Delivery Items shall be delivered to Lender at Producer's cost.

The elements contained in Paragraphs A.1 to A.3 shall conform to the final version of the Picture approved by Producer, and all photography contained in Paragraph A.4 shall have obtained the necessary approvals by all persons appearing in or performing services in connection with the Picture (collectively, the "Artists").

Where the following provides for Lender to have laboratory access or access or be given by an access letter, such access shall be given to Lender by Producer via a laboratory access letter that is substantially in the form of Schedule 1 attached hereto.

EXHIBIT "A"

MANDATORY DELIVERY ITEMS

1.   FEATURE 35MM PRINT ELEMENTS

a.   <u>Access to Original Negative</u>. Irrevocable access to the original negative of the Picture and the trailer.

b.   <u>Interpositive</u>. One 35mm interpositive of the Picture, fully color-timed and conformed, to be manufactured in first generation from the original Picture negative referred to in Paragraph A.1.a above after the final answer print has been approved by Producer.

c.   <u>Internegative</u>. One 35mm internegative of the Picture produced from a first generation 35mm interpositive of the Picture referred to in Paragraph A.1.b above, fully color-timed and conformed to the final version of the Picture.

d.   <u>Checkprint</u>. One complete final sample 35mm composite positive checkprint of the Picture and the trailer from the internegative of the Picture referred to in Paragraph A.1.c above.

e.   <u>Textless Backgrounds</u>. Color background textless sections (i.e., without any superimposed lettering) interpositive, internegative and checkprint of the main and end titles and all descriptive titles, including the backgrounds for inserts, if any, in the Picture and the trailer and of any other parts of the Picture feature which contain superimposed lettering.

2.   FEATURE SOUND ELEMENTS

a.   Optical Sound Negative. Delivery of one (1) 35mm Dolby stereo (SR/SR-D) original optical soundtrack negative of the Picture and the trailer, in good physical condition, fully cut, edited, scored and assembled and conformed in all respects to the final version of the Picture.

b.   3 or 4 Track Mono Magnetic Sound Master. Irrevocable access to the 35mm 3 or 4 track monaural full coat magnetic sound master, containing separate dialogue, music and sound effects tracks fully conformed to the final version of the Picture.

c.   Stereo Print Master. Delivery of one 35mm Dolby stereo 2-track full coat magnetic sound master fully conformed to the final version of the Picture. If the picture is prepared in Dolby SR-D, access to the 35mm six track printmaster.

d.   Magneto Optical Disc. If the Picture is prepared in Dolby SR-D, access to one magneto optical disc conformed to the final version of the Picture and with the correct logo music to be used in connection with the exploitation of the Picture.

e.   Music and Effects Tracks. If the Picture is prepared in Dolby SR-D, delivery of a six track discrete Dolby SR-D music and effects master of the Picture. In addition, delivery of a six-track Dolby SR-D music and effects master of the Picture containing a stereo configuration of left/center/right/surround, optional material on track 5 and a complete discrete dialogue stem on track 6. If the aforesaid six track Dolby music and effects master does not exist, then delivery of a 35mm 4 track Dolby stereo combined music and effects master fully conformed to the final version of the Picture and the trailer with a stereo configuration of left/right/center/surround and a separate 35mm single stripe monaural dialogue guide track.

3.   VIDEO MASTERS: Must be direct film to tape transfers (conversions not acceptable).

a.   Digital PAL Masters. Delivery of D-1 PAL videotape masters of the Picture mastered directly from a 35mm interpositive of the Picture and the trailer, in the fully panned and scanned and letterbox formats, with stereo composite mix on channels 1 and 2 and stereo music and effects tracks only on channels 3 and 4 and the textless background sections (if applicable) included after the Picture and the trailer.

  b. <u>Digital NTSC Masters</u>. Delivery of D-1 NTSC videotape masters of the Picture mastered directly from a 35 mm interpositive of the Picture and the trailer in each of the fully panned and scanned and letterbox formats, with stereo composite mix on channels 1 and 2 and stereo music and effects tracks only on channels 3 and 4 and the textless background sections (if applicable) included after the Picture.

4. <u>PUBLICITY ITEMS</u>

  a. <u>Press Kit</u>. One press kit containing: (i) production notes relating to the production of the Picture; (ii) a list of the cast and crew used in the production of the Picture; (iii) biographies of all key Artists, including the cast members in the Picture, director, writer, Producer and the director of photography; (iv) available feature stories and interviews, whether written or tape recorded; and (v) copies of available reviews of the Picture.

  b. <u>Black & White Photography</u>. Irrevocable access to all original black and white negatives approved by Producer and any other person or entity with approval rights and delivery to Lender of one set of 75 8x10 inch dupe negatives and two 8x10 inch prints of each of the 75 stills, both sets approved by any person (Artists, etc.) with a right of approval over same. All of said stills shall be of reproductive quality and suitable for advertising and publicity purposes. Each such photograph shall bear notations identifying the persons and subject matter.

  c. <u>Color Photography</u>. Irrevocable access to a set of all original color transparencies, color prints and negatives for such prints and/or color contact sheets taken or photographed in connections with the Picture and delivery a set of not less than 125 dupe color transparencies produced therefrom depicting various aspects of the production and location of the Picture. Each dupe color transparency shall be approved by Producer and any other person or entity having approval over same and shall have annexed to it notations which identify the personnel and subject matter appearing therein, and shall be suitable for reproduction for advertising and publicity purposes.

5.   DOCUMENTS

        a.   <u>Continuity Script and Spotting List</u>. Delivery of a clearly legible typewritten copy of the detailed, final language dialogue and action continuity of the Picture with spotting list ("Dialogue/Continuity List"). The Dialogue/Continuity List shall contain all the dialogue, narration, song vocals, main and end title credits, as well as a cut-by-cut description of the Picture action, conforming exactly to the photographic action and soundtrack of the final version of the Picture in such form as to be suitable for transmittal to censorship authorities and for use in connection with dubbing and subtitling the Picture. The Dialogue/Continuity List shall include a statement as to the "action to action" length of each reel of the Picture.

        b.   <u>Copyright Certificates</u>. When available, delivery of copies of the copyright certificates for the Picture and screenplay thereof in the United States, to be delivered promptly after the issuance of the initial certificates by the United States Copyright Office provided, however, that if said certificates are not available to Producer at the time of Delivery, a copy of the copyright applications (Forms PA), accompanied by proof of payment of the copyright application fees, will be delivered to Lender at the time of Delivery with a copy of the original copyright certificates being delivered to Lender when available.

        c.   <u>Copyright Notice</u>. Delivery of a statement in English indicating the correct copyright notice for the Picture.

        d.   <u>Final Credits</u>. Delivery of complete statements of the final credits to be accorded on the screen in the main and end titles in connection with the Picture. Such statements shall be rendered in customary form and shall include the names of all persons who are given a credit and shall contain excerpts from any such agreements defining or describing the form and nature of such required screen credits.

        e.   <u>Statement of Dubbing Restrictions</u>. Delivery of a statement setting forth in detail any restrictions as to the dubbing of the voice of any actor or actress into foreign languages.

        f.   <u>Statement of Distribution Restrictions and Obligations</u>. Delivery of a statement detailing any restrictions and/or obligations set forth in the agreements with the director and actors in the Picture or any other third parties which will effect Lender's exploitation of the Picture.

g.   E & O Insurance. Delivery of errors and omissions insurance certificates from an insurance Producer pre-approved by Lender with liability limits of not less than US$1,000,000 per occurrence and US$3,000,000 in the aggregate with a maximum deductible of not greater than US$10,000 naming Lender and its officers, employees, representatives, attorneys, successors, and assigns as additional named insureds to be in place for a minimum of three years from the date of commencement of principal photography. Producer shall, upon request, from time to time, furnish Lender with certificates of insurance, naming relevant subdistributors as separate additional insured parties on such policy. The errors and omissions policy shall not be subject to termination or amendment without the prior written consent of Lender and the certificate issued naming such parties as additional insureds shall include a statement to this effect.

h.   Paid Advertising Credits. Delivery of a complete statement of final credits to be accorded in paid advertising in connection with the Picture. Such statement shall be rendered in a customary form and shall include the names of all persons who are contractually required to receive a credit in any paid advertising, publicity or exploitation of the Picture and shall contain excerpts from any such agreements defining or describing the form and nature of such required paid advertising credits.

i.   Music Cue Sheet. Delivery of one copy of the music cue sheet of the Picture and any other materials delivered to Lender hereunder which contain music, setting forth, (i) the titles of the musical compositions and sound recording, if applicable; (ii) the name(s) of the composer(s) and their performing rights society affiliation; (iii) names of recording artists; (iv) the nature, extent and exact timing of the uses made of each musical composition in the Picture; (v) the name and address of the Producer of the copyright of each musical composition and sound recording; (vi) the name and address of the publisher and Producer which controls the sound recording; and (vii) all copyright in formation with respect to each such musical composition and sound recording, including the date thereof and of any extensions or renewals.

j.   Music Licenses. Delivery of all music licenses or customary reliance letters for all synchronization and performance rights for all music embodied in the picture and all pre-existing master recordings embodied in the Picture.

k.   Key Agreements: Duplicate originals of all agreements or other documents relating to the engagement of personnel in connection with the Picture, including those for all Artists, including individual Producer(s), the director, screenwriters, principal actors, composer(s) and musical performing artists.

6.   ADDITIONAL DELIVERY ITEMS

   a.   Coverage. Laboratory access to the original negative, answer print, work print, magnetic soundtracks, filled music and effects tracks and the original sound recordings, of all available alternative takes, cover shots, looped dialogue lines and other materials (hereinafter collectively referred to as "coverage") for the purpose of conforming to rating requirements, broadcast standards and practices, and censorship.

   b.   Music Licenses. Notwithstanding anything to the contrary in paragraph A.5.j above, copies of: (i) all synchronization and performance licenses issued in connection with all music embodied in the Picture; and (ii) all master use licenses issued in connection with the pre-existing master recordings embodied in the Picture, to be delivered as they become available, as a non-Mandatory Delivery Item.

   c.   Television Version. If a television version is created by Producer, laboratory access to the Interpositive, Internegative, work print, magnetic sound transfer, music and effects, continuity script and spotting list, editor's lined cutting script, and music cue sheets and digital masters with respect to any television version of the Picture, suitable for exhibition on free television during prime time.

   d.   Laboratory List. A list of the names and addresses of all laboratories used and to be used for production and post-production of the Picture (including, without limitation, sound labs, optical labs, special effects labs, etc.) and a list of all physical elements of the Picture which will be in the possession of each such laboratory.

   e.   Additional Documents. Any additional documents that may be reasonably requested by Lender.

SCHEDULE 1

LABORATORY ACCESS LETTER
(ON PRODUCER'S LETTERHEAD)

Date:
Technicolor Laboratories, Inc.
321 W. 44th Street
New York, NY 10036

Attn: Ray Chung
Re: "Advice From A Caterpillar"

Gentlemen:

Caterpillar Productions ("Producer") has entered into that certain Inter-Party Agreement (the "Agreement") with Foundry Film Partners II, LLC ("Lender"), UGC International, Film Finances, Inc. ("Guarantor"), Andrew Sicilian under which Agreement Lender has been granted certain rights in and to the film entitled "Advice From A Caterpillar" (the "Picture").

For good and valuable consideration, receipt of which is hereby acknowledged, it is hereby agreed, for the express benefit of Lender, as follows:

You and Producer represent to Lender that we have now entered into arrangements whereby you hold in your possession and your control at your offices located in New York all of the materials listed on the attached List of Materials relating to the Picture (the "Materials").

From such time as this letter shall be delivered to you, Lender, Guarantor, and its designees shall at all times have complete and free access to said Materials. If you receive notification from Guarantor that Guarantor has taken over the Film, then you shall only follow instructions of Guarantor, and Producer's right of access to the Materials shall be terminated.

You will at all times perform all laboratory services requested by Lender or its designees relating to the Picture which laboratory services will be performed by you at prevailing rates at Lender's sole expense.

THE BIZ

274

Neither Lender nor Producer shall have any liability for any indebtedness to you incurred by the other.

You presently have no claim or lien against the Picture or the Materials nor insofar as Lender is concerned will you assert any claim or lien against the Picture or the Materials except for your charges for services rendered for and documents furnished to Lender.

Except upon Lender's prior written consent, you shall not allow the Materials to be removed from your facility nor in any way revoke, rescind or modify any representations, rights or agreements granted in favor of Lender hereunder.

This Agreement is irrevocable and may not be altered or modified except by a written instrument executed by Lender and Producer.

Please signify your agreement to the foregoing by signing where indicated below.

Very truly yours,

Caterpillar Productions, LLC

By:_____

Its:_____

AGREED TO:

Technicolor Laboratories, Inc.

By: _____

Its: _____

AGREED TO:

Foundry Film Partners II, LLC

By: _____

Its: _____

EXHIBIT "B"

NOTICE OF ASSIGNMENT AND DISTRIBUTOR'S ACCEPTANCE
This Notice of Assignment and Distributor's Acceptance (the "Notice of Assignment") is made and entered into this ___ day of _____, 1998, by and
among Caterpillar Productions, LLC ("Producer"), _____ ("Distributor"),
Foundry Film Partners II, LLC ("Lender") and UGC International ("Agent").

1. Definitions. All capitalized words used herein shall have the meanings
set forth in the opening paragraph hereof or as specified below:
        b.   "Distribution Agreement" means that certain Distribution
Agreement as it may be amended or modified, dated as of _____, 1998,
by and between Agent, as agent for Producer, and Distributor relating to the
exploitation of the Picture.
        c.   "Lender Assigned Receipts" means all amounts payable by
Distributor pursuant to the Distribution Agreement, including the Minimum
Guarantee and all other payments due thereunder.
        d.   "Minimum Guarantee" means all minimum guarantee or
advance amounts payable by Distributor to Producer pursuant to the Distribution Agreement as modified by this Notice of Assignment.
        e.   "Notice of Availability" shall mean the notice attached hereto
as Schedule 1.
        f.   "Picture" means the full length-theatrical motion picture ten-
tatively entitled "Advice From a Caterpillar," or whatever title under which
this picture may be exploited.
        g.   "Rules" has the meaning set forth in Paragraph 4(g).

2.   Notice of Assignment. Producer and Agent hereby notify Distributor that, notwithstanding anything to the contrary in the Distribution Agreement, all Lender Assigned Receipts are hereby irrevocably assigned to Lender
until written notification from Lender to the contrary.

3.   Payment of Lender Assigned Receipts. Notwithstanding anything
to the contrary in the Distribution Agreement, Distributor agrees to pay

the Lender Assigned Receipts, including the Minimum Guarantee, exclusively to Lender in accordance with Schedule 1 attached hereto and incorporated herein by this reference. Distributor hereby agrees that notwithstanding anything to the contrary contained in the Distribution Agreement, (i) the balance of the Minimum Guarantee shall be payable upon receipt of the Notice of Availability. Distributor acknowledges and agrees that it shall immediately pay all Lender Assigned Receipts (without offset, set-off, deduction or withholding of any kind or nature) to Lender via wire transfer to the following account (or such other account as Lender may notify to Distributor in writing):

> IBJ Schroder Bank & Trust
> One State Street
> New York, NY 10004
> Account Name Foundry Film Partners II:
>   "Advice From A Caterpillar"
> Account No. 41687756
> ABA No. 026007825

4.   Miscellaneous

a.   No Amendment. Producer, Agent and Distributor acknowledge and agree that the Distribution Agreement is in full force and effect enforceable against the parties thereto in accordance with its terms, and that the Distribution Agreement shall not be amended, modified or terminated absent the prior written consent of Lender.

b.   Inspection. Distributor shall afford Lender all rights of audit and inspection with respect to Distributor's books and records pertaining to the Picture that are granted to Producer under the Distribution Agreement.

c.   Notices. Distributor shall furnish Lender duplicates of all notices and statements from Distributor to Producer or Agent.

d.   Condition Precedent. The timely payment of all Lender's Assigned Receipts, including the Minimum Guarantee, in accordance with the terms and conditions of this Notice of Assignment, constitutes an express continuing condition precedent to the grant of rights to Distributor pursuant to the Distribution Agreement.

e.   No Refund. Once the Lender Assigned Receipts have been paid to Lender, the same shall not be subject to refund or return to Distributor by Lender for any reason whatsoever.

f.   No Assumption. Lender has taken assignment only of the Lender Assigned Receipts, and Lender has not assumed any obligations or liabilities of Producer or Agent under the Distribution Agreement. Distributor shall look solely to Producer for the performance and discharge of such obligation and liabilities.

g.   Arbitration. Each of the parties hereto agrees that any dispute under the Distribution Agreement or this Notice of Assignment shall be resolved by mandatory binding arbitration under the American Film Marketing Association Rules of International Arbitration (the "Rules") in effect as of the date the request for arbitration is filed. The arbitration will be held in New York, New York. Each of the parties hereto submits to the exclusive jurisdiction of the courts of the state and country of such forum as an appropriate place for compelling arbitration or giving legal confirmation of any arbitration award. Each of the parties agrees to accept service of process for all arbitral proceedings in accordance with the Rules and to accept service of process for any judicial or other proceedings by registered mail. The prevailing party and Lender in any such actions shall be entitled to prompt payment of costs and fees, including reasonable attorneys' fees.

h.   Override. For the avoidance of doubt, in the event of any inconsistency between this Notice of Assignment and the Distribution Agreement, the provisions of this Notice of Assignment shall control.

i.   Counterparts. This Notice of Assignment may be executed in counterparts and transmitted by facsimile copy, each of which shall constitute an original but, when taken together, shall constitute one instrument.

j.   Governing Law. This Notice of Assignment and the rights and obligations of the parties hereunder shall be construed in accordance and governed by the laws of the State of New York and the federal laws of the United States of America applicable to contracts entered to be wholly performed within said state without reference to the principles of conflict of laws thereof.

IN WITNESS WHEREOF, the parties have executed this Notice of Assignment to be effective as of the date first above written.

CATERPILLAR PRODUCTIONS, LLC

By: _____

Title: _____

FOUNDRY FILM PARTNERS II, LLC

By: _____

Title: _____

[Distributor]

By: _____

Title: _____

UGC INTERNATIONAL

By: _____

Title: _____

SCHEDULE 1

Minimum Guarantee: U.S. $_____ payable as follows:
[Specify Payment Schedule]

FORM E

"SAMPLE FILM" COMPLETION GUARANTY AGREEMENT

1. Definitions

2. Conditions Precedent

3. Failure of Delivery

4. Excess Costs

5. Excluded Risks

6. Excluded Costs

7. Mutual Cooperation

8. Producer's Agreement

9. Notices

10. Governing Law

11. Interpretation

12. Entire Agreement

13. Attorney Fees

14. Assignment

15. Counterparts

1.   <u>Definitions</u>. As used herein, all capitalized words shall have the meanings as set forth below:

   a.   "Advances" has the meaning set forth in the Loan Agreement.

   b.   "Agreement" means this "Sample Film" Completion Guaranty Agreement.

   c.   "Beneficiary" means _____.

   d.   "Commitment Amount" means $_____.

   e.   "Delivery" has the meaning set forth in the Inter-Party Agreement.

   f.   "Delivery Date" has the meaning set forth in the Inter-Party Agreement.

   g.   "Excluded Costs" has the meaning set forth in Paragraph 6.

   h.   "Excluded Risks" has the meaning set forth in Paragraph 5.

   i.   "Guarantee Fee" means a fee payable to Guarantor in consideration of entering into this Agreement in the amount of $_____.

   j.   "Guarantor" means _____.

   k.   "Inter-Party Agreement" means the "Sample Film" Inter-Party Agreement entered into by and among Producer, Beneficiary, Guarantor, and _____.

   l.   "Loan" has the meaning set forth in the Loan Agreement.

   m.   "Loan Agreement" means the "Sample Film" Loan and Security Agreement entered into by and between Beneficiary and Producer for purposes of funding production of the Picture.

   n.   "Picture" means the motion picture tentatively entitled "Sample Film."

   o.   "Producer" means _____.

   p.   "Producer's Agreement" means the "Sample Film" Producer's Completion Agreement entered into by and between Producer and Guarantor.

2.   <u>Conditions Precedent</u>. Guarantor's obligations under this Agreement are subject to the continuing conditions precedent of:

   a.   Receipt by Guarantor of a fully executed copy of the Producer's Agreement, Loan Agreement, and Inter-Party Agreement.

   b.   The Receipt by Guarantor of binders evidencing all policies of insurance relating to the Picture reasonably requested by Guarantor, and the maintenance in force of such insurance.

c.   Beneficiary making Advances under the Loan Agreement up to the Commitment Amount.

d.   Payment to Guarantor of the Guarantee Fee.

e.   Beneficiary's non-interference with Guarantor's efforts to effect Delivery.

3.   Failure of Delivery. Subject to the conditions precedent set forth in Paragraph 2, if Delivery of the Picture does not occur by the Delivery Date (other than due to Excluded Risks as provided in Paragraph 5), Guarantor shall promptly pay Beneficiary the lesser of (a) the then outstanding amount of the Loan (net of any amounts received and retained by Beneficiary from insurance policies relating to the Picture) or (b) the Commitment Amount. Guarantor may elect at any time, by written notice to Beneficiary, to abandon pursuing Delivery of the Picture, in which case Guarantor's liability hereunder will be limited to the lesser of (a) the outstanding amount of the Loan (net of any amounts received and retained by Beneficiary from insurance policies relating to the Picture) at the time of such abandonment or (b) the Commitment Amount. To the extent that Guarantor makes any payment to Beneficiary under this Paragraph 3, Guarantor shall automatically be subrogated to all of Beneficiary's rights, claims, causes of action, and security interests relating to the Picture to the extent of such payment, and Beneficiary shall execute any documents reasonably requested by Guarantor to evidence and effect such subrogation.

4.   Excess Costs. Subject to the conditions precedent set forth in Paragraph 2, if Delivery does occur by the Delivery Date, Guarantor shall pay or be liable for all costs paid or incurred in connection with completion and Delivery of the Picture in excess of the Commitment Amount, if such excess costs were incurred at the request of, or with the consent of, Guarantor (other than Excluded Costs as provided in Paragraph 6).

5.   Excluded Risks. Guarantor shall not be liable to Beneficiary under Paragraph 3 for failure of Delivery attributable directly or indirectly to any of the following (referred to herein as the "Excluded Risks"):

a.   Any defect in any intangible rights (including, without limitation, copyrights and trademarks) relating to any aspect of the Picture (other than music rights to the extent music is required to effect Delivery).

b.   Any infringement by the Picture on the rights of third parties, including, without limitation, copyrights, trademarks, right of publicity, defamation, and invasion of privacy.

c.   Any censorship, rating, or similar requirements of any organization, except that Guarantor shall be obligated to deliver the Picture with a rating from the Motion Picture Association of America, Inc. of not more restrictive than "R".

d.   Any hostile or warlike action by any governmental power or instrumentality thereof.

e.   Any detonation of any atomic or radioactive weapon.

f.   Any insurrection, rebellion, revolution, act of terrorism, civil war, usurped power, or action taken by governmental authority in response thereto.

g.   Any seizure, destruction, confiscation, or quarantine by any governmental entity or instrumentality thereof.

h.   Any claim relating to the artistic quality of the Picture.

i.   Any nuclear reaction, nuclear radiation, or radioactive contamination.

j.   The bankruptcy or insolvency of Beneficiary or any dishonest, fraudulent, or criminal act of any representative of Beneficiary.

k.   Any actions undertaken by the guilds, including, without limitation, strikes, work-stoppages, slow-downs, or the failure to clear the Picture for commencement of production due to the failure of the Producer to post any required deposits, bonds, or escrows to secure any payments to the guilds or their members, including residuals.

l.   Imposition of taxes, including, without limitation, social security taxes, national insurance taxes, withholding taxes, value added taxes, tax indemnity payments, and the like, except to the extent set forth in the Approved Budget.

m.   Currency fluctuations.

n.   Any failure or inability of Distributor to make payments required upon Delivery for any reason.

6. <u>Excluded Costs</u>. In no event shall Completion Guarantor be liable under Paragraph 4 for the following (referred to herein as the "Excluded Costs"):

    a.   Any costs relating to Excluded Risks.

    b.   Any costs incurred after Delivery.

    c.   Any costs of providing, supplying, or delivering items not required to effect Delivery.

    d.   Legal fees and related costs of the Producer.

    e.   Any costs that were not paid or incurred either at Guarantor's request or with Guarantor's written consent.

    f.   Any costs that do not relate to the completion and Delivery of the Picture.

    g.   Any payments that are contingent on revenues generated by the Picture, including participations, residuals, and deferments.

7. <u>Mutual Cooperation</u>. Guarantor shall notify Beneficiary in writing if Guarantor takes over production of the Picture pursuant to the Producer's Agreement, and Beneficiary shall cooperate with all reasonable requests of Guarantor provided such requests neither require Advances by Beneficiary beyond the Commitment Amount nor expose Beneficiary to liability to third parties. Beneficiary shall accelerate the making of Advances if requested by Guarantor. The parties will cooperate with each other in pursuing any claims against third parties responsible for delaying the delivery of, or otherwise increasing the cost of, the Picture.

8. <u>Producer's Agreement</u>. Any action or inaction by Producer under the Producer's Agreement shall not constitute a defense to Guarantor's obligations hereunder.

9. <u>Notices</u>. All notices shall be given in writing by registered mail, return receipt requested, or by facsimile and shall be sent to the respective addresses for notices listed below, or to such other addresses as each party may notify to the other from time to time. A notice sent by registered mail shall be deemed received on the date inscribed in the official return receipt. A notice sent by facsimile shall be deemed received on the next business day.

Addresses for Notice:
Beneficiary:
Guarantor:
With a Copy to:

10.   <u>Governing Law</u>. This Agreement shall be governed by the internal laws of the state of California (i.e., without regard to its conflict of law principles).

11.   <u>Interpretation</u>. This Agreement has been fully negotiated by both parties and their advisors and shall be construed as a whole according to its fair meaning and not strictly for or against either party.

12.   <u>Entire Agreement</u>. This Agreement constitutes the entire agreement between the parties hereto relating to the subject matter hereof and supersedes any and all prior negotiations, term sheets, or agreements. This Agreement may not be modified or amended except by a writing executed by both parties hereto.

13.   <u>Attorney Fees</u>. If any action is commenced relating to this Agreement, the prevailing party shall, in addition to any other relief to which that party is entitled, be entitled to recover its reasonable attorneys' fees and costs.

14.   <u>Assignment</u>. Guarantor may not assign its rights or obligations under this Agreement without the written consent of Beneficiary. Beneficiary may assign its rights under this Agreement in conjunction with any assignment (in whole or in part) of the Loan, provided the assignee assumes Beneficiary's obligations under Paragraph 7 of this Agreement.

15.   <u>Counterparts</u>. This Agreement may be executed in counterparts and transmitted by facsimile copy, each of which shall constitute an original.

IN WITNESS WHEREOF, the parties hereto have executed this Agreement effective as of _____.

[BENEFICIARY]

By: _____

Title: _____

[GUARANTOR]

By: _____

Title: _____

FORM F

"SAMPLE FILM" PRODUCER'S COMPLETION AGREEMENT

1.   <u>Definitions</u>. All capitalized words used in this Agreement shall have the meanings as set forth below:

a.   "Advances" has the meaning set forth in Paragraph 12.

b.   "Agreement" means this "Sample Film" Producer's Completion Agreement and all Exhibits attached hereto.

c.   "Approved" means approved in writing by Producer, Guarantor, and Beneficiary.

d.   "Beneficiary" means _____.

e.   "Budget" means the final Approved budget for the Picture.

f.   "Cash Flow Schedule" means the final Approved cash flow schedule for the Picture.

g.   "Collateral" means all property that is subject to the Security Interest.

h.   "Completion Guaranty" means the "Sample Film" Completion Guaranty Agreement for the Picture entered into by and between Beneficiary and Guarantor.

i.   "Delivery" has the meaning set forth in the Inter-Party Agreement.

j.   "Delivery Specifications" means the specifications for the Approved Picture set forth in Section II of Exhibit "A" attached hereto.

k.   "Distribution Agreement" means the "Sample Film" Distribution Agreement entered into by and between Producer and Distributor with respect to distribution of the Picture.

l.   "Distributor" means _____.

m.   "Event of Default" has the meaning set forth in Paragraph 13(a).

n.   "Guarantor" means _____.

o.   "Guarantor's Approval" means advance written approval by Guarantor, which shall be subject to Guarantor's good-faith discretion.

p.   "Inter-Party Agreement" means the "Sample Film" Inter-Party Agreement entered into by and among Producer, Beneficiary, Guarantor, and _____.

q.   "Loan" means the aggregate of all Advances by Guarantor plus interest thereon at the Prime Rate plus 1.5 percentage points.

r.   "Physical Film Elements" means all tangible personal property embodying any visual or audio aspects of the Picture, such as film negatives and sound tracks.

s.   Picture" means the motion picture to be produced tentatively titled "Sample Film."

t.   "Prime Rate" means the prime rate as published in The Wall Street Journal on the first business day of each calendar month, for purposes of calculating interest on the portion of the Loan outstanding at the beginning of such calendar month. For Advances made during a calendar month, "Prime Rate" shall be the same rate as published on the first business day preceding the date the Advance is made, for purposes of calculating interest on that Advance for the balance of that calendar month.

u.   "Producer means _____.

v.   "Production Bank Account" means the bank account receiving the proceeds of the production loan from Beneficiary for purposes of financing production of the Picture.

w.   "Production Elements" means the Approved production elements for the Picture set forth in Section I of Exhibit "A" attached hereto.

x.   "Production Schedule" means the Approved production schedule for the Picture.

y.   "Relevant Documents" means this Agreement, the Budget, the Cash Flow Schedule, the Production Schedule, the Screenplay, the Production Elements, the Delivery Specifications, the Inter-Party Agreement, the Distribution Agreement, the production loan agreement, and all other contracts relating to the Picture, collectively.

z.   "Screenplay" means the final Approved screenplay for the Picture.

aa.   "Security Interest" means the security interest in the Collateral granted to Guarantor pursuant to the Mortgage of Copyright and Security Agreement attached hereto as Exhibit "G-2".

2.   Production. Producer shall produce and effect Delivery of the Picture in conformance with the Relevant Documents. Producer shall require the director to cover all scenes necessary for a television version, including, but not limited to, preparation of alternative takes, cover shots, and looped dialogue lines, and Producer shall deliver the negative, film, and sound materials containing same to Distributor as necessary to effect Delivery. Any variations from production of the Picture strictly in accordance with the

Relevant Documents, including, without limitation, any modification or enhancement to the Picture, may be undertaken only with Guarantor's Approval, which may be subject to such conditions as Guarantor requires, such as additional deposits to the Production Bank Account or the payment of an additional fee to Guarantor to compensate it for any additional risk incurred. While the Completion Guaranty is in effect, Producer shall not grant any consent rights to any third parties under any agreements relating to the Picture, waive or release any default or obligation thereunder, or agree to any modification or termination thereof, without Guarantor's Approval. Guarantor shall have the right to counter-sign all checks drawn on the Production Bank Account and to receive and approve, pursuant to the Cash Flow Schedule, all draw-downs on production loans or other financing agreements.

3.   <u>Production Bank Account</u>. Producer shall use its best efforts to obtain from the bank holding the Production Bank Account the Production Account Takeover Letter in the form attached hereto as Exhibit "B". Guarantor may at any time (upon written notice to Producer) require that Guarantor be a necessary joint signatory for the disbursement of any funds from the Production Bank Account.

4.   <u>Insurance</u>
        a.   <u>Policies</u>. Producer has obtained and shall maintain all insurance coverages as may be reasonably requested from time to time by Beneficiary, Distributor, or Guarantor, and shall produce for Guarantor, upon request, all policies of insurance and cover notes therefor and the receipts for premiums paid. Evidence of the insurance policies presently in effect is attached hereto as Exhibit "C".
        b.   <u>Additional Insured</u>. Guarantor shall be named as an additional insured and as joint loss payee with Producer, Beneficiary, and Distributor (as required by their respective agreements with Producer) in all of the insurance policies obtained by Producer in connection with the Picture.
        c.   <u>Maintenance in Effect</u>. Producer shall use its best efforts to maintain all such insurance policies in effect, and shall avoid taking or permitting any action or inaction that may void such policies. Producer shall

immediately advise Guarantor of any action or inaction that may void such policies by any party.

    d.   <u>Default</u>. If Producer shall fail to obtain any such insurance policies, Guarantor may, but shall not be obligated to, obtain such policies, and any premiums paid by Guarantor for such policies shall be treated as an Advance hereunder.

    e.   <u>Settlement and Payment of Proceeds</u>. No insurance claim shall be settled without Guarantor's Approval. All payments under any insurance policy shall be applied as provided in the Inter-Party Agreement.

5.   <u>Laboratory Access Letter</u>. Concurrently with the execution of this Agreement, Producer shall execute and deliver to Guarantor the Laboratory Access Letter in the form attached hereto as Exhibit "D" and shall use its best efforts to have the relevant laboratory execute and return to Guarantor such Laboratory Access Letter.

6.   <u>Notice of Irrevocable Assignment and Distributor's Acceptance</u>. Upon execution hereof, Producer shall execute and deliver to Distributor the Notice of Irrevocable Assignment attached hereto as Exhibit "E". Producer shall use its best efforts to have Distributor execute and return to Guarantor the Distributor's Acceptance attached hereto as Exhibit "F".

7.   <u>Contracts</u>. Producer has entered or will enter into written agreements with all personnel comprising the Production Elements, and the form of such contracts, and any amendments thereto, shall be subject to Guarantor's Approval. No such agreements shall contain any "stop dates" as such term is commonly understood in the motion picture industry. All of such contracts shall be strictly in accordance with the Relevant Documents.

8.   <u>Distribution Agreement</u>. The Distribution Agreement has been or will be duly executed by Producer and Distributor and is or will be in full force and effect by commencement of principal photography for the Picture. Producer shall deliver to Guarantor a copy of the fully executed Distribution Agreement.

9. <u>Guilds</u>. Producer has or will become a signatory to the Basic Agreements with the Directors Guild of America and the Screen Actors Guild no later than thirty days prior to commencement of principal photography of the Picture. Producer has budgeted for, or has made financial arrangements acceptable to all guilds regarding, the payment of residuals for the Picture including, where necessary, providing for a bond, deposit, or escrow within the Budget.

10. <u>Reports, Inspection, and Monitoring Production</u>
    a. <u>Reports</u>. During production of the Picture, Producer shall:
        i. Keep Guarantor fully informed as to the progress of production and all plans for continuing and completing production of the Picture;
        ii. Prepare daily progress reports and weekly cost statements and trial balances and supply copies thereof to Guarantor;
        iii. Supply Guarantor with copies of all bank statements issued in connection with the Production Bank Account;
        iv. Submit to Guarantor for inspection all estimates of future expenditures or statements of costs incurred that Guarantor may reasonably require;
        v. Promptly inform Guarantor of any actual or potential Events of Default, all matters potentially affecting Producer's credit and financial standing, all threatened or pending claims or actions against Producer, and the ongoing status of such claims and actions; and
        vi. Furnish Guarantor with any other information requested by Guarantor from time to time.
    b. <u>Inspection</u>. Producer shall maintain complete and accurate books and records relating to the Picture, and Guarantor shall have the unlimited right to inspect and copy such books and records, including access to all computer hardware and software necessary to inspect any books and records kept on computers. Guarantor shall also have the right to inspect any Collateral.
    c. <u>Monitoring Production</u>. Guarantor may at all times be entitled to observe and otherwise monitor production of the Picture, including being on the set and talking to production personnel regarding the progress of the

Picture. Producer shall promptly respond to any request for information from Guarantor and shall attend any reasonably scheduled meetings or, if geographically unfeasible, participate in telephone conference calls. Producer shall use its best efforts to cause any other personnel requested by Guarantor to attend such meetings to discuss the Picture and shall give full consideration to the views and proposals put forward by Guarantor in order to decide upon any steps to be taken to remove any risks perceived by Guarantor.

11. <u>Additional Representations, Warranties, and Covenants</u>. Producer represents, warrants, and covenants to Guarantor as follows:

    a.   Producer shall at all times own all rights in and to the Screenplay and the Picture.

    b.   There are no existing Events of Default.

    c.   Producer shall promptly notify Guarantor of any of the following: (a) any actual or pending Event of Default, (b) any change to the location of Producer's chief executive office, (c) any change to the name or trade name of Producer, (d) any change in the location of any laboratory holding any Physical Film Elements, or (e) any change to the name of the Picture.

    d.   All Physical Film Elements shall be kept in laboratories approved by Guarantor.

    e.   Producer shall promptly register the Picture with the United States Copyright Office upon completion of the Picture.

    f.   Producer shall maintain all policies of insurance covering the Picture as shall be required by Guarantor.

    g.   Producer shall execute such further documents, and take such further actions, as shall be reasonably requested by Guarantor to implement the provisions of this Agreement or to evidence, attach, perfect, or enforce the Security Interest.

    h.   Producer shall not amend any of the Relevant Documents without Guarantor's Approval.

12. <u>Loan</u>. All payments made by Guarantor pursuant to this Agreement or the Completion Guaranty, including, without limitation, all payments made by Guarantor to complete and effect Delivery of the Picture (collectively, the

"Advances") shall be treated as part of the Loan to Producer, which shall be repayable by Producer to Guarantor on demand. The Loan shall bear interest at the Prime Rate plus 1.5 percentage points.

13. <u>Events of Default</u>

   a.   <u>Occurrence</u>. An "Event of Default" hereunder shall be caused by the occurrence of any of the following:

   i.   The failure by Producer to produce or effect Delivery of the Picture in conformance with the Relevant Documents, or any material breach by Producer of any provision of this Agreement or the Relevant Documents.

   ii.   If Guarantor, in its good-faith discretion, determines that either (a) there is a reasonable risk of failure of Delivery or (b) Guarantor may have to advance additional funds in order to effect Delivery (such as production of the Picture being behind the Production Schedule or expenditures being over the Cash Flow Schedule).

   iii.   Any event or claim which, in Guarantor's good-faith discretion, results in, or may with the passage of time result in, any material impairment to (1) the existence, attachment, priority, or perfection of the Security Interest, (2) the value of the Collateral, (3) the effectiveness of any of the Relevant Documents, or (4) Producer's ability to perform its obligations under the Relevant Documents.

   iv.   The creation or attachment of any security interest, lien, or encumbrance against the Collateral other than liens in favor of Beneficiary, guilds, or laboratories.

   v.   Any lawsuit being filed against Producer for more than $25,000 that is not dismissed within thirty days.

   vi.   The placement of any Physical Film Elements in any laboratory that is not approved by Guarantor.

   vii.   Any actual or pending consolidation, merger, or dissolution of, or sale of Collateral by, Producer.

   viii.   Any insolvency or bankruptcy filing or material adverse change with respect to any insurance companies insuring any aspect of the Picture.

ix.   Any insurance company that is insuring any aspect of the Picture denying or failing to affirm any of its obligations.

x.   Producer giving Guarantor false or misleading information or representations or not disclosing all material facts that might be relevant to Guarantor.

xi.   Guarantor being required to make any Advance.

b.   Consequence. Upon the occurrence of any Event of Default, the following consequences shall occur:

i.   The Loan shall become immediately due and payable.

ii.   Guarantor shall have the election to take over production of the Picture in accordance with the provisions of Paragraph 14.

iii.   Guarantor may immediately commence enforcement of the Loan, including by foreclosing on the Security Interest, and Guarantor may exercise all of the rights and remedies of a secured creditor under applicable law.

iv.   Guarantor shall automatically hold all of the Collateral for Producer, and may take any action, including taking possession of, licensing, or disposing of the Collateral, as Guarantor in its good-faith discretion deems appropriate, including the settlement or compromise of any claims relating to the Collateral. Producer does hereby waive any claim for damages it might otherwise have against any third parties (as express third party beneficiaries) who handle, acquire, license, or dispose of the Collateral in accordance with the instructions of Guarantor operating pursuant to the provisions of this subparagraph.

v.   Guarantor shall be entitled to the appointment of a receiver to take immediate possession of the Collateral.

vi.   Guarantor shall have the right to apply any cash or deposits held by Producer against the Loan.

14.   Takeover

a.   Exercise of Rights. If Guarantor exercises its takeover rights, it shall be deemed to have been irrevocably appointed as the manager and agent of Producer for such purpose, and Producer shall place at the disposal of, and under the control of, Guarantor the Production Bank Account and all persons, premises, and equipment employed or used by Producer in connection with production of the Picture. Producer shall, without additional remuneration, cooperate fully with Guarantor to facilitate the takeover with the minimum possible disruption to production of the Picture and shall furnish all information and render all reasonable and customary production services as Guarantor shall request. Producer shall advise Guarantor in all respects as to all items of production information within the knowledge or access of Producer.

    b.   <u>Scope of Authority</u>. Guarantor may take any and all actions as it reasonably deems necessary in its sole discretion in order to complete the Picture and effect Delivery, including, without limitation, deferring the payment of all producer's fees. Guarantor may take any action as Guarantor in its good-faith discretion deems appropriate, including disposition of the Collateral and the settlement or compromise of any claims relating to the Collateral.

    c.   <u>No Liability</u>. Guarantor shall incur no liability to Producer attributable to any actions that Guarantor undertakes for and on behalf of Producer pursuant to Guarantor's takeover rights. Producer hereby waives any claim for damages it might otherwise have against Guarantor or any third parties (as express third-party beneficiaries) as a result of any actions Guarantor takes pursuant to its takeover rights.

    d.   <u>Termination</u>. Guarantor shall terminate exercise of its takeover rights and revest control of production of the Picture with Producer upon the occurrence of either of the following events:

    i.   Producer contributing additional funds to the Production Bank Account in an amount that, in the good-faith discretion of Guarantor, adequately protects Guarantor from incurring any liability under this Agreement or the Completion Guaranty, without prejudice to the rights of Guarantor to re-exercise its takeover rights upon a subsequent Event of Default; or

    ii.   Prior to the time that Guarantor has made any advances (or after repayment of the Loan in full), Beneficiary provides an irrevocable written release of all of Guarantor's obligations under the Completion Guaranty, which release does not affect Guarantor's right to retain its guaranty fee.

e. <u>Takeover Agreement</u>. In order to evidence Guarantor's takeover rights, upon execution of this Agreement Producer shall execute and deliver to Guarantor the Takeover Agreement attached hereto as Exhibit "H".

f. <u>Other Actions</u>. In lieu of a complete takeover, upon any Event of Default Guarantor may take any actions that it would have been entitled to in a complete takeover, including deferring all or part of any producer's fees as necessary to complete the Picture and effect Delivery.

15. <u>Grant of Security Interest</u>. In order to secure all of Producer's obligations and Guarantor's rights under this Agreement, including repayment of the Loan, upon execution of this Agreement Producer shall execute and deliver to Guarantor (a) the UCC-1 Statement attached hereto as Exhibit "G" (to which shall be attached the description of the Collateral attached hereto as Exhibit "G-1") and (b) the Mortgage of Copyright and Security Agreement attached hereto as Exhibit "G-2". Guarantor may immediately or at any time hereafter file and record such documents whether or not Guarantor has made any Advances. Such filing shall be terminated if no portion of the Loan is outstanding and either Delivery has occurred or Guarantor is irrevocably released from all of its obligations under the Completion Guaranty. The Security Interest granted to Guarantor shall be prior to all other liens and encumbrances other than liens in favor of Beneficiary or laboratories. At the request of Guarantor, Producer shall execute and deliver all such further reasonable documents consistent herewith as Guarantor may deem necessary or appropriate to perfect the Security Interest.

16. <u>Power of Attorney</u>. Upon execution of this Agreement, Producer shall execute and deliver to Guarantor the Power of Attorney attached hereto as Exhibit "H-1".

17. <u>Acknowledgment of Subrogation</u>. Producer acknowledges that if Guarantor repays any financing provided by Beneficiary pursuant to the Completion Guaranty then, in addition to its other rights and remedies hereunder, Guarantor shall automatically be subrogated to all the rights of Beneficiary with respect to such financing, including the security interest of Beneficiary.

18. <u>No Third Party Beneficiary Status</u>. Producer hereby acknowledges that it is not a third-party beneficiary under the Completion Guaranty.

19. <u>No Assignment</u>. Neither party may assign or delegate its rights or obligations under this Agreement to any other party.

20. <u>Credit</u>. Guarantor shall be entitled to a credit in the end titles of all positive prints of the Picture, which shall be on a single card and shall read as follows: "Completion Guaranty Provided Through _____." Failure to do so shall not be an Event of Default, but Producer shall use reasonable efforts to prospectively cure any such failure.

21. <u>Guarantor's Representatives</u>. Any action that may be undertaken by Guarantor hereunder may be undertaken by any of Guarantor's agents or representatives.

22. <u>Waivers</u>. No waiver by Guarantor of any Event of Default or any of the obligations or covenants of Producer shall act as a subsequent waiver of the same matter or as a waiver of any other matter.

23. <u>Rights or Remedies</u>. All the rights and remedies of Guarantor under this Agreement or by operation of law shall be cumulative and shall not be exclusive of any other rights or remedies available.

24. <u>Notices</u>. All notices shall be given in writing by registered mail, return receipt requested, or by facsimile and shall be sent to the respective addresses for notices listed below, or to such other addresses as each party may notify to the other from time to time. A notice sent by registered mail shall be deemed received on the date inscribed in the official return receipt. A notice sent by facsimile shall be deemed received on the next business day.

    <u>Addresses for Notice:</u>
    <u>Producer:</u>

Guarantor:

With a Copy to:

25. Governing Law. This Agreement shall be governed by the internal laws of the state of California (i.e., without regard to its conflict of law principles).

26. Interpretation. This Agreement has been fully negotiated by both parties hereto and their advisors and shall be construed as a whole according to its fair meaning and not strictly for or against either party.

27. Entire Agreement. This Agreement and the Inter-Party Agreement constitutes the entire agreement between Guarantor and Producer with respect to the subject matter hereof, and supersedes all prior negotiations, term sheets, or agreements relating to such subject matter. This Agreement may not be modified or amended except by a writing executed by both parties hereto.

28. Attorney Fees. If any action is commenced relating to this Agreement, the prevailing party shall, in addition to any other relief to which that party is entitled, be entitled to recover its reasonable attorneys' fees and costs.

29. Jurisdiction. Guarantor and Producer hereby consent to Los Angeles, California, as a non-exclusive location for jurisdiction and venue of any legal actions brought relating to this Agreement and waive any objection they might otherwise have to such jurisdiction and venue, including for non-convenient forum.

30. Counterparts. This Agreement may be executed in counterparts and transmitted by facsimile copy, each of which shall constitute an original.

IN WITNESS WHEREOF, the parties hereto have executed this Agreement effective as of _____.

[PRODUCER]

By: _____

Title: _____

[GUARANTOR]

By: _____

Title: _____

This Sales Agent Agreement ("Agreement") is entered into as of
_____, by and between _____ ("Owner") and
_____ Inc. ("Agent").

1. Definitions

      a.   The "Pictures" means the motion pictures to be produced by Owner tentatively titled "_____", "_____ " and "_____. "

      b.   The "Territory" shall mean the United States and Canada.

      c.   The "Term" of this Agreement shall continue indefinitely unless terminated by either party upon 30-days advance written notice to the other.

      d.   "Agent Procured License Agreements" shall mean agreements for distribution of the Pictures in the Territory that are solicited and negotiated by Agent during the Term as long as they are entered into at any time prior to six months after the end of the Term.

e.   "Agent Gross Receipts" shall mean all gross receipts actually received by Owner (whether paid during or after the Term) attributable to Agent Procured License Agreements.

2.   Agent Services. Owner hereby engages Agent during the Term to act as Owner's sales representative in connection with soliciting and negotiating Agent Procured License Agreements. Agent shall not own, or be a licensee of any rights to, the Pictures, and Agent shall be acting as the Agent of Owner. All Agent Procured License Agreements must be approved and executed by Owner, which approval and execution it may withhold arbitrarily in its sole discretion. Agent agrees to exert its best-efforts to obtain offers from distributors and to negotiate the same on terms advantageous to Owner. However, Agent makes no representations or warranties regarding the terms of offers, if any, which will be made.

3.   Expenses. Each party shall bear their own expenses relating to this Agreement. Agent shall not have any authority to enter into any contract imposing liability on Owner for any costs or expenses without the prior consent of Owner.

4.   Payments. All Agent Gross Receipts shall be paid into a separate escrow account, with joint escrow instructions executed by Agent and Owner. The escrow instructions shall provide that 10% of all Agent Gross Receipts shall be paid promptly to Agent, with the balance paid to Owner. In the event that any Agent Gross Receipts are paid directly to Owner, Owner shall remit all commissions due Agent (together with detailed explanatory statements) within 30 days of the close of the month of receipt of such Agent Gross Receipts.

5.   Representations and Warranties. Owner hereby represents and warrants that it does or will own or control all of the distribution and exploitation rights for the Pictures in the Territory. Owner agrees to indemnify

Agent and its employees from all losses, claims, and expenses, including reasonable attorneys' fees, arising from any breach of the foregoing representation and warranty.

6.   Arbitration. In the event of any dispute between the parties as to any part of this Agreement, such dispute shall be submitted to the American Arbitration Association in Los Angeles, California. The award rendered shall be binding upon the parties and may be entered in any court having jurisdiction of the subject matter.

7.   Governing Law. This agreement is made in, and shall be governed and interpreted in accordance with the internal laws of, the State of California.

IN WITNESS WHEREOF, the parties hereto have executed this Agreement as of the date first written above.

[OWNER]

By: _____
Title: _____

[AGENT]

By: _____
Title: _____

FORM H

PRO-LICENSOR LICENSE AGREEMENT

1. <u>DEFINITIONS</u>

License:	This License Agreement
Licensor:	_____
	_____
	_____
	_____
Licensee:	_____
Territory:	_____
Term:	_____ years from the date hereof.
Rights:	The [non-exclusive/exclusive] right to exploit the Picture through the Media in the Territory for the Term.
Media:	(a) The right to manufacture and sell video units (cassette or disc).
	(b) The right to exploit the Picture through free television.
	(c) The right to exploit the Picture through pay television (cable, satellite, or pay-per-view).
Picture:	" _____ "

2. <u>LICENSE OF RIGHTS</u>

Licensor hereby licenses the Rights to Licensee. Licensor shall deliver or make available (by lab access letter or otherwise) the underlying materials (including copies of existing art work) necessary for Licensee to exploit the Rights licensed hereunder. All of such underlying materials shall remain at all times solely owned by Licensor.

3. <u>PAYMENTS</u>

In consideration for Licensor's entering into this License, Licensee agrees to pay Licensor the following:

a.   A non-refundable advance payment of $_____ (the "Advance"), payable upon execution hereof. Receipt of the Advance by Licensor is a condition precedent to this License and all of Licensor's obligations hereunder.

b.   Prompt reimbursement to Licensor of all costs and expenses incurred by Licensor (at Licensor's actual cost) in connection with performing its obligations under this License, including costs of shipping, delivering, or making available the underlying materials pursuant to Section II. In addition, Licensee shall directly pay all costs owed to third parties relating to exploitation of the Rights under this License, including any payments for guilds, music clearances, or participations.

c.   A royalty, recoupable against the Advance only, equal to ___% of the gross receipts received by Licensee or any of its affiliates or related parties attributable to exploitation of the Rights.

[FOR VIDEO:]

d.   A royalty, recoupable against the Advance only, equal to the greater of (1) __% percent of the gross receipts from all sales of video units of the Picture less only the sum of sales taxes and actual cash refunds (not reserves) for returns or (2) U.S. $_____ per video unit sold.

4.   ACCOUNTING AND AUDIT RIGHTS

Royalty payments shall be made to Licensor within 45 days of the end of each calendar quarter, accompanied by a detailed accounting statement setting forth the amount and sources of all gross receipts, **[for video]** including the number of video units sold, the sales price for each video unit, the applicable sales taxes, and return refunds. All payments shall be in U.S. dollars based on the currency conversion rate in effect at the time payment is owed. All payments by Licensee to Licensor shall be owed on a gross basis, without withholding of any kind, and Licensee shall be solely responsible for any required withholding, including withholding taxes. Upon request by Licensor, Licensee shall promptly furnish any additional information relating to Licensee's exploitation of the Rights. Once per calendar year, Licensor shall have the right to have its agents or representatives inspect the books, records, and tax returns of Licensee upon five-days' advance written notice.

5.   LIMITATION ON EXPLOITATION

The Rights granted hereunder must be exercised directly by Licensee, and may not be sublicensed or assigned to any third party.

[FOR VIDEO:]

The royalty is calculated on the basis that Licensee will be responsible for all costs of manufacture and marketing of the video units, and Licensee may not enter into an arrangement whereby a third party bears such costs and expenses. Licensee may not exploit the Rights by combining or tying the Rights with any other product owned by Licensee. The Rights may not be exploited as a discount item.

6.   CREDITS AND LABELING

Licensee will not alter or delete any of the titles or credits on the Picture, including the copyright notice. All packaging and advertisements shall prominently display the copyright notice, trademark, and logo of Licensor, and Licensor shall own at all times the underlying intangible property relating to the Rights and the Picture, including all trademarks and copyrights.

7.   TERMINATION

This License shall automatically terminate, with a reversion of the Rights to Licensor, upon the occurrence of any of the following events:

a.   Licensee's failure to account and pay any amounts owed under Section III within thirty days of any payment date.

b.   Licensee's failure to comply with any of its other material obligations under this License.

c.   Licensee's failure to use its best efforts in connection with exploitation of the Rights.

d.   Licensee's paying royalties of less than U.S. $_____ to Licensor with respect to any calendar quarter.

e.   Licensee's failure to generate or report any gross receipts attributable to the Rights in any calendar quarter.

f.   Licensee's ceasing to engage in its current business activities.

g.   The filing of a voluntary or involuntary petition in bankruptcy with respect to Licensee.

In order to secure Licensor's reversion rights in the case of termination of this License, Licensee hereby grants Licensor a security interest in the Rights.

[FOR VIDEO:]

Upon termination of this License, whether at the end of its stated Term or pursuant to this Section VII, Licensee shall have a three-month period to sell-off video units that it has in stock on the date of termination, but the number of video units sold may not exceed the number of video units sold during the three-month period preceding such termination.

8. GOVERNING LAW AND JURISDICTION

This License shall be governed by the internal laws of California (i.e., without regard to conflict of law principles). Both parties agree and consent to personal and subject matter jurisdiction in any state or federal courts in California, and both parties consent to Los Angeles, California as a non-exclusive location for jurisdiction and venue of any dispute brought relating to this License. Licensee hereby irrevocably appoints Licensor as Licensee's agent for service of process for litigation hereunder, and Licensor shall send a copy of any such process to Licensee by fax or regular mail.

9. GUARANTY

All of Licensee's obligations under this License are hereby unconditionally guaranteed by _____.

IN WITNESS WHEREOF, the parties hereto have executed this License effective as of the ____ day of _____, ____.

LICENSOR:

_____

_____

By: _____

Title: _____

LICENSEE:

_____

By: _____

Title: _____

AGREED TO AND ACCEPTED
WITH RESPECT TO THE
GUARANTY IN SECTION IX:

_____

FORM I

PRO-LICENSEE SHORT FORM AGREEMENT

In consideration of the timely payment by Licensee of the License Fee, Licensor hereby grants to Licensee the exclusive Rights in the Film for exploitation in the Territory during the Term (all as defined herein).

1. "Licensee": _____

                                     _____

                                     _____

                                     _____

2. "Licensor": _____

                                     _____

                                     _____

                                     _____

3. "Film": _____

4. "Rating": _____

5. "Budget": _____

6. "Key Elements": At the election of Licensee, this Short Form Agreement is conditioned upon the following Key Elements appearing in or providing services in connection with the Film:

                   Actors: _____

                                  _____

                                  _____

Director: _____
Producer: _____
Writer: _____

7. "Territory":   _____

                       _____

8. "Language": Original version and dubbed, subtitled, synchronized, or simulcast in _____.

9. "Rights":   Rights means the exclusive right to exploit the Film in the Territory during the Term in the Language in any and all media whether now known or hereinafter devised, including, but not limited to, the following:

Rights Granted	Yes
Theatrical Rights	_____
Non-Theatrical Rights	_____
Video Rental Rights (including DVD)	_____
Video Sell Through Rights (including DVD)	_____
Television Rights	_____
Ancillary Rights	_____

10. "Term":   _____ years from the later of the date of acceptance of Delivery Materials by Licensee or the date of availability in all listed media of exploitation.

11. "License Fee": U.S. $_____. The License Fee shall be payable as follows:

               ___% upon execution of the License Agreement
               ___% upon commencement of principal photography
               ___% upon completion of principal photography

___% upon acceptance of delivery of the initial
Delivery Materials in accordance with the terms
and conditions of Licensee's standard delivery
schedule (the "Delivery Schedule")

___% upon acceptance of and access to the secondary
Delivery Materials in accordance with Licensee's
Delivery Schedule

12. "Minimum Guarantee":   ___% of the License Fee.

13. "Buyout":   ___% of the License Fee as a flat buyout of the
following Rights: _____.

14. Withholding: All payments by Licensee to Licensor shall be subject
to applicable withholding requirements.

15. "Royalty":

     a.   Theatrical and Non-Theatrical Rights Gross Receipts less
Distribution Expenses shall be payable as follows: ___% to Licensor and
___% to Licensee. Once Licensee has fully recouped the Minimum Guarantee and Distribution Expenses, ___% to Licensor and ___% to Licensee.

     b.   Video Rental Rights Gross Receipts less Distribution Expenses shall be payable as follows: ___% to Licensor and ___% to Licensee.

     c.   Video Sell Through Rights Gross Receipts less Distribution Expenses shall be payable as follows: ___% to Licensor and ___% to Licensee.

     d.   Gross Receipts less Distribution Expenses from the exploitation of all other Rights (not subject to the Buyout) shall be payable as follows: ___% to Licensor and ___% to Licensee.

     e.   Licensee shall maintain a reserve not to exceed 25% of video Gross Receipts to cover anticipated returns, which reserve shall be liquidated within twelve months.

     f.   Licensee shall be entitled to recoup the Minimum Guarantee from Licensor's share of all Gross Receipts.

     g.   No Royalty shall be payable by Licensee to Licensor with respect to Gross Receipts derived from exploitation of any Rights subject to the Buyout.

16. "Distribution Expenses":   All costs paid, incurred or accrued by Licensee relating to the exploitation of the Rights.

17. "Gross Receipts":   All revenues actually received by Licensee from exploitation of the Rights in the specified media.

18. "Delivery Materials":   As specified in Licensee's Delivery Schedule, to be delivered to Licensee at sole cost and expense of Licensor.

19. "Delivery Date":   Delivery Date means _____, ____, time being of the essence.

20. Governing Law and Jurisdiction: The terms, conditions and performance of this Agreement shall be governed by the laws of _____. Any dispute between the parties relating to this Agreement shall be resolved exclusively in the courts of _____.

21. U.S. Theatrical Release: No later than _____ months prior to the Delivery Date, the Film shall have been theatrically released in the United States on no less than ___ screens with direct prints and advertising expenditures of no less than U.S. $_____.

22. Additional Terms: _____

Licensor and Licensee intend to enter into a License Agreement (the "License Agreement"), consistent with Licensee's current standard terms and conditions. However, if the License Agreement is not executed, this Short Form Agreement shall constitute a binding and enforceable agreement between the parties with respect to the matters contained herein.

LICENSEE: LICENSOR:

_____   _____

By: _____   By: _____
Its: _____   Its: _____
Date: _____   Date: _____

FORM J

PRO-LICENSEE LICENSE AGREEMENT

d.   Indemnities

e.   Sell-Off Period

f.   Agent

g.   Taxes

h.   Governing Law; Jurisdiction

i.   Further Assurances

j.   Bank Charges

k.   Blocked Funds

l.   Set-Off

m.   Execution in Counterparts

EXHIBITS:

A   Distribution Expenses

B   Delivery Schedule

C   Short Form Mortgage of Copyright

D   Power of Attorney

This License Agreement is entered into as of _____, ____, by and between:

_____

_____

_____

_____

(the "Licensee")

and   _____

_____

_____

_____

(the "Licensor")

1.   Definitions. As used herein, the following terms shall have the meaning set forth below:

a.   "Budget" has the meaning set forth in the Short Form Agreement.

b.   "Buyout" has the meaning set forth in the Short Form Agreement.

c.   "Delivery" has the meaning set forth in paragraph 7 hereof.

d.   "Delivery Date" has the meaning set forth in the Short Form Agreement, time being of the essence.

e.   "Delivery Materials" has the meaning set forth in the Delivery Schedule.

f.   "Delivery Schedule" means the Delivery Schedule attached hereto as Exhibit "B", together with all attachments thereto.

g.   "Distribution Expenses" means all costs paid, incurred, or accrued by Licensee relating to the exploitation of the Rights, including without limitation those items set forth on Exhibit "A" hereto.

h.   "Film" means the full-length, live-action, theatrical film tentatively titled "_____," the screenplay and final shooting script thereof together with all modifications, synopses, and treatments, the trailer thereof, and the copyright in and to any of the foregoing.

i.   "Key Elements" has the meaning set forth in the Short Form Agreement.

j.   "Language" has the meaning set forth in the Short Form Agreement.

k.   "License" means this License Agreement and the Short Form Agreement, both together with any exhibits or schedules attached thereto.

l.   "License Fee" has the meaning set forth in the Short Form Agreement.

m.   "Licensee" has the meaning set forth in the introduction.

n.   "Licensor" has the meaning set forth in the introduction.

o.   "Minimum Guarantee" has the meaning set forth in the Short Form Agreement.

p.   "Rating" has the meaning set forth in the Short Form Agreement.

q.   "Rights" has the meaning set forth in the Short Form Agreement.

r.   "Royalty" has the meaning set forth in the Short Form Agreement.

s.   "Short Form Agreement" means the Short Form Agreement entered into by and between Licensor and Licensee with respect to the Film, which Short Form Agreement is incorporated herein by this reference.

t.   "Term" has the meaning set forth in the Short Form Agreement.

u.   "Territory" has the meaning set forth in the Short Form Agreement, together with any and all airplanes, ships, trains, or other installations (including governmental, military or industrial) registered in or flying the flag of any country included in the Territory.

2.   Grant of Rights. Subject to the terms and conditions of this License, Licensor hereby irrevocably grants to Licensee the Rights, including the right to:

a.   Use (other than by sale) written summaries of the Film with biographies of Key Elements not to exceed 7,500 words in length.

b.   Use the name, tradename, trademark, and logo of Licensor in connection with Licensee's exploitation of the Rights.

c.   Use all still photographs delivered to Licensee by Licensor pursuant to the Delivery Schedule in connection with Licensee's exploitation of the Rights.

d.   Use excerpts of the Film for any purpose including advertisement and promotion of the Film.

e.   Institute and prosecute actions or proceedings in the name of Licensee or Licensor or both which Licensee determines, in its sole and absolute discretion, are necessary or convenient to preserve Licensee's rights under this License, and to defend any action or proceeding brought against Licensee relating to Licensee's rights under this License.

f.   Authorize, in Licensee's sole and absolute discretion, any other person to exploit the Rights, including the terms and conditions of any distribution agreement, sub-distribution agreement, license agreement, or assignment.

3.   <u>Licensor's Representations, Warranties, Covenants, and Agreements</u>. Licensor hereby represents, warrants, covenants, and agrees that:

a.   Licensee shall own all right, title, and interest in and to the Rights without limitation, restriction, or encumbrance whatsoever, and during the Term the Rights shall remain free and clear of all encumbrances mortgages, pledges, liens, hypothecations, participations, and demands.

b.   Licensor has the full and complete corporate and legal right and authority to (i) enter into this License and (ii) grant the Rights to Licensee.

c.   Licensor has not licensed, and during the Term will not license, or otherwise permit the exploitation of, the Film in the Language (other than in the original version, without subtitling or dubbing) by any other person other than Licensee pursuant to this License, nor will Licensor take any other action or fail to take any other action that would adversely affect Licensee's exploitation of the Rights.

d.   Licensor has paid, and will during the Term continue to pay, all obligations arising in connection with the Film, including salaries, copyright fees, residuals, deferments, participations, guild payments, union payments, and synchronization, mechanical, and performance fees and royalties payable in connection with the production, manufacture, and exploitation of the Rights.

e.   The Film is entirely original and does not violate or infringe any trademark, tradename, copyright, patent, intellectual property right, literary right, artistic right, dramatical right, musical right, personal right, or moral right of any person.

f.   The Film is not slanderous, libelous, or defamatory, and does not violate the privacy of any person.

      g.   There are no threatened or actual claims, causes of action, or disputes which would in any way affect Licensee's full and unfettered right to exploit the Rights.

      h.   In its present form, without alteration or edit, the Film will be acceptable to governmental censors in each country of the Territory, and the Film has a rating no more restrictive than the Rating.

      i.   Licensor shall not, and shall not authorize or permit any other person to, exploit the television rights in the Film outside the Territory where such exploitation is capable of being received in or transmitted to the Territory.

      j.   The Film contains all the dramatic elements and characters contained in, and is in substantial conformance with, the screenplay approved by Licensee. The Film is in color, has a running time of not less than _____ minutes and not more than ____ minutes (exclusive of main and end titles), is in spoken English, and incorporates the services of the Key Elements.

      k.   Licensor has obtained all rights, releases, clearances, and licenses with respect to all materials and elements embodied in and all persons appearing in, or performing services in connection with, the Film.

      l.   Licensee shall have the unfettered right, which right shall not infringe the right of any person, to adapt, edit, cut, augment, translate, change the title of, synchronize, sub-title, dub, or otherwise alter the Film for any reason, including to comply with governmental censorship authorities.

      m.   Licensee may use, and may authorize others to use, the names, voices, likenesses, and biographies of all persons appearing in or performing services in connection with the Film for the purpose of publicity, advertising, or promotion relating to the Film.

      n.   The Film does not incorporate stock footage in the aggregate in excess of sixty seconds.

    4.   <u>Licensee's Representations, Warranties, Covenants and Agreements</u>. Licensee hereby represents, warrants, covenants, and agrees that:

      a.   Licensee has the full and complete corporate and legal right and authority to enter into this License.

b.   Licensee shall include on each copy of the Film, and on each videogram, credits included therein by the Licensor at the time of Delivery, which credits Licensor hereby represents and warrants are true, complete and accurate; provided, however, Licensee shall be permitted to add such credits as Licensee deems necessary, including Licensee's logo.

5.   Royalty. All Royalties shall be calculated in accordance with the Short Form Agreement.

6.   Accounting. Within sixty days following each calendar quarter during the first two years of the Term and within sixty days following each calendar six month period thereafter, Licensee shall furnish to Licensor reasonably detailed statements setting forth the amount of any royalty due Licensor, including the calculation thereof, together with any payment due to Licensor; provided, however, no statement shall be furnished and no payment shall be made until such time as the aggregate amount owed by Licensee to Licensor during a given accounting period exceeds U.S. $500. All statements furnished to Licensor hereunder together with all payments made in connection therewith shall be permanently binding on Licensor for all purposes unless, within twelve months of the receipt of each such statement, Licensor notifies Licensee in writing that Licensor objects to such statement and sets forth in detail the reason why Licensor so objects. Licensee shall maintain separate books of account with respect to its exploitation of the Rights and, no more than once per calendar year, on thirty days prior written notice, Licensor may, at Licensor's sole cost and expense, designate a chartered accountant to review such separate books and records of Licensee. Such chartered accountant must not be employed on a contingency basis and must, prior to commencing the audit, execute such documents Licensee may reasonably request in order to secure the confidentiality of Licensee's books and records. The audit shall be limited to the separate books of account maintained with respect to the twelve months preceding the commencement of the audit.

7.   Delivery. Licensor shall deliver, at Licensor's sole cost and expense,

the initial Delivery Materials no later than the Delivery Date, which initial Delivery Materials shall be in accordance with Licensor's representations and warranties in Paragraph 4 and shall be subject to acceptance by Licensee. Once written notice of acceptance has been furnished to Licensor by Licensee, delivery shall be deemed complete ("Delivery").

8.   Security Interest. In order to secure Licensee's rights under this License and the representations, warranties, covenants, and agreements of Licensor under this License, Licensor hereby grants a security interest to Licensee in and to the Film the form of which is attached hereto as Exhibit "C". In connection with such security interest, Licensor hereby grants to Licensee an irrevocable power of attorney, coupled with an interest, to execute and deliver all documents and take all actions necessary or convenient to enforce the terms of this License and to secure Licensee's rights hereunder, the form of which Power of Attorney is attached as Exhibit "D".

9.   Censorship. Licensee shall have the unfettered right to adapt, edit, cut, augment, translate, change the title of, synchronize, subtitle, dub, or otherwise alter the Film in order to comply with the censorship requirements of any governmental authority having control over Licensee's exploitation of the Rights. Licensor and Licensee covenant and agree that, if the Film (whether or not edited) is disapproved by any governmental authority having control over Licensee's exploitation of the Rights, the License Fee shall immediately be reduced by the following amounts:

Country	Percentage
_____	__%
_____	__%
_____	__%

If, prior to such disapproval, Licensee previously has remitted any part of the License Fee to Licensor, Licensor shall immediately refund that portion of the License Fee which corresponds to the above-referenced percentages. Notwithstanding the foregoing, if, in Licensee's sole and absolute discretion, the editing of the Film required by any governmental authority having control over Licensee's exploitation of the Film would adversely impact Licensee's ability to exploit the Film, Licensee may (but shall not be obligated to) treat this License as terminated at which point Licensor shall immediately refund the License Fee in full together with all of Licensee's costs and expenses, including attorneys' fees.

10. <u>Termination by Licensor.</u> This License shall terminate on the earlier of (a) expiration of the Term, or (b) failure by Licensee to pay the License Fee as and when due. No other breach or default by Licensee shall result in the termination of this License. Notwithstanding anything to the contrary herein, Licensee shall not be in breach of this License until such time as (y) Licensor has delivered and Licensee has received written notice of Licensee's alleged breach and (z) Licensee has not cured such breach within thirty days of receipt of Licensor's written notice. Following payment by Licensee of the License Fee in full, if Licensee does in fact breach this License or is otherwise in default hereunder, Licensor's sole remedy shall be an action at law for money damages.

11. <u>Termination by Licensee.</u> If the Film, as determined by Licensee in its sole and absolute discretion, materially deviates from the Budget or the Key Elements, or if Licensor breaches this License, including any representation or warranty contained herein, then Licensee has the right to terminate this License. If Licensee terminates this License pursuant to this paragraph, Licensor shall immediately refund the License Fee in full together with all of Licensee's costs and expenses, including attorneys' fees.

12. <u>Budget.</u> The parties acknowledge that Licensee has entered into this License based on Licensor's representations and warranties concerning the Budget. In the event that Licensor produces the Film with a final approved budget (or actually spends) less than the amount stated in the Budget, Licensee shall have the right either to terminate this License or to reduce the License Fee proportionately. If Licensee terminates this License pursuant to this paragraph, Licensor shall immediately refund the License Fee in full together with all of Licensee's costs and expenses, including attorneys' fees.

Licensor shall provide a certificate of the final cost of production to Licensee at the time of Delivery, together with a certificate (certified by an officer of Licensor) verifying that the amount shown is at least 95% (ninety-five percent) of the Budget. Licensor shall maintain separate books of account with respect to its production of the Film and, within one year of receipt of the foregoing certificates, on thirty days prior written notice, Licensee may designate a chartered accountant to review such separate books and records of Licensor.

13.   Miscellaneous

a.   Notice. Any notice or other communication required to be given pursuant to this License shall be sent to the parties at the addresses specified in the introduction, or to such alternative addresses notified by the parties in accordance with this paragraph. All notices or other communications must be in writing and shall be either personally delivered or sent via registered mail, pre-paid, return receipt requested, both accompanied by a facsimile copy. Notice or other communications sent by personal delivery shall be deemed received on the day delivered. Notice or other communications sent by registered mail shall be deemed received on the date inscribed in the official return.

b.   Assignment; Binding on Successors and Assigns. Licensor shall not assign this License prior to Delivery without the prior written consent of the Licensee. Upon receipt of such written consent, this License shall be binding on Licensor's successors and assigns.

c.   Merger; Amendment. This License (including the Short Form Agreement) supersedes any prior written or oral statement, representation, warranty, agreement, or understanding and contains the entire agreement of the parties hereto with respect to the subject matter hereof. This License may not be modified or amended except by an agreement in writing signed by both parties hereto. In the event of any conflict between this License Agreement and the Short Form Agreement, this License Agreement shall prevail.

d.   Indemnities. Licensor will at all times defend, indemnify and hold harmless Licensee from and against any and all claims, damages, costs, liabilities, and expenses, including reasonable attorneys' fees, arising out of or caused by (i) Licensor's production of the Film, (ii) any matter, aural or visual, contained in the Film, or (iii) breach by Licensor of any representation, warranty, covenant, or agreement made by Licensor hereunder. Licensor will provide Licensee with the necessary documents that Licensee requires to obtain a standard distributor's errors and omissions insurance policy with respect to the Film and covenants and agrees to name Licensee as an additional named insured on any policy of insurance obtained by Licensor with respect to the Film. Licensee will at all times defend, indemnify and hold harmless Licensor from and against any and all claims, damages, costs, liabilities, and expenses, including reasonable attorneys' fees, arising out of or caused by any breach by Licensee of any of its obligations hereunder.

     e.   <u>Sell-Off Period</u>. Upon the expiration of the Term of this License:

     (i) Licensee shall cease exploiting the Rights and shall, at Licensor's request and cost, within ninety days of such expiration or termination, deliver or destroy, at Licensor's election, all physical materials in Licensee's possession embodying the Rights; and

     (ii) Licensee shall have the sole and exclusive right to dispose of by sale or otherwise all videograms for a period commencing upon expiration or sooner termination of the Term and ending six months thereafter, and at the end of such sell-off period, Licensee shall destroy all remaining videograms in its possession; provided, however, if Licensee receives orders during such sell-off period for more videograms than it has in stock, Licensee shall be entitled to manufacture and sell videograms sufficient to comply with such orders.

     f.   <u>Agent</u>. Where, with Licensee's prior written consent, Licensor is acting as the agent of some other person, Licensor represents and warrants to Licensee that Licensor has full authority to execute this License on behalf of itself and such other person, that such other person, together with Licensor, will be jointly and severally bound by the terms and conditions of this License, and that such other person shall execute such document or documents requested by Licensee guarantying its and Licensor's performance of this License.

     g.   <u>Taxes</u>. All payments to be made by Licensee to Licensor hereunder, including the License Fee, shall be reduced by any applicable withholding tax. Licensee covenants and agrees to take reasonable steps to assist Licensor in obtaining an exemption, if available, from withholding, from the appropriate taxing authorities in the Territory. All payments, fees, and royalty calculations shall be reduced by any value added tax or similar tax.

      h.   Governing Law; Jurisdiction. The terms, conditions, and performance of this License shall be governed by the laws of _____. Any dispute between the parties relating to this License shall be resolved exclusively in the courts of _____.

      i.   Further Assurances. Licensor will take all steps and execute all documents necessary or convenient to consummate the transactions contemplated hereby and to protect and evidence the rights of Licensee pursuant hereto.

      j.   Bank Charges. Any bank or similar charges payable in connection with the remittance of any payment to Licensor hereunder, including the License Fee, shall be borne solely by Licensor.

      k.   Blocked Funds. Licensee shall have no obligation to report, or otherwise make payments with respect to, any blocked funds.

      l.   Set-Off. Licensee shall have the continuing right to deduct from any payment owed to Licensor, including the License Fee, any amounts owed or otherwise payable by Licensor to Licensee hereunder or otherwise.

      m.   Execution in Counterparts. This License may be executed in counterparts and transmitted by facsimile copy, each of which shall constitute an original and which when taken together shall constitute the License.

IN WITNESS WHEREOF, the parties have executed this License Agreement to be effective as of the date first above written.

LICENSOR:

By: _____

Title: _____

LICENSEE:

By: _____

Title: _____

EXHIBIT "A"

DISTRIBUTION EXPENSES

(a) <u>Advertising</u>. Advertising, marketing, promoting, exploiting and publicizing the Firm including as follows:

i) Publications, such as trade publications, fan magazines, newspapers, organization publications, and other space and display advertising, national and local.

ii) Cooperative advertising and advertising allowances to exhibitors (whether effected by credits against or deductions from film rentals, by direct reimbursement, or otherwise).

iii) Commercial tie-ups.

iv) Radio and television advertising, including cost of time and program and commercial preparation, recording and prints and tapes.

v) Tours and personal appearances directly connected with the Film of persons substantially involved in the Film.

vi) Previews and screenings.

vii) Entertainment, such as of press and personalities.

viii) Art work, cuts and engravings.

ix) Promotional material, such as souvenirs, and the preparation, manufacture and dissemination of press books, and of any other advertising accessories or materials, for free distribution.

x) Production of trailers and the manufacture of prints of such trailers for the Film utilizing scenes from the Film or material from other sources.

(b) <u>Checking</u>. Checking percentage engagements and licenses of the Film.

(c) <u>Claims and Litigation</u>. Notwithstanding anything to the contrary elsewhere, the gross amount paid for the settlement of any claims (or an account of any judgment or decree in any litigation relating to any claims), such as for infringement, unfair competition, violation of any right of privacy, right of publicity, defamation, or breach of contract, or arising out of other matters in connection with distribution of the Film (such as the literary, dramatic or musical material on which the Film is based), or the distribution, exploitation or exhibition thereof, including all expenses, court costs and reasonable attorneys' fees in connection with any such claims or litigation, or in connection with the investigation, assertion, prosecution or defense of any other claims or litigation relating to the Film or its distribution, exhibition or exploitation. Any net sums (after first deducting court costs and attorneys' fees) received from the settlement of claims (or from judgments) for any unpaid amounts shall be treated in the same manner in which a payment from the respective person would have been treated in the absence of a claim or action.

(d)   Collections. Costs incurred in connection with collections, including attorney and auditor fees and costs.

(e)   Conversion. Costs, discounts, and expenses incurred in obtaining remittances collections received in a foreign currency, including costs of contesting the imposition of restrictions which result in restricted funds.

(f)   Copyright. Copyright, trademark, and patent costs in connection with the Film and protection thereof.

(g)   Delivery. The cost of Delivery, if applicable.

(h)   Dubbing. Costs of subtitling, dubbing and synchronizing the Film.

(i)   Insurance. All costs for insurance of any and all risks of loss with respect to the Film and any components thereof.

(j)   Prints and Physical Properties. Prints, replacement prints, master discs and records; laboratory work; titles; dupe negatives and fine grain prints, redubbed tracks and foreign versions, including a version or versions synchronized with music or sound effects; substandard reductions; re-editing, recutting, rerecording and changes of or in the Film. If the methods or media of exhibition, transmission, projection or communication, or procedures, techniques or practices in connection with any of the foregoing, should be modified or changed, the corresponding costs of the new, substitute or changed methods, media, procedures, techniques, or practices shall be Distribution Expenses.

(k) <u>Third-Party Royalties and Guild Payments</u>. If Licensee pays any of the following, synchronization, recording, performing, patent and trademark royalties, and all other required payments to any person, including any participations or residuals for or with respect to the exploitation of the Film.

(l) <u>Taxes</u>. Taxes, excises and imposts (and payments and expenses in contesting, compromising or settling any of them), imposed by any taxing authority (regardless of any doubt as to the legality or applicability of any of them, and regardless of how they may be designated or characterized by the respective taxing authority or any other taxing authority, including, on or with respect to:

   xi) The Film.

   xii) Any prints and physical properties of the Film.

   xiii) Advertising accessories, for free distribution, relating to the Film.

   xiv) Exhibition, distribution or other use of the Film.

   xv) Any receipts or other revenues or credits from the Film or trailers thereof, or from the exploitation of the Film, or the remittance of payment of all or any portion thereof.

   xvi) All taxes on personal property, turnover, sales, use, film hire, excise, stamp, gross income and receipts taxes, and taxes computed on a portion of receipts or revenues.

(m) <u>Trade Associations</u>. Dues, fees and contributions paid to trade organizations.

(n) <u>Transportation, Duties and Censorship</u>. Freight, shipping, transportation, reels and containers, storage, duties, tariffs, customs charges, import taxes and censorship (including voluntary and involuntary censorship, classification and rating by governmental bodies or other persons, such as religious, ethnic and veteran's groups and organizations, and networks and other exhibitors or groups and organizations of exhibitors).

(o) <u>Video Costs</u>. Manufacturing, shipping and packing, marketing and/or exploitation of video discs and/or video cassettes or similar audio visual devices for the exhibition of the Film in the home.

(p) <u>Licenses</u>. All licenses, duties, fees or any other amounts required to permit exploitation of the Film.

(q) Record Costs. If applicable, all costs relating to creation of or distribution of the soundtrack, including artwork development and painting, copyright registration and enforcement, manufacturing, shipping, marketing, promotion, scrap, recording, mixing, editing, record royalties, mechanical copyright royalties, union fees for recording, sales, guild- mandated changes, etc.

(r) Music Publishing Costs. All costs relating to music publishing, including costs of collection, copyright registration and enforcement, costs of goods, royalties to composers, royalties to songwriters and subpublisher fees.

(s) Manufacturing Costs. Manufacturing costs relating to exploitation of the Rights.

EXHIBIT "B"

DELIVERY SCHEDULE

[ATTACH LICENSEE'S FORM]

EXHIBIT "C"

SHORT-FORM MORTGAGE OF COPYRIGHT

For good and valuable consideration, receipt of which hereby is acknowledged, _____ ("Licensor") hereby grants a security interest to _____ ("Licensee") in all of Licensor's right, title, and interest in and to the film tentatively titled "_____" in order to secure Licensor's obligations to Licensee pursuant to that certain License Agreement dated as of _____, ___, by and between Licensor and Licensee (the "License").

Dated: _____, _____.

LICENSOR:

_____

By: _____

Title: _____

EXHIBIT "D"

POWER OF ATTORNEY

_____ ("Licensor") hereby grants to _____ ("Licensee") an irrevocable power of attorney, coupled with an interest, to execute and deliver all documents, and to take all actions necessary or convenient, to enforce the provisions of the License Agreement dated as of _____, _____, by and between Licensor and Licensee.

Dated: _____, ____.

LICENSOR:

_____

By: _____
Title: _____

FORM K

"SAMPLE FILM" PRODUCTION/ DISTRIBUTION AGREEMENT

1.   Definitions. As used in this Agreement, the following terms shall have the meanings set forth below:

a.   "Affiliate" means with respect to any party an entity that has at least 25% ownership of, is owned at least 25% by, or is directly or indirectly owned at least 25% by the same entity that also has at least a 25% ownership of such party. For purposes of this definition, ownership includes ownership through other Affiliates.

b.   "Collection Account" means a bank account in the name of the Foreign Parties, which account shall be designated in writing by the

Foreign Parties to Studio from time to time, as set forth in the Inter-Party Agreement.

        c.   "Co-Production Agreement" means the "Sample Film" Co-Production Agreement entered into by and among the Foreign Parties relating to their respective ownership and distribution of the Picture.

        d.   "Delivery" means Sales Agent's actual or deemed acceptance pursuant to Paragraph 5 of Studio's delivery to Sales Agent of all the items relating to the Picture that are set forth on the Delivery Schedule.

        e.   "Delivery Items" means all Primary Delivery items and Secondary Delivery items.

        f.   "Delivery Schedule" means the delivery schedule attached hereto as Exhibit "A".

        g.   "Distribution Costs" means all reasonable and customary costs (net of discounts, refunds and rebates allocable to the Picture) paid, incurred, or accrued (to the extent hereafter provided) by either party or their respective Affiliates to third parties (and not to Affiliates) relating to Exploitation of the Rights including, without limitation, the list of Distribution Costs set forth on Exhibit "C". Except as set forth in the next sentence, Distribution Costs shall be calculated by aggregating all Distribution Costs of Affiliates, and any and all inter-Affiliate transactions, fees, charges or licenses shall be disregarded. Notwithstanding the foregoing, Distribution Costs shall include all payments to Affiliates for Distribution Costs if such Affiliates regularly either (a) receive similar payments from third parties or (b) manufacture tangible property for ultimate sale, lease, or distribution to the public. Distribution Costs shall not include any financing costs or interest (other than as included in Picture Cost) or overhead allocation. Any Distribution Costs allocable to more than one motion picture shall be fairly allocated to the Picture, with no overlapping or duplicate allocation. There shall be no double deduction of Distribution Costs. Distribution Costs must be calculated based only on (a) expenses paid or (b) expenses that are accrued (applying generally accepted accounting principles in the motion picture industry).

        h.   "Distribution Fee" means a distribution fee equal to 30% of Gross Receipts derived from Exploitation of the Rights, except as provided below:

i)   The Distribution Fee shall be 15% for (a) soundtrack and music publishing rights, (b) Merchandising Exploitation and (c) Studio's television output deal used by _____ pursuant to Paragraph 11.

ii)   In the Sales Agent Territories, the Sales Agent's Distribution Fee shall be 15%.

iii)   Other than as set forth in paragraph 1(h)(i)(c), the Distribution Fee on Studio's television output deals shall be subject to negotiation as provided in Paragraph 11.

i.   "Domestic Rights" means the Rights in the Domestic Territory.

j.   "Domestic Territory" means the United States and Canada, their respective territories and possessions (including without limitation, the U.S. Virgin Islands, Puerto Rico, Guam, Saipan, the Caroline Islands, and American Samoa), their military posts and government installations, wherever located, all airlines flying the flag of the United States or Canada, and all ships primarily serviced out of the United States or Canada, and the Territories of Nassau, Bahamas, Bermuda, and Freeport.

k.   "Draw Down" means the payment to Studio under the Letter of Credit upon Primary Delivery.

l.   "End User" means an entity the revenue of which constitute:

i)   Advertising revenue, subscription dues, or viewing fees in the case of Television Exploitation or Radio Exploitation;

ii)   Retail sales or rentals to the general public and/or mail club sales in the case of Video Exploitation;

iii)   Exhibition charges to and concession or ride receipts from the general public in the case of Theatrical Exploitation;

iv)   Wholesale sales to retailers or retail sales and/or mail order club sales in the case of Merchandising Exploitation; or

v)   Receipts from the general public in the case of amusement or theme park Exploitation of the Picture.

For the avoidance of doubt, with respect to Gross Receipts derived from Exploitation of the Rights, End Users shall include any person or entity distributing the Picture for purposes other than exhibition in theaters or by television stations; exhibitors or others who may actually exhibit the

Picture to the public; amusement/theme parks; radio or television broadcasters and other transmitters; cable operators; television program services including, without limitation, pay television and basic cable; book and music publishers; and persons or entities making Wholesale or retail sales of video discs, video cassettes or similar devices, books, sheet music, phonograph records merchandise, etc. whether or not any of the foregoing are subsidiaries, divisions or Affiliates of a party and, accordingly, the Gross Receipts derived therefrom shall not be deemed Gross Receipts hereunder.

      m.   "Exploit" or "Exploitation" means any and all manner of exploitation, reproduction, distribution, sale, manufacturing, use, performance, display, licensing, or other manner of dissemination, but subject to compliance with the third party obligations set forth on Exhibit "E".

      n.   "First Installment" means all but $180,000 of the Investment Amount.

      o.   "Foreign Distributors" means collectively _____ _____.

      p.   "Foreign Parties" means collectively the Foreign Distributors and Producer.

      q.   "Foreign Rights" shall mean the Rights in the Foreign Territory.

      r.   "Foreign Territory" means the entire world, excluding the Domestic Territory, including, without limitation, all airlines flying the flag of any constituent part of the Foreign Territory and all ships primarily serviced out of the Foreign Territory.

      s.   "Gross Receipts" means all revenues, monies, or other consideration actually received by or credited to a party or its Affiliates (excluding End Users) in freely remittable currency attributable to any Exploitation of the Rights. Thus, Gross Receipts shall be calculated by aggregating the Gross Receipts of all Affiliates (excluding Affiliate End Users), and any and all inter-Affiliate transactions, fees, charges, or licenses shall be disregarded other than with respect to Affiliate End Users. If a party hereto or its Affiliates is an End User with respect to any Exploitation, Gross Receipts shall be calculated on an arm's-length basis at fair market value (i.e., as though there was a license between the party and a third party with respect to such Exploitation). Gross Receipts shall be calculated using the cash method except for reasonable reserves that are accrued applying generally accepted accounting principles in the motion picture industry. Gross Receipts shall not include (a) amounts collected as taxes or for payment of taxes such as admission, sales, use or value added taxes, (b) film rental contributed to charitable organizations, (c) receipts from remakes, sequels, or TV series, and (d) de minimis salvage value receipts received from print stocks, stock footage, stills, props, sets, wardrobe, or other Picture Cost items (provided, however, any material sums received from the sale of stock footage or the sale of cars purchased in connection with or allocated to the Picture shall be included in Gross Receipts without Distribution Fee).

t. "Interactive Media" means all media involving the viewer's ability to change, modify, or control the sequence or performance of the presentation in a non-linear manner (including, without limitation, CD-rom, videogames, arcade games, and pinball games), excluding Videograms.

u. "Inter-Party Agreement" means the "Sample Film" Inter-Party Agreement entered into by the Foreign Parties and other parties relating to the allocation and payment of revenues relating to the Picture.

v. "Investment Amount" means $__ million which amount shall be paid without setoff, cross-collateralization, counterclaim or defense.

w. "Letter of Credit" means the letter of credit substantially in the form attached hereto as Exhibit "D."

x. "Media" means Television Exploitation, Theatrical Exploitation, Video Exploitation, Video on Demand Exploitation, and Merchandising Exploitation.

y. "Merchandising Exploitation" means Exploitation of tangible personal property (excluding Videograms) using or incorporating the characters (whether human or otherwise) in the Picture and/or the trademark or copyright relating to the Picture, including (a) Interactive Media, (b) any books, music or other published materials and (c) records and tapes.

z. "Net Receipts" means Gross Receipts after deduction and recoupment by each party of Distribution Fees and Distribution Costs from their respective Rights.

aa.   "Participations" means all participations, deferments, bonuses, or other amounts payable to third parties in connection with the Exploitation of the Rights, excluding Residuals.

bb.   "P&A" (prints and advertising) means Distribution Costs for Theatrical Exploitation attributable to (1) costs of advertising, promotion and publicity for the Picture and (2) costs for positive prints, internegatives, magnetic and optical sound tracks, trailers and other copies of the Picture together with shipping costs and insurance relating to prints.

cc.   "Sales Agent Territories" means the countries where Sales Agent acts as Sub-Distributor for the Foreign Parties pursuant to the Co-Production Agreement.

dd.   "Picture" means a single live-action theatrical motion picture tentatively titled "Sample Film," the screenplay, story, and shooting script upon which the Picture is based, the soundtrack and music for the Picture, all marketing material relating to the Picture, all ancillary rights relating to the foregoing, and the copyright to any of the foregoing, but subject to compliance with the third party obligations set forth on Exhibit "E".

ee.   "Picture Cost" means all costs (net of discounts, refunds, rebates, and the like allocable to the Picture and proceeds of sale of property and equipment that are not included in Gross Receipts) paid, incurred or accrued (to the extent hereafter provided) by Studio or its Affiliates to third parties (and not to Affiliates) that relate directly to the development or production of the Picture as long as such expenses are not included in Distribution Costs. Picture Cost shall be calculated by aggregating all Picture Costs of Affiliates, and any and all inter-Affiliate transactions, fees, and charges shall be disregarded. Notwithstanding the foregoing, Picture Cost shall include all payments to Affiliates (using Studio's standard rate card or charges) for Picture Cost if such Affiliates regularly receive similar payments with respect to services rendered for third parties. Picture Cost shall be calculated based only on (a) expenses paid or (b) expenses that are incurred or accrued (applying generally accepted accounting principles in the motion picture industry). Picture Cost shall not include (a) any overhead allocation or (b) any completion bond fee. Studio shall be entitled to interest on the unrecouped portion of Picture Cost at 1% over the prime rate. All Picture Costs are subject to audit pursuant to Paragraph 17 hereof.

     ff. "Primary Delivery" means Delivery of all items set forth on Exhibit "B" hereto (excluding the Short-Form Assignment if the Letter of Credit is not issued) by _____.

     gg. "Proportionate Share" means [allocation].

     hh. "Recoupment" means:

     i) For Studio, the point at which it has recouped (a) the Picture Cost minus (b) the Investment Amount from the aggregate Net Receipts it retains or is paid pursuant to this Agreement.

     ii) For Foreign Distributors, the point at which payments are owed to Studio pursuant to Paragraph 10(c)(4)(ix) of the Inter-Party Agreement.

     ii. "Reporting Date" means:

     i) For Foreign Parties, (a) the end of each calendar month commencing one month following the date of initial general theatrical release of the Picture in the Domestic Territory for the first twelve months after such release, (b) the end of each calendar quarter for the next three years and six months, and (c) the end of each semi-annual period thereafter.

     ii) For Studio (a) the end of such Studio Fiscal Month commencing one Studio Fiscal Month following the date of initial general theatrical release of the Picture in the Domestic Territory for the first twelve months after such release, (b) the end of the last Studio Fiscal Month of each quarter for the next three years and six months, and (c) the end of the last Studio Fiscal Month of each semi-annual period thereafter.

     jj. "Residuals" means all residuals, supplemental market payments, and similar payments required by any guilds and local rights societies, such as ASCAP, required under applicable bargaining agreements, contingent upon revenues from Exploitation of the Rights (including mechanical and performance copyright royalties).

     kk. "Rights" means the irrevocable, perpetual, exclusive right to own and Exploit the Picture (including all customary publicity rights) throughout the Universe by all media of Exploitation whether now known or hereafter discovered, including, without limitation, in the Media.

ll. "Secondary Delivery" means Delivery of all items set forth on the Delivery Schedule but not referenced on Exhibit "B" hereto.

mm. "Second Installment" means $180,000 of the Investment Amount.

nn. "Short-Form Assignment" means the Short-Form Assignment attached as Schedule 1 to the Delivery Schedule.

oo. "Signature Date" means the date this Agreement is fully executed by all parties.

pp. "Studio Fiscal Month" means the fiscal month used by Studio (i.e., generally ending on the last Saturday of the month).

qq. "Sub-Distribution Agreements" means any licenses, sales, distribution agreements, or sales agent agreements of or for the Rights, excluding (a) inter-Affiliate transactions and (b) transactions with End Users in their capacity as End Users.

rr. "Sub-Distributor" means a licensee, purchaser, distributor, or sales agent under any Sub-Distribution Agreements.

ss. "Television Exploitation" means Exploitation of the Rights by all means, methods, or devices, whether now known or hereafter developed of free, pay, closed-circuit, over-the-air, microwave, laser, pay-per-view, cable, satellite, telecommunications (including exhibition of the entire Picture in a linear manner on telephone and computer networks), or terrestrial broadcast, as those terms are commonly understood in the entertainment industry.

tt. "Theatrical Exploitation" means Exploitation of the Rights by all means, methods, or devices, whether now known or hereafter developed of cinematic exhibition (e.g., theatrical, public video, and non-theatrical, including exhibition in hotels and on ships and airlines), as those terms are commonly understood in the entertainment industry.

uu. "Video Exploitation" means Exploitation of the Rights by all means of Videograms, including home video and commercial video, as those terms are commonly understood in the entertainment industry (excluding Interactive Media and any Exploitation included within Theatrical, Television, or Video On Demand Exploitation).

vv. "Videograms" means video cassettes, laser discs, CD-rom, and video CD and any other similar device embodying the Picture in a linear form only, excluding specifically any Interactive Media.

ww. "Video On Demand Exploitation" means Exploitation of the Rights by video on demand and near video on demand, as those terms are and will be from time to time commonly understood in the entertainment industry, including without limitation where the viewer can access through cable, satellite, or telecommunication a film on demand and control or choose the approximate timing thereof.

xx. "Wholesale" means the purchase of inventory from manufacturers or producers and the sale of that inventory to retailers by an entity that regularly performs such activity and that adds value through its marketing and distribution functions. For the avoidance of doubt, "Wholesale" does not include any direct sales to retailers by a party or its Affiliates under its current practices.

2. <u>Ownership</u>. The purpose of this Agreement is to provide for the co-production, co-ownership, and Exploitation of the Rights. The parties shall own the following rights:

a. Studio shall own (i) the Domestic Rights and (ii) the copyright to the Picture in the Domestic Territory.

b. Subject to the condition precedent of payment in full of the First Installment to Studio, Foreign Parties shall own (i) the Foreign Rights and (ii) the copyright to the Picture in the Foreign Territory.

3. <u>Payment of Investment Amount</u>. The Foreign Distributors hereby agree to pay Studio the Investment Amount upon Delivery. To secure this obligation, the Foreign Distributors shall deliver the Letter of Credit to Studio within thirty days after the Signature Date. The Letter of Credit shall provide for payment of all but $180,000 of the Investment Amount on Primary Delivery, and the remaining $180,000 payable on Secondary Delivery. Studio will deliver to the bank item C(11) on the Delivery Schedule as a condition precedent to issuance of the Letter of Credit.

4.   Production. Studio shall be responsible for producing the Picture and funding the Picture Cost, including all cost overruns, whether or not due to enhancements or unforeseen difficulties, and shall have the right to make all production decisions in its sole and absolute discretion.

5.   Delivery. Each Delivery Item shall be delivered to Sales Agent at its address for notices as provided in this Agreement. Sales Agent shall have fifteen business days from the actual receipt of all Delivery Items (applied separately for Primary Delivery first and then Secondary Delivery) to evaluate such items for any technical or other material defects, and Delivery shall be deemed to occur at the end of such time period unless Sales Agent has objected by that time pursuant to Schedule 2 to the Delivery Schedule. All disputes as to Delivery shall be resolved in accordance with the arbitration provisions set forth in Schedule 2 to the Delivery Schedule, which resolution shall be binding on the parties. No item shall be deemed delivered to Sales Agent until such time as such item is released from Customs in England into Sales Agent's actual possession. Secondary Delivery shall be completed within 120 days of Primary Delivery (except that (a) item A(12)(b) shall be delivered within 45 days of Primary Delivery, (b) item A(17) shall be delivered within ninety days of Primary Delivery unless delayed due to the director or the lab, but not to extend beyond 120 days after Primary Delivery, and (c) items C(3) and C(7)(a) shall be delivered when received by Studio). Studio shall pay all costs of Delivery, but such costs shall be treated as Distribution Costs.

6.   Access to Material. Commencing from the Signature Date, Studio and Foreign Distributors (by obtaining such items through Sales Agent only) shall have reciprocal free access to all alternative versions, foreign language tracks, trailers, teasers key art, slides, color transparencies, TV spots, electronic press kits, and other marketing and publicity materials that are created by each other when and if made (including during production), but duplication thereof shall be at their own cost and expense (with no charge for overhead or any internal costs by the other party). In the Sales Agent Territories, Studio shall only have access to the foregoing materials on the same terms and conditions that Sales Agent has access to such materials. Foreign Distributors shall be entitled to have access to the Picture film footage in order to make promo reels or other marketing material during production.

7.   <u>Modification and Credits</u>. Studio and Foreign Distributors shall not alter, edit, cut, add to, or modify the Picture except as required for censorship or other regulatory requirements and television broadcast or airline requirements and in response to any actual or threatened legal claims. Foreign Distributors shall comply with all contractual credit obligations of which they have written notice and shall be deemed to have notice once such notice is delivered by Studio to Sales Agent. In the Domestic Territory, (a) the first card shall read "Paramount Pictures Presents"; (b) the second card shall read "In Association With Producer"; and (c) Foreign Distributors shall be entitled to an end credit reading substantially in the form: "Produced in association with _____." Throughout the Foreign Territory (a) the first card shall read "Producer and"; (b) the second card shall read "_____ Present" and (c) the third card shall read "In Association with Paramount." However, the local Sub-Distributor in Sales Agent Territories will be entitled to a first position presentation credit at Sales Agent's option.

8.   <u>Distribution</u>. Studio and Sales Agent (on behalf of the Foreign Distributors) shall consult in good faith in advance to coordinate (a) the initial release patterns and dates and advertising campaign for their respective Rights and (b) Exploitation of Interactive Media. Foreign Distributors shall not release the Picture theatrically in the Foreign Territory prior to the earlier of (a) the initial general theatrical release of the Picture in the Domestic Territory or (b) _____. Sales Agent shall not (and shall not authorize any third party to) exhibit in Mexico an English language version of the Picture via any means of Television Exploitation. Foreign Distributors may present the Picture at film festivals in the Foreign Territory at any time after the earlier of (a) the initial general theatrical release of the Picture in the Domestic Territory or (b) _____. Subject to Studio's rights hereunder, Sales Agent has commenced licensing the Picture in Sales Agent Territories, but Studio shall have a fifteen day right of first negotiation with Sales Agent with respect to allowing Studio to act as the distributor of any rights in the Sales Agent Territories where there is no minimum guarantee or advance. In the event that Studio and Sales Agent do reach agreement with respect to any such distribution, the receipts

and expenses of Studio with respect to such distribution shall not be subject to this Agreement and shall not be treated as Gross Receipts or Distribution Costs, respectively. All transactions shall be on an arm's-length basis and shall be in accordance with standard industry practice and pricing for other comparable theatrical motion pictures. In the event the Rights are exploited as a package with one or more other films, the Gross Receipts shall be allocated based on the packaging party's respective reasonable, good-faith business judgment. If Sales Agent enters into a Sub-Distribution Agreement in Sales Agent Territories without an advance or minimum guaranty, the aggregate Distribution Fee of Sales Agent and the Sub-Distributor shall not exceed 30% without Studio's approval.

9.   Theatrical Exploitation by Studio. Studio shall release the Picture on a number of screens, with a P&A expenditure, commensurate with other films of a similar budget and genre, subject to Studio's reasonable business judgment. However, Studio shall initially release the Picture on a minimum of _____ screens in the Domestic Territory and will spend a minimum of $__ million on P&A for the Picture by the end of the first four weeks after the initial general theatrical release of the Picture in the Domestic Territory.

10.   Soundtrack and Music Publishing Exploitation by Studio. Foreign Parties hereby appoint Studio as their agent to Exploit soundtrack and music publishing rights in the Foreign Territory. The Net Receipts attributable to such rights in the Foreign Territory shall be paid in accordance with the provisions of Paragraph 15(a) and the Net Receipts attributable to such rights in the Domestic Territory shall be paid in accordance with the provisions of Paragraph 15(b). Sales Agent shall have a fifteen day right of first negotiation to license soundtrack rights prior to Studio licensing such rights to a non-Affiliated third party, but only if such right of first negotiation does not cause any adverse impact (in Studio's opinion) on the creative aspects of the soundtrack.

11.   Television Exploitation by Foreign Distributors. Subject to availability, Foreign Distributors and Studio may mutually agree to the use of

Studio's television output deals by Foreign Distributors for the Picture on mutually agreeable terms and conditions, including Studio's Distribution Fee.

12.   Piracy. Each party agrees to employ customary measures to protect their respective Rights from piracy. In the event that any third parties infringe on either party's respective Rights (including copyright infringement), that party shall use reasonable efforts to prevent such infringement.

13.   Residuals. Foreign Distributors shall promptly reimburse Studio for any residuals actually paid by Studio attributable to Studio's receipt of the Investment Amount, payable upon Studio's delivery to Sales Agent, on behalf of the Foreign Distributors, of evidence of payment and the calculation thereof, supported by the applicable statements rendered to the guilds. For purposes of calculating Residuals, however, Foreign Parties shall provide Studio with an appropriate allocation, and Residuals with respect to Video Exploitation and Television Exploitation shall not be treated as payable prior to nine months or fifteen months, respectively, after Primary Delivery. Upon written demand therefor, Foreign Distributors shall promptly reimburse Studio for any Residuals actually paid by Studio attributable to the Foreign Territory upon Studio's delivery to Sales Agent, on behalf of the Foreign Distributors, of evidence of payment and the calculation thereof. For the avoidance of doubt, Foreign Distributors shall have ultimate liability for, and shall indemnify Studio from, all Residuals attributable to the Foreign Territory, but Studio and Foreign Distributors shall mutually cooperate to minimize Residuals attributable to the Foreign Territory. Foreign Distributors shall have the right, at their sole cost and expense, to timely defend any allocation of Residuals attributable to the Foreign Territory, subject to Studio's mutual participation and approval.

14.   Participations. Except as set forth below, all Participations shall be paid by Studio and Foreign Parties shall not be obligated to pay any amount of the Participations, but the Participations shall be treated as one of the Studio's recoupable Distribution Costs. The allocation and calculation of Participations as between the parties hereto shall not impact the ac-

tual calculation of such Participations as between Studio and the third party participants, who shall not be third party beneficiaries of this Agreement.

15. <u>Allocation of Net Receipts</u>. All Net Receipts shall be applied in the following order on a continuing and cumulative basis:

(a) Net Receipts attributable to the Foreign Rights shall be paid in the following continuing order of priority:

i) First, 100% to Foreign Distributors until Foreign Distributors have reached Recoupment.

ii) Next, once all the Foreign Distributors have reached Recoupment and if Studio has not reached Recoupment, 100% to Studio until Studio has reached Recoupment.

iii) Next, once both parties have reached Recoupment, 50% to Studio and 50% to Foreign Parties.

(b) Net Receipts attributable to Domestic Rights shall be paid as follows:

i) First, 100% to Studio until Studio has reached Recoupment.

ii) Next, once Studio has reached Recoupment and if Foreign Distributors have not reached Recoupment, 100% to Foreign Distributors until all the Foreign Distributors have reached Recoupment.

iii) Next, once both parties have reached Recoupment, 50% to Foreign Parties and 50% to Studio.

16. <u>Accounting and Payment</u>. In order to determine and calculate Gross Receipts, Net Receipts, and the calculation and allocation of Residuals and Participations, Studio and Foreign Parties shall report to each other within sixty days after the end of each Reporting Date which report from the Studio to Foreign Parties shall include a specific calculation of Participations. The reports shall contain sufficient detail to permit Studio to comply with its obligations to, and agreements with, third parties. Within thirty business days after delivery of the accounting statements by both parties, Studio shall send Foreign Parties a combined accounting statement setting forth the calculation of any amounts owed by one party to the other. Any payments

owed by one party will be offset by payments owed by the other party, and the net amount owed by one party to the other pursuant to such statement shall be paid by Studio to the Collection Account or from the Collection Account to Studio by bank wire transfer within ten days of receipt of the accounting statement. All payments owed to the other party shall be in U.S. dollars. Any foreign currency shall be converted into U.S. dollars at the exchange rate prevailing at the date of conversion. The parties shall cooperatively work together to attempt to minimize withholding taxes to the extent permissible by law. Any payments owed by Studio to Foreign Parties shall be paid to the Collection Account.

17.   Audit Rights. Once per calendar year, each party shall have the right to have its reputable certified public accountant, which certified public accountant shall be subject to the other parties' approval, which approval shall not be unreasonably withheld, inspect and copy the books and records of the other party to verify Gross Receipts, Distribution Costs, Picture Costs, and the status of Recoupment, upon a mutually agreeable time. The parties hereby represent and warrant to each other that they permit audits to be performed in the order of requests received and that within five days of the auditing party's notice under this Paragraph, the party to be audited shall inform the auditing party (a) of the number of audits to be performed prior to the noticed audit and (b) the approximate time at which the auditing party can go forward with its audit. Each party shall keep for at least four years full, true, and accurate separate books and records of accounts relating to their Exploitation of the Rights. Upon request by either party, the other party may promptly furnish any additional information relating to their Exploitation of the Rights.

18.   Producer. In consideration for its services, Producer shall be paid an executive producer fee of $_____, payable by the Studio, $_____ on the date of delivery of the Letter of Credit to Studio (or payment of both the First and Second Deposit) and $_____ on the date of Draw Down (or payment of the First Installment). Producer (or its designee) may take, at its election, either, neither, or both a presentation credit pursuant to Paragraph 7 (on a separate card immediately after Studio's) and an exclusive

executive producer credit. Such on-screen credits shall be substantially similar in all respects to the "Produced By" credit (except that each such credit on screen shall run for the time of one of the two "Produced By" credit cards on screen), and the executive producer credit shall appear above (and otherwise shall be substantially similar in all respects to) the "Produced By" credit whenever and wherever the "Produced By" credit appears, such as on paid advertising.

19.   <u>Derivative Rights</u>. Notwithstanding anything to the contrary herein, all derivative rights to the Picture that are not included within the Rights shall remain owned by Studio. Thus, Studio shall own all sequel, prequel, theme park, and television rights (excluding Television Exploitation of the Picture itself) with respect to the Picture. If within fifteen years of the date hereof, Studio elects to produce a theatrical motion picture remake, sequel, or prequel to the Picture, Studio shall so notify Foreign Parties, and the Foreign Parties shall have a thirty-day right to elect to acquire the rights to such prequel or sequel in the Foreign Territory on the same terms and conditions as provided herein.

20.   <u>Representations and Warranties of Studio</u>. Studio hereby represents and warrants to Foreign Parties the following:
        a.   This Agreement shall be valid, binding, and enforceable in accordance with its terms with respect to Studio, and the performance of Studio's obligations hereunder will not breach any other agreement to which Studio is a party.
        b.   Upon Delivery, the Rights shall be free and clear of all liens and encumbrances of every kind, excluding all mechanic's liens, guild liens and similar liens. Foreign Parties shall have quiet enjoyment of the Foreign Rights upon Draw Down (or payment of the First Installment), and Exploitation of the Rights will not infringe the rights of any third parties including, without limitation, copyright (whether literary, dramatic, musical or otherwise), trademark, tradename, contract rights, property or personal rights, right of privacy, or right of publicity, and will not give a cause of action for defamation (including libel or slander) to any person.

c.   Studio will not enter into any agreements that conflict with this Agreement.

d.   The Picture shall have an initial general theatrical release in the Domestic Territory prior to _____.

e.   All credits on the Picture and all credit obligations furnished to Sales Agent by Studio shall be complete and accurate and shall correspond to all contractual and guild requirements in all material respects.

f.   Studio shall make Primary Delivery of the Picture on or before the earlier of (a) sixty days following completion of the Picture by Studio or (b) _____.

21.   Representations and Warranties of Foreign Parties. Foreign Parties hereby represent and warrant to Studio the following:

a.   This Agreement shall be valid, binding, and enforceable in accordance with its terms with respect to Foreign Parties, and the performance of Foreign Parties' obligations hereunder will not breach any other agreement to which Foreign Parties are a party.

b.   Foreign Parties will not enter into any agreements that conflict with this Agreement.

c.   No third parties shall be granted any rights of approval or control over Studio's Exploitation of the Domestic Rights.

d.   The payments from the Collection Account under Paragraph 10(c) of the Inter-Party Agreement prior to payments to Studio will be bona fide, actual payments that conform to the definition of Distribution Costs and the other provisions of this Agreement (e.g., such payments do not reflect overhead).

e.   The Inter-Party Agreement will not be amended except by a writing executed by all the required parties thereto and the Studio (to the extent such amendment affects the interests of the Studio). If a proposed amendment does not affect the interests of Studio, Studio shall have fifteen days to review the proposed amendment before it is effective.

f.   As of the date the conditions precedent set forth in Paragraph 28 are met, the Inter-Party Agreement and the Co-Production Agreement shall be in full force and effect and shall constitute a binding obligation of the parties to each such agreement.

g.   The Collection Account mechanism provided in the Inter-Party Agreement will remain in effect pursuant to the terms of the Inter-Party Agreement unless amended or terminated with the prior consent of Studio (where such amendment affects the interests of Studio).

h.   Foreign Distributors will comply with all third party obligations set forth on Exhibit "E", except that Studio shall be responsible for any costs associated with (i) any dubbing or editing rights of any such third parties (with Studio having the exclusive right to decide whether such rights apply) and (ii) any costs of complying with restrictions of which Studio first gives notice after Delivery.

22.   <u>Assignment</u>. Neither party may assign their rights or obligations under this Agreement without the consent of the other except as follows:

a.   Either party may freely assign their rights to payments from the other party hereunder.

b.   Either party may assign or delegate any of their rights or obligations under this Agreement to (i) any Affiliate, although the original party shall remain primarily liable hereunder, or (ii) to any entity with or into which such party may merge or consolidate, or which may succeed to all or substantially all of their distribution related assets.

c.   Either party may enter into Sub-Distribution Agreements (including, without limitation, soundtrack and music publishing licenses) in accordance with the provisions hereof.

d.   The Foreign Parties may assign their rights under this Agreement to a bank as security for financing of only the Picture under the provisions of the Inter-Party Agreement.

23.   <u>Entire Agreement</u>. This Agreement constitutes the entire agreement among the parties hereto relating to the Picture, and this Agreement supersedes all prior correspondence, negotiations, term sheets, letter agreements, or understandings relating to the Picture. In the event of any conflict between the provisions of this Agreement and the provisions of the Inter-Party Agreement or the Co-Production Agreement, the provisions of this Agreement shall prevail.

24.   Notices. All notices to be given by any party to any other party pursuant hereto shall be in writing by registered mail return receipt requested or by facsimile and shall be sent to the respective addresses for notice listed below or to such other addresses as each party may notify to the others from time to time. A notice sent by registered mail shall be deemed received on the date inscribed in the official return receipt. A notice sent by facsimile shall, in the absence of proof to the contrary, be deemed received on the next business day.

Addresses for notice:

25.   Further Assurances. All parties shall take all steps and execute all documents reasonably necessary to protect and evidence the rights of the other party pursuant to this Agreement. Studio shall obtain and furnish to Foreign Parties any required documentation necessary to register the Picture with any foreign government, such as the CNC in France.

26.   Obligations of Foreign Distributors. All of the obligations of Foreign Distributors hereunder shall be separate, not joint and several, except that their obligation to pay Residuals and Participations pursuant to Paragraphs 13 and 14 shall be joint and several and the obligations of Toho-Towa and Marubenni shall be joint and several.

27.   Amendment. This Agreement may not be amended except by a writing executed by all the parties hereto.

28.   Conditions Precedent. A conditions precedent to the effectiveness of this Agreement is the complete execution of this Agreement (with the signature of either Toho-Towa or Marubeni eliminating the requirement of signature of the other). Within a reasonable period of time, an Inter-Party Agreement substantially in the form currently under negotiation (with any changes thereto subject to the approval of Studio which approval shall not be unreasonably withheld) shall be executed by the parties thereto. In no event will the Foreign Rights vest in Foreign Distributors until Studio has received the full First Installment.

29.   Governing Law. This Agreement shall be governed by the internal laws of state of California (i.e., without regard to its conflict of law principles).

30.   Execution in Counterparts. This Agreement may be executed in counterparts and transmitted by facsimile copy, each of which shall constitute an original and which taken together shall constitute the Agreement.

31.   Claims

       a.   If any person, firm or corporation shall do or perform any acts which Studio believes constitute a copyright infringement in the Domestic Territory of the Picture, or of any of the literary, dramatic or musical material contained in the Picture, or constitute a plagiarism, or violate or infringe any right of Studio therein, or if any person, firm or corporation shall do or perform any acts which Studio believes constitute an unauthorized or unlawful distribution, exhibition or use thereof, then and in any such event, Studio may and shall have the right, without the obligation, to take such steps and institute such suits or proceedings as Studio may deem advisable or necessary to prevent such acts and conduct and to secure damages and other relief by reason thereof, and generally can take such steps as may be advisable or necessary or proper for the full protection of the rights of the parties. Prior to taking any such action, Studio shall consult in good faith with Producer as to the appropriate action to be taken. Studio may take such steps or institute such suits or proceedings in its own name (or in the name of Foreign Parties or in the names of the parties jointly, but only with respect to Studio's derivative rights under Paragraph 19). Studio shall be entitled to recoup from the Gross Receipts of the Picture its reasonable costs and expenses (including reasonable outside attorneys' fees) paid or incurred in connection with the foregoing; provided, however, that if any collections are affected by compromise or judgment, such expenses shall first be deducted from such collections. The remainder of such collections, if any (except such collections arising out of the failure or breach of any of the warranties, representations or agreements of the Foreign Parties hereunder), shall be included in Gross Receipts. Studio's decisions in connection with the settlement of any suits or proceedings shall be final. Nothing herein contained shall be deemed a limitation or restriction of the Foreign Parties' obligation to indemnify and hold harmless Studio pursuant to Paragraph 32(a) below.

b.   If any person, firm or corporation shall do or perform any acts which Foreign Parties believe constitute a copyright infringement in the Foreign Territory of the Picture, or of any of the literary, or dramatic material contained in the Picture, or constitute a plagiarism, or violate or infringe any right of the Foreign Parties therein, or if any person, firm or corporation shall do or perform any acts which Foreign Parties believe constitute an unauthorized or unlawful distribution, exhibition or use thereof, then and in any such event, Foreign Parties may and shall have the right, without the obligation, to take such steps and institute such suits or proceedings as Foreign Parties may deem advisable or necessary to prevent such acts and conduct and to secure damages and other relief by reason thereof, and generally can take such steps as may be advisable or necessary or proper for the full protection of the rights of the parties. Prior to taking any such action, the Foreign Party initiating such action shall consult in good faith with Studio as to the appropriate action to be taken. Foreign Parties may take such steps or institute such suits or proceedings in their own name. The Foreign Parties shall be entitled to recoup from the Gross Receipts of the Picture their reasonable costs and expenses (including reasonable outside attorneys' fees) paid or incurred in connection with the foregoing; provided, however, that if any collections are affected by compromise or judgment, such expenses shall first be deducted from such collections. The remainder of such collections, if any (except such collections arising out of the failure or breach of any of the warranties, representations or agreements of Studio hereunder), shall be included in Gross Receipts. The Foreign Parties' decisions in connection with the settlement of any suits or proceedings shall be final. Nothing herein contained shall be deemed a limitation or restriction of the Studio's obligation to indemnify and hold harmless Foreign Parties pursuant to Paragraph 32(c).

32.   Indemnity

a.   The Foreign Parties shall forever defend, indemnify and save harmless Studio and its distributors, directors, officers, employees, agents, and attorneys and their respective successors, assigns and licensees (sometimes referred to hereafter as the "Studio Indemnitees"), against all claims, actions, causes of action, losses, liabilities, costs, expenses, damages, judgments, and settlements including reasonable outside attorneys' fees and court costs, which may be suffered, made or incurred by Studio or its distributors, or its or their respective successors, assigns or licensees, arising out of or in connection with any breach of any representations, warranties, undertakings or agreements of any nature whatsoever made or entered into herein or hereunder by the Foreign Parties.

      b.   Studio shall give the Foreign Parties prompt written notice of the institution of any action or the making of any claim alleging a breach of the Foreign Parties' agreements, representations or warranties hereunder, and Studio may, at its election, be represented by outside counsel retained by Studio and the reasonable costs of such representation may be charged against the Gross Receipts of the Picture; it being understood and agreed that the right to make such charge shall in no way limit the Foreign Parties' obligation to pay such costs to Studio upon Studio's demand.

      c.   Studio shall forever defend, indemnify and save harmless the Foreign Parties and their distributors, directors, officers, employees, agents and attorneys and their respective successors, assigns and licensees (sometimes referred to hereinafter as the "Foreign Parties' Indemnitees"), against all claims, actions, causes of action, losses, liability, costs, expenses, damages, judgments, and settlements including reasonable outside attorneys' fees and court costs, which may be suffered, made or incurred by the Foreign Parties or their distributors, or their respective successors, assigns or licensees, arising out of or in connection with any breach of any representations, warranties, undertakings or agreement of any nature whatsoever made or entered into herein or hereunder by Studio.

      d.   The Foreign Parties shall give Studio prompt written notice of the institution of any action or the making of any claim alleging a breach of Studio's agreements, representations or warranties hereunder, and the Foreign Parties may, at their election, be represented by outside counsel retained by the Foreign Parties and the reasonable costs of such representation may be charged against the Gross Receipts of the Picture; it being understood and agreed that the right to make such charge shall in no way limit Studio's obligation to pay such costs to the Foreign Parties upon the Foreign Parties' demand.

IN WITNESS WHEREOF, the parties hereto have executed this Agreement effective as of the Signature Date.

                          _____

Date: _____   By: _____

                              Title: _____

Date: _____   By: _____

                              Title: _____

Date: _____   By: _____

                              Title: _____

Date: _____   By: _____

                              Title: _____

EXHIBIT "C"

DISTRIBUTION COSTS

(a) <u>Advertising</u>. Advertising, marketing, promoting, exploiting and publicizing the Picture exclusively as follows:

i) Publications, such as trade publications, fan magazines, newspapers, organization publications, and other space and display advertising, national and local.

ii) Cooperative advertising and advertising allowances to exhibitors (whether effected by credits against or deductions from film rentals, by direct reimbursement, or otherwise), excluding any share paid by third parties.

iii) Commercial tie-ups.

iv) Radio and television advertising, including cost of time and program and commercial preparation, recording and prints and tapes.

v) Tours and personal appearances directly connected with the Picture of persons substantially involved in the Picture.

vi) Previews and screenings.

vii) Entertainment, such as of press and personalities.

viii) Art work, cuts and engravings.

ix) Promotional material, such as souvenirs, and the preparation, manufacture and dissemination of press books, and of any other advertising accessories or materials, for free distribution.

x) Production of trailers and the manufacture of prints of such trailers for the Picture utilizing scenes from the Picture or material from other sources.

(b) Checking. Checking percentage engagements and licenses of the Picture.

(c) Claims and Litigation. Notwithstanding anything to the contrary in the Production/Distribution Agreement, the gross amount paid for the settlement of any claims (or an account of any judgment or decree in any litigation relating to any claims), such as for infringement, unfair competition, violation of any right of privacy, right of publicity, defamation, or breach of contract, or arising out of other matters in connection with distribution of the Picture (such as the literary, dramatic or musical material on which the Picture is based), or the distribution, exploitation or exhibition thereof, including all expenses, court costs and reasonable outside attorneys' fees in connection with any such claims or litigation, or in connection with the investigation, assertion, prosecution or defense of any other claims or litigation relating to the Picture or its distribution, exhibition or Exploitation but excluding the costs and expenses of any claims and litigation between the parties hereto. With respect to any claim covered by insurance for which premiums are charged to the Picture under the preceding sentence (or with respect to which an equivalent charge is made as provided in the preceding sentence), deductions may be made under the preceding sentence only to the extent that the respective amounts deducted exceed the covered amount. Any net sums (after first deducting court costs and outside attorneys' fees) received from the settlement of claims (or from judgments) for any unpaid amounts constituting (or which, if paid, would constitute) Gross Receipts shall be treated in the same manner in which a payment from the respective person would have been treated in the absence of a claim or action.

(d)   Collections. Costs incurred in connection with collection of Gross Receipts, including attorney and auditor fees and costs.

(e)   Conversion. Costs, discounts, and expenses incurred in obtaining remittances of Gross Receipts received in a foreign currency, including costs of contesting the imposition of restrictions which result in restricted funds.

(f)   Copyright. Copyright, trademark, and patent costs in connection with the Picture and protection thereof.

(g)   Delivery. The cost of Delivery.

(h)   Dubbing. Costs of subtitling or dubbing the Picture.

(i)   Insurance. All costs for insurance of any and all risks of loss with respect to the Picture and any components thereof.

(j)   Prints and Physical Properties. Prints, replacement prints, master discs and records; laboratory work; titles; dupe negatives and fine grain prints, redubbed tracks and foreign versions, including a version or versions synchronized with music or sound effects; substandard reductions; re-editing, recutting, rerecording and changes of or in the Picture. If the methods or media of exhibition, transmission, projection or communication, or procedures, techniques or practices in connection with any of the foregoing, should be modified or changed, the corresponding costs of the new, substitute or changed methods, media, procedures, techniques, or practices shall be Distribution Costs.

(k)   Third-Party Royalties and Guild Payments. Synchronization, recording, performing, patent and trademark royalties, and all other required payments to any person, including any Participations or Residuals for or with respect to the Exploitation of the Picture.

(l)   Taxes: Taxes, excises and imposts (and payments and expenses in contesting, compromising or settling any of them), imposed by any taxing authority (regardless of any doubt as to the legality or applicability of any of them, and regardless of how they may be designated or characterized by the respective taxing authority or any other taxing authority, but excluding income taxes), on or with respect to:

i) The Picture and any trailers thereof.

ii) Any prints and physical properties of the Picture.

iii) Advertising accessories, for free distribution, relating to the Picture.

iv) Exhibition, distribution or other use of the Picture, trailers thereof or physical properties thereof.

v) Any Gross Receipts or other revenues or credits from the Picture or trailers thereof, or from the Exploitation of the Picture, or the remittance of payment of all or any portion thereof.

vi) All taxes on personal property, turnover, sales, use, film hire, excise, stamp, gross income and Gross Receipts taxes, and taxes computed on a portion of receipts or revenues.

(m) <u>Trade Associations</u>. Dues, fees and contributions (to the extent reasonably allocable to the Picture or the distribution thereof) to MPAA, AMPTP and MPEA or any similarly constituted or substitute authorities or organizations, or their respective successors, wherever located, and fees for industry public relations activities and for protection against copyright infringements.

(n) <u>Transportation, Duties and Censorship</u>. Freight, shipping, transportation, reels and containers, storage, duties, tariffs, customs charges, import taxes and censorship (including voluntary and involuntary censorship, classification and rating by governmental bodies or other persons or organizations, such as religious, ethnic and veteran's groups and organizations, and networks and other exhibitors or groups and organizations of exhibitors).

(o) <u>Video Costs</u>. Manufacturing, shipping and packing, marketing and/or Exploitation of video discs and/or video cassettes or similar audio visual devices for the exhibition of the Picture in the home.

(p) <u>Licenses</u>. All licenses, duties, fees or any other amounts required to permit Exploitation of the Picture.

(q) <u>Record Costs</u>. All costs relating to creation of or distribution of the soundtrack, including artwork development and painting, copyright registration and enforcement, manufacturing, shipping, marketing, promotion, scrap, recording, mixing, editing, record royalties, mechanical copyright royalties, union fees for recording, sales, guild-mandated changes, etc.

(r)   <u>Music Publishing Costs</u>. All costs relating to music publishing, including costs of collection, copyright registration and enforcement, costs of goods, royalties to composers, royalties to songwriters and subpublisher fees.

(s)   <u>Manufacturing Costs</u>. Manufacturing costs relating to Exploitation of the Rights such as Merchandising and Interactive Media.

There shall be no double deduction of any Distribution Costs. Accordingly, no Distribution Costs that have been deducted under any paragraph shall be deducted under any other paragraph or under the Agreement as a whole, and no item which has been included in cost of production shall be deducted as a Distribution Cost. In no event may there be any deduction on account of any Distribution Cost attributed to any payments to Foreign Distributors or any revenue item which is not includable in Gross Receipts hereunder. All Distribution Costs must relate directly to the Exploitation of the Rights.

FORM L

SHORT-FORM DEFINITION OF NET PROFITS

Participant shall be entitled to __% of 100% of "Net Profits," which shall mean the amount of "Gross Receipts" (defined below) remaining, if any, after deducting therefrom, on a continuing basis the sum of (a) all expenses paid by Company in connection with the acquisition, development, production, or distribution of the Picture, (b) interest at 7% on the amount of such expenses from the date incurred to the date of recoupment, and (c) a distribution/sale/overhead fee to Company of 10% of all Gross Receipts. "Gross Receipts" shall mean all nonrefundable cash revenues actually received in U.S. currency by Company attributable to the Picture. Each payment hereunder shall be made within 30 days of the end of each calendar quarter, accompanied by an accounting statement setting forth the calculation thereof. Participant's representatives shall have the right to audit the books and records of the Company once per calendar year as to the calculation of Net Profits. In no event will the definition, calculation or payment of Net Profits to Participant be less favorable than that provided to any other participant.

ABOUT THE AUTHOR

Schuyler M. Moore is a partner in the corporate entertainment department at the Los Angeles office of the national law firm of Stroock & Stroock & Lavan, LLP. Mr. Moore has been practicing in the entertainment industry since 1981, and he represents a broad spectrum of clients throughout the entertainment industry, including producers, sales agents, foreign distributors, and financiers.

Mr. Moore holds his undergraduate degree from UCLA (Phi Beta Kappa, Summa Cum Laude) and his law degree also from UCLA (first in his class). He is the author of *Taxation of the Entertainment Industry*, published by Panel Publishers. He is an adjunct professor for the UCLA Law School, teaching Entertainment Law, and a frequent speaker and writer on a wide variety of entertainment subjects.